NO CRYSTAL STAIR

NO CRYSTAL STAIR

Visions of Race

and Gender in

Black Women's Fiction,

Revised and Updated

Gloria Wade-Gayles

The Pilgrim Press
Cleveland, Ohio

To the memory of Toni Cade Bambara,
an authentic sister who continues to be our light

The Pilgrim Press, Cleveland, Ohio 44115
© 1997 by Gloria Wade-Gayles

All rights reserved. Published 1997

Langston Hughes, "Mother to Son" from *Selected Poems by Langston Hughes,* copyright 1926 by Alfred A. Knopf, Inc., and renewed 1954 by Langston Hughes. Used by permission of the publisher.

Printed in the United States of America on acid-free paper

02   01   00   99   98   97   5   4   3   2   1

Library of Congress Cataloging-in-Publication Data

Wade-Gayles, Gloria Jean.
    No crystal stair : visions of race and gender in Black women's
fiction / Gloria Wade-Gayles. — Rev. and updated ed.
        p.   cm.
    Includes bibliographical references and index.
    ISBN 0-8298-1151-6 (alk. paper)
    1. American fiction—Afro-American authors—History and criticism.
2. American fiction—Women authors—History and criticism.   3. Afro-
American women in literature.   4. Afro-Americans in literature.   5. Race
relations in literature.   6. Sex roles in literature.
    I. Title.
    PS153.N5W26   1996
    813.009'9287—dc21   96-47198
                                                         CIP

Well, son, I'll tell you:
Life for me ain't been no crystal stair.
It's had tacks in it,
And splinters,
And boards torn up,
And places with no carpet on the floor—
Bare.
But all the time
I'se been a-climbin' on,
And reachin' landin's,

And turnin' corners,
And sometimes goin' in the dark
Where there ain't been no light,
So boy, don't you turn back.
Don't you set down on the steps
'Cause you finds it's kinder hard.
Don't you fall now—
For I'se still goin', honey,
I'se still climbin',
And life for me ain't been no crystal stair.

—Langston Hughes, "Mother to Son," 1926

CONTENTS

Acknowledgments   ix

Introduction to the Revised Edition   xi

Introduction to the First Edition (Beverly Guy-Sheftall)   xxiii

A Personal Response (Zillah Eisenstein)   xxix

To the Reader   xxxiii

1   The Narrow Space of Race, the Dark Enclosure of Sex: 1
    The Case for This Book

2   A Historical Overview: 17
    Black Women in White America, 1946–1976

3   The Halo and the Hardships: 45
    Black Women as Mothers and Sometimes as Wives

4   "Going Nowhere Immediate":   97
    Black Women of Hopelessness

5   "Journeying from Can't to Can" and   127
    Sometimes Back to "Can't":
    Black Women of Challenge and Contradiction

6   Giving Birth to Self: 165
    The Quests for Wholeness of Sula Mae
    Peace and Meridian Hill

7   The Space and the Enclosure: 195
    The Collective Vision of Black Women

Afterword (Alton Hornsby Jr.)   219

Notes   223

Selected Bibliography   237

Index   249

ACKNOWLEDGMENTS

I want to thank my colleagues at Spelman College for their various expressions of support and encouragement: Angela Getter and Fleda Jackson, whose gifts of assistance are too numerous to mention; Jean Billingslea-Brown, whose reading of No Crystal Stair as a "discrete text for the early eighties" shaped my arguments for this second edition; Beverly Guy-Sheftall, whose research in black feminist thought provided the historical lens for my revisiting of the book; and Candace Raven, whose expertise in completing tasks well and on time inspired me to meet deadlines for this revision. Several bright and disciplined Spelman students were no less supportive: Jennifer McZier guided me into the Internet for bibliographic information; Asha Almo and Tahra Edwards made filing sense of my many notes; and Zenobia Connor analyzed the appropriateness of the book's controlling metaphor—"the narrow space and the dark enclosure"—to a group of recently published black women's novels.

In a special way, I want to thank the many English teachers who for over a decade have opened well-used copies of the first edition of No Crystal Stair in courses on black women's fiction. They kept the book alive. Pilgrim Press now gives it new breath.

To all those at Pilgrim who made it happen, most especially Richard Brown and Kelley Baker, I owe my deepest gratitude.

INTRODUCTION TO THE REVISED EDITION

Revisiting *No Crystal Stair* more than a decade after its publication in 1984, I see with greater clarity my cautious dance around the term "black feminist criticism": I identified myself as a feminist who was using a feminist lens to study selected black women's novels written between 1946 and 1976, but I wrote that the book was not a "platform for black feminism" or an attempt to explain "black feminist theory or criticism." Rather it was "a *literary* study that interfaced the novels with history and sociology."[1] I saw no contradiction at the time between being a black feminist and writing a book on black women's fiction that was something other than black feminist criticism. Beverly Guy-Sheftall placed "black feminist criticism" where I had written "literary study" and attributed my caution to the elusiveness of the term in the early eighties.

In 1976, I began working on the manuscript that would later become *No Crystal Stair*. The first theoretical essay on black feminist criticism appeared a year later, in 1977. Written by Barbara Smith and titled "Towards a Black Feminist Criticism," it was a "painstaking definition"[2] of the term and a passionate call for black women to understand the "absolute necessity" of creating a body of scholarship that "embodies the realization that the politics of sex as well as the politics of race and class are crucial interlocking factors" in black women's literature.[3] In 1980, a second pioneering essay, Deborah McDowell's "New Directions for Black Feminist Criticism," reiterated the call and suggested ways by which black women critics could respond. In 1981, the publication of Barbara Christian's *Black Women Novelists: The Development of a Tradition, 1892–1976*, the first book on a group of black women's novels studied through the lens Smith had described, could be considered the debut of black feminist criticism. Christian's brilliant analysis not only proved the existence of a tradition in black women's fiction, but also grounded that tradition deep in feminist soil. Her book was of inestimable value to me during the final stages of my writing, sending me back to reassess interpretations I had written before it appeared.

Several essays and one or two books did not, however, constitute a body of scholarship. Therefore, while I am gratified that Guy-Sheftall considered *No Crystal Stair* "black feminist criticism par excellence,"[4] I believe my cautious dance in 1984 was both wise and justified. I was certain that "black feminist criticism," when it became a body of scholarship, would be recognizable not only by the use of a feminist lens, but also by the application of a distinctive theory and language. I could not claim that which did not exist.

In retrospect, I realize that my decision to interface the novels with history and sociology was more risky than my use of "black feminist criticism" would have been. Making such a connection could be misconstrued as an equating of literature and sociology, an error that, as Ralph Ellison rightly observed, does disservice to literature. Needless to say, that was not my intent. At the time, given the fact that there was no body of feminist analyses of black women in real life, an interdisciplinary approach to the study of race, sex, and class was appropriate. Like black feminist criticism, this scholarship made its debut at the beginning of the decade of the eighties. Angela Davis's *Women, Race, and Class* and bell hooks's *Ain't I a Woman*, pioneering works in this area, appeared in 1981. Patricia Hill-Collins's *Black Feminist Thought*, an extensive interdisciplinary analysis of black womanhood using feminist theory, would not appear until 1990. In the absence of such scholarship and theory, interfacing black women's literature with history and sociology, I argued, could instruct us in the complexity of black womanhood in real life. My reasoning was evocative of Barbara Smith's belief that black women writers have much to tell us about black womanhood, for we can assume, Smith wrote, that "little has stood between the black woman and the telling of her story."[5]

On a more personal level, an interdisciplinary approach was the only one my feminist politics allowed me to take, shaped as they were by Toni Cade Bambara, the only black feminist speaking at national podiums whom I knew personally. Bambara's anthology, *The Black Woman*, published in 1970, was the first collection of essays by black women that examined black womanhood through a feminist lens and, therefore, was credited with ushering in the black feminist movement of the seventies. An authentic and passionate black feminist, Bambara recognized no line between what we say and what we do, between what we see in real life and what we find in art, between theory and praxis, between "feminist" and "revolutionary." For her, black feminism was "an embrace of the community and a hardheaded attempt [on the part of black women] to get basic with each other." Black women had to do that, she wrote, because "we are involved in a struggle for liberation."[6] She believed, and acted out her belief, that a black feminist was daily involved in shaping a black feminist platform and in moving that platform from the printed page and the amplified podium into the lives of real black women. Influenced by her ideology, I believe that interfacing the novels with information about black women in real life was, subconsciously, my attempt to do what I wrote I was *not* attempting to do: "set forth a black feminist platform."[7]

When I prepared a bibliography of recent titles for this revised edition of *No Crystal Stair*, I became aware of the significance of 1984 in the development of black feminist writing. Books that would become definitive texts were published in that year, most notable among them Audre Lorde's *Sister Outsider: Essays and Speeches*; Paula Giddings's *When and Where I Enter: The Impact of Black Women on Race and Sex in America*; Mari Evans's *Black Women Writers*; Gloria Hull's *Give Us Each Day: The Diary of Alice Dunbar-Nelson*; and bell hooks's *Feminist Theory: From Margin to Center*. In 1984, black feminist scholarship was buttressed by the founding of *Sage*, "the first explicitly black feminist periodical devoted exclusively to the experi-

ences of women of African descent in the United States and throughout the world."[8]

These developments explain why, in 1984, *Black American Literature Forum*, a major scholarly journal, sent out a call for papers on
black feminist criticism. The call read: "To what extent is a specifically feminist criticism of Afro-American writing desirable, or even
necessary?"[9] Black feminist scholars had already answered the question and would continue to do so during the remaining years of the
decade. Those scholars included Mary Helen Washington, Nellie
McKay, Frances Foster, Trudier Harris, Miriam DeCosta-Willis,
Deborah McDowell, JoAnne Braxton, Sherley Ann Williams, Sandra
Govan, Hortense Spillers, Cheryl Wall, Barbara Christian, and Hazel
Carby.

Three years later, in 1987, scholars of African American literature
gathered at the Center for the Study of Black Literature and Culture
at the University of Pennsylvania to "discuss the past and future of
the field."[10] Both the papers and the responses given at the conference, published as *Afro-American Literary Study in the 1990s*, gave
evidence that scholarship on African American literature would no
longer be dominated by attention to male writers. It would make
ample room for black feminist criticism, which would be recognized
as some of the most exciting and brilliant scholarship in the decade.

If Toni Cade Bambara's *The Black Woman* predicted that black
feminists were serious about the business of liberation, responses to
Alice Walker's *The Color Purple* indicated that the nation would not
mute their voices of empowerment. The novel was published in 1983,
outside the dates of my analysis, but I felt justified in commenting on
the new directions it suggested for black women's fiction. Not only
did Walker receive the Pulitzer Prize for the novel, but, in 1985, the
film adaptation, directed by Steven Spielberg, was a box-office success, receiving several Academy Award nominations. The film, however, was as controversial as it was successful. Black men, joined by
more than a few black women, picketed the film's debut and wrote
numerous articles charging Alice Walker with hatred for black men
or with "male bashing." Negative responses to the film, which according to some feminist critics reflected Spielberg's twisting of

Walker's vision, constituted a dress rehearsal for conflicts between black men and black women that would take place in the eighties; these conflicts reached a crescendo in 1991 in responses to the Clarence Thomas nomination or, more precisely, to Anita Hill's allegations of sexual harassment.

The charge that black women were willing participants in a national conspiracy against black men was not new to the black feminist struggle. As I explain in the historical overview in *No Crystal Stair*, it gave shape in the seventies to heated dialogues between black women and black men, both from the podium and on the printed page. What distinguished the eighties from the seventies was not the charge, but rather black feminists' refusal to permit the charge to distract them from the important business of producing feminist scholarship. They wrote about black male–female issues, but only in the context of theory and only for the purpose of explaining systems of oppression in white America that all groups designated as "Other" needed to work to dismantle. Analysis of the concept of the Other was one of the distinguishing characteristics of the new scholarship.

To study this scholarship is to see black feminists brilliantly moving the uniqueness of black womanhood from "theme" to "theory" and creating a space in which only they could/would speak for themselves. This meant continuing to challenge sexism in the black community and most especially the oath of loyalty to black men that black women were expected to take. Paula Giddings spoke for black feminists when she wrote in "The Last Taboo," an essay on the Thomas–Hill debacle, that racial unity is not racial solidarity.[11]

Given the tilling and harvesting taking place in black feminist thought, it is not surprising that the eighties saw a new naming word for black feminists that differentiated them in a number of ways from white feminists. Whereas in the seventies they were *black feminists*, many now called themselves *womanists*. As Alice Walker defines the word in her preface to *In Search of Our Mothers' Gardens*, published in 1983, a year before *No Crystal Stair*, "Womanist is to feminist as purple is to lavender."[12] It is the stronger term. In *Words of Fire* (1996), the first anthology of black feminist writings from the nineteenth century to the present day, Guy-Sheftall points to the emergence of the word in the works of a number of major scholars: "Scholars such as Cheryl Gilkes, Katie Cannon, Jacquelyn Grant, Delores Williams, Renita Weems, and Emily Townes . . . self-identify as 'womanist' theologians as a way of differentiating themselves from white feminist theologians."[13]

Theology, philosophy, sociology, history, biography, autobiography, poetry, drama, art, fiction, ancient studies, meditation, sex therapy, meditation, journals, self-therapy . . . black women explored a multitude of subjects and articulated their genius in every genre. They created a new literary canon and became a community of black women writers with high visibility in the nation. The proliferation, and quality, of their writing, along with national attention on issues of gender, opened doors in the academy that had been traditionally closed to black women. To be sure, black women began their challenge of white and male control of the academy in the seventies, but it was not until the eighties that the challenge bore fruit. The increase in courses, seminars, conferences, papers at scholarly proceedings, and articles in reputable journals that examined the black woman as writer and as subject was dramatic and unprecedented in our history.

Black women's scholarship published after *No Crystal Stair* is impressive not because it is larger or more diverse in subject matter, but rather because it is immersed more deeply in the soil of black feminist analysis and, using a new angle of analysis, it reveals truths not examined in the seventies. Of necessity, new truths create a new language. In the late seventies, black feminists wrote about the impact of race, *sex*, and class on black women's reality. Today, they write about the interlocking of race, *gender*, and class. The understanding now, as Hill-Collins explains in *Black Feminist Thought*, is that "sex is a biological category attached to the body—humans are born female or male. In contrast, gender is socially constructed."[14] In the late seventies, black feminists wrote about racism, sexism, and classism as egregious ills in white America. Today, they write about patriarchy, a word that means not simply male (white) domination, but the system of oppression in which all Others are violated in various ways. In the past, they wrote about family and community. Today they write about the social construct of gender and of race, black women's spirituality, female bonding, womanist theology, black female subjectivity, and homophobia. In the seventies, they wrote about black women and white women. Today, they write about women of color, moving their analyses into the arena of diversity. I do not mean to suggest that these subjects and these terms never appeared in writings during the seventies and early eighties. They did. Homophobia, for example, was central to "A Black Feminist Statement," the pioneering essay written by the Combahee River Collective, organized in 1974. But without the existence of a body of scholarship into which the new knowledge could be incorporated, they were present in an isolated way. The creation of a black feminist dictionary, so to speak, and a black feminist encyclopedia registers them, counts their syllables, contextualizes them, explains them, highlights them, and makes them accessible to students and scholars in the field.

When I study pages that are of particular significance to literary criticism, I am made more keenly aware of differences between *No Crystal Stair* and today's new scholarship. Though feminist in that it examines the interlocking of race, gender, and class, my analysis is essentially thematic and, of course, interdisciplinary in focus. The new scholarship is theoretical and attached to different schools, among them postmodern, poststructuralist, postcolonial, or Marxist. *No Crystal Stair*, in language and in subject/focus, is a product of the time in which it was written, and yet it reaches beyond the year of its publication into the study of black women's literature being conducted in the nineties. Thus do I suggest several reasons why a revised edition is significant and necessary.

1. Although we have reason to celebrate the flourishing of black women's scholarship begun in the eighties, when we turn our attention from quality to quantity, we realize that the *number* of resources is large only when we compare it to what we once had. Books on literature written by black men and on literature written by whites, regardless of gender, far outnumber books on literature written by black women. The truth is that in ten short years we could not have succeeded in correcting an imbalance that has existed for over a century.

Some attention is appropriate here to the rumor that black women writers now control black scholarship. Even with the flourishing of black women's writing, men remain the most influential of scholars—even when the subject is black women's literature. Nor is it true, as another rumor suggests, that black women have power in the academy. The truth is that black men are power brokers in black studies and white women in women's studies. We have made great strides in moving from the margin to the center, but we are not yet the center.[15] This fact, I submit, makes the shelving of any feminist analysis of black women's literature unwise and out of consonance with the goal of creating a *body* of scholarship to help correct the imbalance of voice and visibility that has been ours for more than a century. We must reclaim, and use, books of scholarship from our immediate past with no less passion than we reclaim texts from the nineteenth century. All of them belong to a tradition in black women's writing.

When we reclaim scholarly texts, we should see them not as "dead" texts important only for historical reasons, but rather as breathing texts that can assist us, in ways we cannot predict, in the continued development of black feminist criticism. *No Crystal Stair* is such a text. Like its sister texts, *No Crystal Stair* resonates with answers to questions fundamental to the field, including the following: In what way is the book in dialogue with other black feminist texts of the period? What does this dialogue teach us about a community of black women scholars then in existence, and how does this information instruct us in community building in the nineties? What aspect of our reality did the language fail to address, and how does this information instruct us in creating a precise and compelling language for the nineties? What did we take with us from the old analysis into the new, and what does this information teach us about continuity and change in black women's literature? The answers to these questions can be instructive in understanding the theoretical complexion we are today preparing for black feminist scholarship in the twenty-first century.

2. Another reason for a second edition of *No Crystal Stair* is a very obvious one: It was the first and remains the only interdisciplinary study of a group of twenty-six novels written by black women dur-

ing periods in history that saw black women moving steadily toward empowerment: post–World War II, the civil rights movement of the sixties, and the beginning of black women's liberation in the seventies. It examines novels that are among the most frequently taught texts in the academy, among them *The Bluest Eye, Sula, Their Eyes Were Watching God, Meridian, The Third Life of Grange Copeland,* and *Quicksand.* More important, however, it examines novels that are often either overlooked or relegated to a list of "suggested readings," among them Sarah Wright's *This Child's Gonna Live,* Dorothy West's *The Living Is Easy,* and Gayl Jones's *Corregidora* and *Eva's Man.* Hence the relevance and significance of the book to today's study of black women's novels.

3. Ironically, the very nature of the new scholarship suggests the need for a second edition of *No Crystal Stair.* I refer here to those books so immersed in complex theory that they are accessible only to a highly select audience of scholars. Such books assume that the reader brings to the scholarship not only a close reading of the novels under study, but also an understanding of the theory that shapes the study. In some cases, the books can become more a study of the critics who formulated the theory than of the black women writers who created the novels. They are seminal and brilliant books, needed scholarship, but they do not reach the larger audience of readers interested in black women's literature: the general reading public outside the academy and the undergraduate population within the academy. Many of these readers have a firm background in the novels and are, therefore, familiar with the characters under study in *No Crystal Stair,* but they are drawn to the type of study in the book for the same reason that I had to write it more than a decade ago and for the same reason that Barbara Smith almost two decades ago wrote about the power of the truth in the black woman's "telling of her story": to celebrate the genius of black women writers and to understand through a study of their novels the interlocking of race, class, and gender in a reality unique to black women in white America.

4. Finally, although scholarship has changed, the axes of power and influence that turned a decade ago turn no less today. This gives a new, fresh meaning to the central metaphor of *No Crystal Stair:*

There are three major circles of reality in our nation, which reflect degrees of power and influence. There is a large circle in which white people, most of them men, experience influence and power. Far away from it is a smaller circle, a narrow space, in which black people, regardless of sex, experience uncertainty, exploitation, and powerlessness. Hidden in this second circle is a third, a small, dark enclosure in which black women experience pain, isolation, and vulnerability. These are the distinguishing marks of black womanhood in white America.[16]

Thirteen years ago, my study of the narrow space and the dark enclosure identified twenty-six major black women's novels written between 1946 and 1976. That the number written in two decades, 1976–1996, far exceeds the number written over four speaks to the flourishing of black women's writing in the eighties and in the nineties. The recent novels are as follows:

1976: Toni Morrison, *Song of Solomon*
1977: Octavia Butler, *Kindred*
1980: Toni Cade Bambara, *Salteaters*
1981: Toni Morrison, *Tar Baby*
1982: Ntozake Shange, *Sassafrass, Cypress, and Indigo*
       Gloria Naylor, *The Women of Brewster Place*
1983: Paule Marshall, *Praisesong for the Widow*
       Alice Walker, *The Color Purple*
1986: Gloria Naylor, *Linden Hills*
       Sherley Anne Williams, *Dessa Rose*
       Marita Golden, *A Woman's Place*
1987: Gloria Naylor, *Mama Day*
       Toni Morrison, *Beloved*
1989: Marita Golden, *Long Distance Life*
       Tina Ansa-McElroy, *Baby of the Family*
       Terry McMillan, *Disappearing Acts*
       Alice Walker, *The Temple of My Familiar*
1991: Paule Marshall, *Daughters*
1992: Alice Walker, *Possessing the Secret of Joy*

Gloria Naylor, *Bailey's Cafe*
Marita Golden, *And Do Remember Me*
Bebe Moore Campbell, *Your Blues Ain't Like Mine*
Terry McMillan, *Waiting to Exhale*
Toni Morrison, *Jazz*
1993:   Tina Ansa McElroy, *Ugly Ways*
Octavia Butler, *Parable of the Sower*
1994:   Louise Meriwether, *Fragments of the Ark*
1995:   Linda Brown, *Crossing Over Jordan*
Bebe Moore Campbell, *Brothers and Sisters*
Ntozake Shange, *Liliane*
Dorothy West, *The Wedding*
A. J. Verdelle, *The Good Negress*

Initially, I gave serious thought to adding a final chapter on the appropriateness of the metaphor—the narrow space and the dark enclosure—to the novels listed above, but they would not cooperate with the brief discussion I attempted to write, and understandably so. To make them appendages to a study written thirteen years ago— to graft them as new skin onto the old—would be counter to the black feminist platform that calls for a close reading of our texts. Hence my decision to list the new novels without discussing them.

Moreover, to remain true to the organizational schema of the book, discussion of the new novels would need to be preceded by an overview of developments in this nation during the late eighties and early nineties that have had a profound effect on black women. Those developments are major indicators of a conservative mood in the nation that jeopardizes the few gains black women have achieved and, as such, they should receive careful attention.

I also gave serious thought to rewriting several sections of the book not only to improve the quality of my writing, but also to take advantage of the insight of recent black feminist scholarship. However, because *No Crystal Stair* is a discrete text of its time and is, therefore, instructive in a number of ways, I resisted the desire to revise.

Early on in my research, I realized that only in a new book could the new novels and the political milieu in which they were created receive the insight of new scholarship as well as the smoother movement of my pen. I believe that this second edition of *No Crystal Stair*, like Barbara Smith's call in 1977 for black women to understand the "absolute necessity" of black feminist criticism, calls for the absolute necessity of an interdisciplinary study of black women's novels written between 1976 and 1996 that examines the interlocking of race, gender, and class in black womanhood in white America. My research on such a needed book has already begun.

INTRODUCTION TO THE FIRST EDITION

Despite Gloria Wade-Gayles's assertion that her study is "not a platform for black feminism" and "doesn't attempt to explain feminist theory or feminist criticism," *No Crystal Stair* is black feminist criticism par excellence. Since the concept of black feminist criticism is elusive, I should like to explore the broader issue of what it means to be a black feminist critic in order to place *No Crystal Stair* in the appropriate context.

In her comprehensive review essay on feminist criticism, Cheri Register argues that the major task of the feminist critic is to illuminate the "female experience." More specifically, "feminist critics look at how literature comprehends, transmits, and shapes female experience and is, in turn, shaped by it."[1] Barbara Desmarais defines feminist criticism as a "corrective, unmasking the omissions and distortions of the past—the errors of a literary critical tradition that arise from and reflect a culture created, perpetuated, and dominated by men."[2] In the first theoretical essay on black feminist criticism, Barbara Smith describes her uneasiness as she attempts to write about black women writers from a feminist perspective, although she acknowledges at the same time that such an approach is urgently needed. Her painstaking definition of black feminist criticism is still useful:

> When Black women's books are dealt with at all, it is usually in the context of Black literature which largely ignores the implications of

sexual politics. When white women look at Black women's works they are of course ill-equipped to deal with the subtleties of racial politics. A Black feminist approach to literature that embodies the realization that the politics of sex as well as the politics of race and class are crucial interlocking factors in the works of Black women writers is an absolute necessity. Until a Black feminist criticism exists we will not even know what these writers mean.[3]

The black feminist critic also works "from the assumption that Black women writers constitute an identifiable literary tradition," which means that "thematically, stylistically, aesthetically, and conceptually Black women writers manifest common approaches to the act of creating literature as a direct result of the specific political, social, and economic experience they have been obliged to share."[4]

Though feminist analysis of women writers became more prevalent during the late 1970s, the need for black feminist criticism became more urgent, according to Deborah McDowell:

Not only have Black women writers been "disfranchised" from the critical works by white women scholars in the "female tradition," but they have also been frequently excised from those on the Afro-American literary tradition by black scholars, most of whom are males. . . . When Black women writers are neither ignored altogether nor given honorable mention, they are critically misunderstood and summarily dismissed.[5]

In her lucid essay on new directions for black feminist criticism, McDowell calls for a clearer definition of "the Black feminist aesthetic" and delineates the major tasks that confront the black feminist critic over the next decade.[6]

Not surprisingly, black women have been more drawn to black women's literature than has any other segment of the population. From the publication of Pauline Hopkins's article "Famous Women of the Negro Race: Literary Workers" (*The Colored American Magazine*, April 1902) to Claudia Tate's recent collection of interviews with black women writers, the black female literary tradition in America has been celebrated in some quarters (although it was ignored, for the most part, by the literary establishment). This celebration has taken place in two phases. The first phase is characterized by efforts to document that such a tradition exists. Frances Collier Durden's master's thesis, "Negro Women in Poetry from Phillis Wheatley to Margaret Walker" (Atlanta University, 1947), is probably the first work that falls into this category. One of the earliest doctoral dissertations to analyze the black female literary tradition (which is different from examinations of images of black women in literature) is Beatrice Horn Royster's "The Ironic Vision of Four Black Women Novelists: A Study of the Novels of Jessie Fauset, Nella Larsen, Zora Neale Hurston, and Ann Petry" (Emory University, 1975). Sharyn Skeeter's "Black Women Writers: Levels of Identity" (*Essence*, May 1973) is better known and reached a broader audience.

The second phase was ushered in by the publication of Mary Helen Washington's scholarly article "Black Women Image Makers" (*Black World*, August 1974). Moving beyond Skeeter's descriptive approach, Washington argued that black women writers are a distinct group not only because of their long history but because unique themes recur in their works. The introduction to her pioneering anthology *Black-Eyed Susans: Classic Stories by and about Black Women* (1975) contains a more detailed analysis of these major themes. Alice Walker's essay "In Search of Our Mothers' Gardens: The Creativity of Black Women in the South" (*Ms.*, May 1974) is perhaps the most eloquent and poignant account of the black woman artist ever written. I should also mention that Walker designed the first course on black women writers, which she taught in 1977 at Wellesley College. Another publication in the second phase was *Sturdy Black Bridges: Visions of Black Women in Literature*, edited by Roseann Bell, Bettye Parker, and Beverly Guy-Sheftall (1979), which was credited with being the "first book-length critical work devoted to a 'minority' literature."[7]

This second phase is also distinguished by the emergence of black feminist literary criticism, notably Smith's and McDowell's work and Barbara Christian's *Black Women Novelists: The Development of a Tradition 1892–1976* (1981), the first full-length study of the novels of black women. The publication of *No Crystal Stair* links Gloria Wade-Gayles to a small but productive body of black feminist critics who "analyze the works of Black female writers from a feminist or political perspective."[8]

No Crystal Stair is a major contribution to the new scholarship on women. It is the first full-length, interdisciplinary study of black women's novels in the contexts of race, sex, and class. Like feminist critics in general, Wade-Gayles analyzes the novels she examines in the context of a particular set of cultural conditions at a given point in time. She subjects these important novels to "rigorous textual analyses," which McDowell argues is essential for the black feminist critic.[9] Although Wade-Gayles focuses on conceptual and thematic similarities rather than on stylistic and linguistic characteristics, *No Crystal Stair* provides fresh insights into the nature of black womanhood during the period 1946–1976.

Moreover, the book is revisionist, according to the author, because it deviates in many ways from previous analyses of black women writers. It does not, for example, make the case, as the critic Mary Helen Washington has done, that black women writers create new, nonstereotypical images of black women.[10] Wade-Gayles demonstrates that the uniqueness of the black woman writer is to be found in her complex treatment of race and sex, which is a manifestation of her more sensitive understanding of black womanhood. Wade-Gayles's approach is more similar to that of Barbara Christian, but it is more interdisciplinary because of its reliance on both history and sociology to analyze black women's visions.

Wade-Gayles's most outstanding contribution to feminist criticism is that she provides a coherent conceptual framework for understanding what it has meant to be black and female (and heterosexual) as this experience is portrayed in the literature of black women of the mid-twentieth century. Her use of two central metaphors—the narrow space and the dark enclosure—to illuminate the double burden of race and sex, which is unique to black women, is stunningly perceptive. She describes three circles, asserting boldly:

> In one circle white people, mainly males, experience influence and power. Far removed from it is the second circle, a narrow space in

which black people, regardless of sex, experience uncertainty and powerlessness. And in this narrow space, often hidden but no less present and real, is a small dark enclosure for black women only. It is in this enclosure that black women experience . . . the unique marks of black womanhood.

Sensitive to the significance of gender, Wade-Gayles departs from traditional approaches to the study of black women that result in exclusively racial interpretations.

This study also reminds us that critical works or anthologies dealing with black or women's literature that fail to include more than token treatment of the writings of black women should be considered inadequate. *No Crystal Stair: Visions of Race and Sex in Black Women's Fiction* seriously challenges the male-focused literary canon. It also calls attention to the white focus, which has developed over the past decade in women's literature. To ignore such novels as Paule Marshall's *Brown Girl, Brownstones,* Toni Morrison's *The Bluest Eye,* and Alice Walker's *The Third Life of Grange Copeland,* which are brilliantly analyzed in *No Crystal Stair,* is to deprive oneself of an extraordinary literary experience. Learning to know Silla Boyce, Pauline Breedlove, and Mem Copeland, to name only a few of the most memorable characters in this study, enables us to understand significant aspects of American culture and many of the most complex dimensions of the human experience.

To be sure, *No Crystal Stair* was written for black women and black men. It deals honestly and sensitively with the issue of sexism within the black community. It lays bare the problematic nature of black male–female relations; however, this thorny issue is always analyzed within the context of a racist, sexist, capitalist social order. *No Crystal Stair* also refuses to idealize relations between black women themselves; while it discusses the importance of bonding among us black women, it reveals the fragile state of black sisterhood. Much too frequently class and color differences separate us and make our relationships painful. I hope that white women will also find *No Crystal Stair* useful, for it illustrates the radical ways in which the lives of black women and white women diverge in America, despite our common gender. Zillah Eisenstein's sensitive comments on the following pages make this point more eloquently. I hope too that black men will agree with Alton Hornsby's acknowledgment in the Afterword that this book is a significant contribution to scholarship and, I add, to dialogue between black men and black women.

Finally, *No Crystal Stair* is a celebration of black women writers and their collective vision of the human condition. They have much to say to all of us.

Beverly Guy-Sheftall
Director
The Women's Resource and
Research Center
Spelman College
Atlanta, Georgia
January 1984

A PERSONAL RESPONSE

Gloria Wade-Gayles's *No Crystal Stair* is an experience with black women writers and black women's literature that takes the reader inside the complex, painful, and struggling reality of black women. It is a study of the visions of black women by black women writers through the inside lens of a black woman. It is a gift to black women and, even more so, to white women because it shares the intimate thoughts, visions, and desires of black women. The intimacy is there to experience. You do not have to build it; you merely have to be willing to feel it. But to receive fully the intimate pain of racism and patriarchy in these black women's lives, we white women have to become conscious of our own white privilege, to be aware that we are part of black women's pain. Even when we do not mean to be, we are part of what denies black women their lives. We, as white women, inevitably are in black women's way as they struggle for their own reality. If we can come really to understand what this means and focus on this tension, we can also build through it, around it, even in it. No (white) feminist has the right not to read this book.

No Crystal Stair was not written for white women but was written with us in mind. It was written in hope of erasing the dominance of white privilege. As such, the white woman is often the outsider, so that the inside of black women's lives can be seen. In order for white women to be able to hear and see black women we must explore these inner realms of black women's lives and accept that we are the outsider. We need to know—or imagine—or try to imagine what it means to be a black woman. It is impossible for a white woman to know what it is to be black or to experience black women's realities exactly as they do, but we can come close. We must try to get as close as possible. *No Crystal Stair* helps us (white feminists) in that endeavor.

Gloria Wade-Gayles's book is a marvelous and much-needed literary study of the peculiar reality of black women as both black and female. The "peculiar" reality is defined by the specific way that both sex and race define black women, as different from, and yet similar to, white women. Wade-Gayles, as well as the authors she analyzes, is often angry at the way white women and their standards limit and define the understanding of what life is like for black women. She, as well as the black women writers she analyzes, has to construct their identity within the confines of racism and patriarchy, but they are never completely determined by the reality. It is the process of *how* they create their reality as black women against the backdrop of racism, patriarchy, and economic class privilege and how they feel about this situation that exemplifies the specific realities of black women. *No Crystal Stair* lets us experience these realities.

No Crystal Stair depicts black women in white America as "twice burdened" and "doubly invisible." They are twice burdened because they are both black and female; they are doubly invisible because of the way a racist, white, patriarchal society tries to erase their presence. "Regardless of class, black women are defined in this nation as a group *distinct* from black men and *distinct* from white people *only* by the double jeopardy of race and sex." Wade-Gayles uses this idea of double jeopardy to present an insider's narrative of black women's lives. She constructs a vision of reality that recognizes and encompasses black women's complexities.

The discussion in *No Crystal Stair* moves back and forth between describing the reality of *the* black woman and constructing the realities of black women. This is done with a keen sensitivity to the way economic class further particularizes black women's experience, often adding to blackness and femaleness the harsh burden of economic need. Although Wade-Gayles's focus is on the way sex and race define each other to limit black women's lives, her discussion always moves further along. She is wonderfully sensitive in her treatment of black motherhood. Black women, as mothers, have various and conflicting feelings about their motherhood—ambivalence, pain, strength, and so on, like Toni Morrison's Eva, in *Sula*, who takes her son's life because "it was too painful for her." Wade-Gayles also discusses black women as domestics who "edge into life through the back door," who are surrounded by the darkness of racism and poverty. In the end she presents us with different visions of black women: those "going nowhere immediately" who lead lives of submission and despair, those who are "giving birth to themselves" and challenge all limitations to do so, and those who try and sometimes make it and other times don't. She gives us a depiction of black womanhood and also makes clear that there is no such abstract category as the black woman.

Gloria Wade-Gayles as a black woman and a feminist lets black women speak for themselves. It is a time when black and white women's lives are becoming more similar. As white women join black women in the labor force and as heads of single-parent families, it is terribly important for us all to understand the specific differences that exist within our similarities.

Black women speak for themselves in this book. White women need to read it, think it, feel it, act on it. It is a gift to us, whether it was meant to be or not.

Zillah Eisenstein
Author of *The Radical Future of Liberal Feminism* (1981)
Ithaca College
January 1984

TO THE READER

This is not a book about joy and comfort, wealth and power, true romance and fairy tales that end with everyone living happily ever after. It is a painful book to read; it was a painful book to write. It is a book about the impact of racism and sexism on the reality of black women in white America and indirectly on the reality of those whom black women love—black children, black men, and other black women. As such it is a book about all of us, for who in this country is not touched in some way by black women's lives? But since it examines black women in literature rather than in real life, perhaps it is only a book about *fiction*. Perhaps.

chapter 1

THE NARROW SPACE OF RACE, THE DARK ENCLOSURE OF SEX

The Case for This Book

> But what's all dis here talkin' about? Dat man ober dar say dat women needs to be helped into carriages, and lifted ober ditches, and to have de best place every whar. Nobody ever help me into carriages, or ober mud puddles, or gives me any best places . . . and ar'nt I a woman? Look at me! Look at my arm! . . . I have plowed, and planted, and gathered into barns, and no man could head me—and ar'nt I a woman? I could work as much as a man when I could get it, and bear de lash as well—and ar'nt I a woman? I have borne five chilern and I seen 'em mos' all sold off into slavery, and when I cried out with a mother's grief, none but Jesus heard—and ar'nt I a woman?
>
> —Sojourner Truth, 1853, in Elizabeth Cady Stanton,
> *History of Woman's Suffrage*, 1881

When black feminists challenge an exclusively racial interpretation of black womanhood, they claim a legacy of struggle and achievement begun in the nineteenth century and passed on from generation to generation of black women. These women knew how to articulate their insistence on change, on liberation, with passion and intensity, for they were rewinding and playing at high octaves the speech Sojourner Truth delivered at a gathering of white women who neglected to see black women as *women*.

Baring her breasts and giving witness to her strength and to her humanity, Sojourner Truth challenged the absence of black women from the roll of new women voters being prepared at the time. The refrain of her question—*"Ar'nt I a woman?"*—resonated for black feminists in the seventies because the axes of power and influence that turned in Sojourner Truth's world were turning, though in different ways, in the seventies and creating three circles of reality in our nation. There is a large circle in which white people, most of them men, experience influence and power. Far away from it is a smaller circle, a narrow space, in which black people, regardless of sex, experience uncertainty, exploitation, and powerlessness. Hidden in this second circle is a third, a small, dark enclosure in which black women experience pain, isolation, and vulnerability. These are the distinguishing marks of black womanhood in white America.

Unlike other groups in white America, black women are twice burdened. Because they are *black*, they are denied the pedestals and petticoated privileges a racist and sexist society assumes to be appropriate "gifts" for women. Because they are *women*, they are denied the power and influence men enjoy as the "natural" (or God-decreed) heads of families and leaders of nations. Black women are thus confined to both the narrow space of race and the dark enclosure of sex. This "double jeopardy" has created a complex, painful, and dehumanizing reality in which they have struggled for both freedom and selfhood. Like the speaker in Langston Hughes's "Mother to Son," black women in real life have found it "kinder hard" to survive and achieve in places "where there ain't been no light," and often they have been able to measure their progress only by the "corners" they turn and the "landin's they reach." Life for them "ain't been no crystal stair."[1]

And yet their unique position in American culture is often ignored or minimized in studies of the impact of race and sex on American values, lifestyles, and economic groupings. In histories of the black experience, for example, the women are either background figures refracted in a monolithic mirror of blackness and maleness, or they are extraordinary leaders such as Sojourner Truth, Harriet Tubman, Charlotte Hawkins Brown, and Frances Harper, who just happened to be women.

The picture is not significantly different in women's history. Works by white scholars—whether men or women—concentrate on the oppression of white women in a male-dominated culture and relegate black women to footnotes that can easily be missed. Even in contemporary feminist scholarship the identity of black women as "women" is less important than their identity as "blacks," for white feminists often compare their own oppression to that of "the Negro." The truth of Gerda Lerner's statement is therefore irrefutable: "belonging as they do to two groups which have traditionally been treated as inferiors by American society—Blacks and women—[black women] have been doubly invisible. Their records lie buried, unread, infrequently noticed and even more seldom interpreted."[2]

If scholarship ignores black women, mythology makes them its most colorful subject. An intricate web of misconceptions and stereotypes defines black women in many roles and, simultaneously, creates the monolithic "black woman." She is

> Sapphire. Mammy. Tragic mulatto wench. Workhorse, can swing an ax, lift a load, pick cotton with any man. A wonderful housekeeper. Excellent with children. Very clean. Very religious. A terrific mother. A great little singer and dancer and a devoted teacher and social worker. She's always had more opportunities than the black man because she was no threat to the white man so he made it easy for her. Curiously enough, she frequently ends up on welfare. Not beautiful, rather hard-looking unless she has white blood, but then very beautiful. The black ones are very exotic though, great in bed, tigers. And very fertile. If she is middle-class, she tends to be uptight about sex, prudish. She is unsupportive of black men, domineering, castrating. Very strong. Sorrow rolls right off her brow like so much rain. Tough, unfeminine. Opposed to women's rights movements, considers herself already liberated.[3]

The problem of understanding the anomalous position of black women in America is further complicated by the tendency to interpret their reality exclusively in racial terms. As incredible as it might seem, images that are unmistakable sexual caricatures or that clearly relate to the sexual roles of wife and mother are often presented as interpretations of blackness, not womanhood. Such a reading of black women is tantamount to suggesting that the age-old problem of "woman's place" never took hold in the black experience. The suggestion is a gross misinterpretation of American history and culture, for race and sex are the main axes on which power and responsibility have always turned in this country. It is fatuous thinking to suggest that racial oppression vitiates the sexual consciousness of black women, for our gender is the first syllable of our name and sexual roles are the very core of our functioning in society.

As Angela Davis explains in *Women, Race, and Class* (1981), class is also an axis, if not the central one, for when groups are denied or given power on the basis of race and sex, the intent and the results are economic in nature.[4] Zillah Eisenstein makes a similar argument when she writes that "capitalist patriarchy requires racial oppression alongside sexual and class oppression." While all women are oppressed in a capitalist patriarchy, Eisenstein writes, "what they share as sexual oppression is differentiated along class and racial lines in the same way that patriarchal history has always differentiated humanity according to class and race." To see "sex or class, or race or class, or sex or race" is to misread the nature of oppression in this country. We must see "the process and relations of power. If we direct ourselves to the process of power we can begin to learn how and why women are oppressed, which is the first step in changing our oppression."[5]

While I agree with Eisenstein, I believe the tendency of scholars to study only the narrow space, which often means the "ghetto," and, therefore, to see black women through the lens of race and class blurs the lines that distinguish them from other groups, i.e., black men, white women, and white men. This calls, I submit, for a shift in emphasis from race and class to race and sex. I do not mean to deemphasize class or, for that matter, to remove it from the equation of oppression. Poverty is the most egregious exploitation. Nor do I mean to suggest that we can always distinguish between class oppression and racial and sexual oppression, for the lines of distinction are sometimes faint or even nonexistent, and, as Eisenstein explains, they are made by the "process and relations of power" that affect the lives of all people in this country. Rather, I am emphasizing a point often missed in studies of the black experience and studies of class oppression: regardless of class, black women are defined in this nation as a group *distinct* from white people and *distinct* from black men *only* because of the double jeopardy of race and sex.

Since American culture is a mosaic of regional differences, I discuss black womanhood as it reflects such differences. Especially for southern black womanhood is this kind of focus necessary. As Beverly Guy-Sheftall explains, the South "has been and continues to be a predominantly bi-racial society. . . . The consequences of this bi-racialism . . . have been exaggerated forms of racial and sexual stereotyping and the creation of strong social constraints along race and sex lines." Moreover, because of the economic condition of the South, black women have been "relegated to a permanent domestic caste."[6] This fact has created tension between black women and white women and conditioned many black women to cope with life as it is rather than struggle to make it what it should be.

Whether they accept or challenge the negative images "others" have of them, black women are not blind to their position in this society, which has "taught" them that "the Negro's skin and the woman's sex are prima facie evidence of subjection,"[7] and they know that theirs is a triple subjection. In Maya Angelou's words, they "are caught in the tripartite crossfire of masculine prejudice, white illogical hate, and Black lack of power";[8] and because they hear the loud thunder of this crossfire repeatedly, many black women have been forced to sacrifice their own creativity and lead severely circumscribed lives.

Writing a book about racism and sexism, two highly charged subjects in American culture, is like navigating between Scylla and Charybdis. When you think you have steered the analysis around the most difficult assumptions about black womanhood, you find yourself faced with new ones. They are many in number, and they are problematic.

One is the parallel between sexual oppression and racial oppression which obliterates differences between them. As early as 1860, Elizabeth Cady Stanton drew such a parallel in the suffrage movement. "Prejudice against *color,* of which we hear so much, is no stronger than that against *sex* [italics added]," she wrote. "It is produced by the same cause, and manifested very much in the same way."[9] Without equating racial and sexual oppression as Stanton did, Gunnar Myrdal, in a special appendix on women in *An American Dilemma* (1944), observed striking similarities between the mistreatment of woman and the mistreatment of blacks. And in the 1970s white feminists made their case with the analogy of "women as niggers."[10] They argued that women and blacks "have shared a collective experience of being assigned a set of attributes and responsibilities on the basis of a physical characteristic and, as a result, each has been denied fundamental rights of citizenship, including access to political, economic, and educational opportunity."[11]

The analogy is problematic in many ways. First of all, it makes women synonymous with being white and black synonymous with being male. Second, it fails to acknowledge major differences between the "attributes and responsibilities" assigned to gender and those assigned to race and, worse, the "attributes and responsibilities" assigned to black women by virtue of their double identity. Third, it fails to acknowledge that differences in the assigned "attributes and responsibilities" translate in different degrees of denial of opportunity. Given their double identity, black women would, of necessity, experience the most grievous denial.

For obvious reasons, white women are implicated in both the narrow space and the dark enclosure. Because of their race, they have identified with the "master" and with the "majority race" that holds power. Because of their gender, they have vicariously experienced power and influence through their husbands and fathers. Indeed, they have participated actively, and without coercion, in the oppression of black men and women. They have been "ladies" who lived in leisure because black women have been "mammies." They have been protected and pampered, while black women have been dehumanized, brutalized, and devalued as blacks and as females. Calvin Hernton writes:

> When any group of women has to submit to ... atrocities, when they are denied the smallest privacy of body, when they have to stand in public before men and women naked on an auction block

and be fingered in the most intimate places, it is absurd to ask
them to esteem themselves. . . . The fiber of the human personality
is not that independent of the milieu in which it has to struggle for
sanity. It was in this way, then, that the Negro woman during
slavery began to develop a depreciatory concept of herself not only
as a female but as a human being as well. She did not have much of
an alternative.[12]

White women were victims of the peculiar institution of slavery,
but they were beneficiaries as well, and it is as beneficiaries that many
black women see them. In fact, the indictment of white women as
racist is so prevalent in the thinking of most black people that even
when white women put their lives on the line for black liberation,
they are seen as the women who sleep with "the man," who give birth
to new generations of "the man," and who socialize each new generation to take power. The metaphorical equation of race and sex, therefore, comes dangerously close to minimizing the sufferings of black
people in general and black women in particular and, in so doing,
loses what relationship it has to truth.

Moreover, national images of white women, though sexist in nature, place an impenetrable barrier between them and their so-called
sisters in oppression. White women are fragrant, dainty, and feminine
ladies whom white America has placed on a pedestal. In the media,
their hair moves like softly blown silk, accentuating blue eyes and chis-
eled features. Even when they are pictured at work ("woman's work,"
of course), they are immaculate in ruffled aprons and manicured nails.
By contrast, black women, imprisoned in the racist images of the obese
mammy, the unkempt welfare mother, and the hip-shaking woman
of the street, are neither dainty nor feminine and certainly not pretty.
White women are "the driving forces behind every man . . . and the
valued sex objects."[13] Black women are devalued sex objects and, as
Sapphires and Caledonias, castrating women who exacerbate the powerlessness of black men. Since the history, present reality, and national
images of black women and white women diverge radically along racial and class lines, it is sometimes necessary to speak of them as "step-
sisters" in one oppression and antagonists in another.

Given the complexity of black womanhood, black men are "brothers" in the narrow space of race, but they can have a very different identity in the dark enclosure of sex. There black women often struggle against them and because of them. However, seeing black men as "enemy" is as flawed a reading of our struggle as white women's analogy of the "woman as nigger." When this becomes our angle of analysis, we render ourselves unable to dislodge, and remove, the distrust of feminism that is evident in the black community. The truth is that for many black women, women's liberation is one thing and feminism is another altogether. The former they believe in; the latter they reject, in part because they see it as a concept created by white women and applicable only to white women's reality, the center of which is hatred for men. White women have ownership in this distrust not only because of the history of their relations with black women, but also because, empowered by their race, they determine how the nation interprets feminism. As a result, their designation of men as "enemy" is attributed to black feminists. When this attitude takes up residence in the thinking of some black women, they have all the reason they need to remain firm in their opposition to feminism. It reinforces the position, not unique to black women, that women who embrace feminism are bitter, wounded-in-love women; power-hungry careerists; confused bisexuals; or latent lesbians.

We see fear of these labels in Marabel Morgan's call for women to be "total" women who, she explains, do not compete with men. They pretty themselves for men, take delight in cooking for men, and make themselves irresistible sex kittens.[14] For black women, being the total woman Morgan describes is an impossibility, requiring as it does a life of leisure, membership in the right bridge clubs, an executive husband, and money for the best in negligees, fragrances, and coiffures.

But black women have also been caught in the either/or game— either you are a "real" (as opposed to a "total") woman, or you are one of the questionable types in our society. When race is added, the game becomes more serious. Black women are often expected to prove that they are "real" women and also that they will stand by their men. Given this attitude, it is not surprising that more than a few black

women, joining their voices with many black men, responded nega-
tively to Ntzoke Shange's *For Colored Girls Who Have Considered Suicide When the Rainbow Is Enuf*. The problem with the play, they explained, was not its depiction of abusive black men, but rather its
failure to place the abuse in the context of racial oppression. We can
understand what happens in the dark enclosure of sex, they argued,
only if we understand what happens in the narrow space of race.
There was, in their opinion, only one reason for the overwhelming
success of the play: it served white people well by giving a white
woman's man-as-enemy reading of black women's pain. Clearly, what
is operative here is black women's sense of loyalty to black men with
whom they experience oppression in the narrow space of race. This
loyalty is, of course, misguided, but the fact that it exists can be instructive to black feminists as we work to win believers. Attention to
the interlocking of race and gender, which precludes a deemphasis of
race and the designation of black men as "enemy," is politically wise.

In truth, since the beginning of the movement in the seventies,
black feminists have focused on the interlocking of race, class, and
sex, not to win recruits or to curry favor with any group, but rather
to speak the truth about the complex reality of black women in white
America. As women in the Combahee River Collective asserted, "No
one before has ever examined the *multilayered* [italics added] texture
of Black women's lives." To do so, they continued, is to realize the
difficulty, if not the impossibility, of separating "race from class from
sex oppression because in our lives they are experienced simultaneously."[15]

This book examines "the multilayered texture" of black women's
lives in selected novels written by black women artists between 1946
and 1976. However, it is not an attempt to explain black feminist criticism or give a theoretical analysis of the novels. Instead, it is a literary
study that interfaces the novels with history and sociology. In lieu of
a feminist study of the interlocking of race, gender, and class in black
women's lives, and even with such a study, fiction by black women
instructs us in and sensitizes us to the complexity of our unique reality, for double jeopardy has been a dominant theme in black women's
fiction since its earliest beginnings. For more than a century, black

women writers have "documented the feminine heart"[16] that beats in an ebony frame. From the publication of Harriet Wilson's *Our Nig* in 1859, the first-known novel written by an American black woman, to the publication of Gayl Jones's *Eva's Man* in 1976, black women writers have created memorable characters who ask, either *sotto voce* or stridently, "Ar'nt I a woman?" and black? Sometimes they speak in metaphors: "De nigger women is de mule uh de world."[17] Other times they release soul-drenched rage: "All I keep hearing is you all talking about the hard time a colored man's got. But what about the *colored woman?* What about her?"[18] Always they are aware that theirs is a double jeopardy.

As I use "feminist" in this book, it means any approach to black womanhood that identifies sexism as a problem, whether major or minor, and calls, either explicitly or implicitly, for wider options for women—for space in which they can create themselves as persons. I believe that the writers whose novels I discuss are feminists in this sense. Writing from the inside, they turn traditional images of black women inside out and upside down, exposing them as poor reflectors of the truths of black women's humanity. The writers take us into the minds of their women characters, where, in the silence of their thoughts, the women define their own humanity as something far larger than the sum total of roles and images created by others.

My examination of black women's literature does not suggest that fiction can substitute for a history of black women in real life. Fiction never equals fact. But it does mirror fact, and in a profound way it is "an interpretation and compilation of history, anthropology, sociology, psychology, and a host of other areas"[19] that puts us in touch with the sound and sense of real life. The highly respected historian William Chafe makes this point emphatically when he defends his use of "the interior perspective of fiction" in *Women and Equality: Changing Patterns in American Culture* (1977). Chafe writes:

> Despite the problems created by using a novel for purposes of
> historical analysis, the interior perspective that is offered outweighs
> the limitations of subjectiveness. . . . In the case of both women and
> blacks, novels provide a vividness of detail and personal experience

necessary to understand the larger processes at work in the society, but for the most part unavailable in conventional historical sources.[20]

Barbara Smith, a black critic whose writing on black women's fiction has significantly raised the consciousness of many black women, uses the same reasoning as Chafe. She writes, "The untraditional methods might be the only way to proceed in a field where there is barely any published data to consult." But unlike Chafe, whose use of fiction by black men betrays either an ignorance of black women writers or a male orientation to scholarship, or both, Smith adds that "books by black women authors are the richest written source [of information on black womanhood] because in the creation of the work, we can assume that little has stood between the black woman and the telling of her story."[21]

It is significant for another reason to understand "the telling of her story": Black women writers, like white women writers, have suffered the "silences" of which Tillie Olsen writes. These "silences" are not

> *natural* silences—that necessary time for renewal, lying fallow, gestation, in the natural cycle of creation. They are unnatural: the unnatural thwarting of what struggles to come into being, but cannot. In the old, the obvious parallels: when the seed strikes stone; the soil will not sustain; the spring is false; the time is drought; . . . the frost comes premature.[22]

Because of double jeopardy, black women have suffered an "unnatural thwarting" of their creativity far more than white women have; only twenty-six major novels by black women have been published over a period of three decades. And when their "seeds" have struck soil rather than "stone" and they have created memorable works, black women writers have been given recognition begrudgingly or not at all. Until the late sixties they were, in fact, second-class citizens in literary scholarship. Like most black male writers, they were excluded from the mainstream of literary scholarship because of their race. And because of their sex, they were not among the privileged few black writers chosen by the system as worthy of some attention. Even when critics began in the late fifties to acknowledge the existence of black women writers, they preferred, as Alice Walker has noted, to "talk about [their] lives . . . , not about what they wrote."[23]

. Heightened interest in women's issues in the late sixties made black women writers legitimate, significant, and worthy of literary awards. In fact, some critics (most of them male) now say that the black woman writer's double jeopardy has become a double asset: she is potentially a major writer in the market of women's literature and in the market of black literature. The question they now ask is, "Where are the black male writers?" Other critics, many of them black women, believe that the new interest in black women's literature is only a fad, just as the celebration of black writers during the Harlem Renaissance of the 1920s was a fad. They are reminded of Langston Hughes's words when the Renaissance ended:

It was the period when the Negro was in vogue.

I was there. I had a swell time while it lasted. But I thought it wouldn't last long. . . . For how could a large and enthusiastic number of people be crazy about Negroes forever?[24]

Many women are concerned that interest in black women writers has not had an impact on the lives of black women in this nation. Again they are reminded of Hughes's observation:

But some Harlemites thought the millennium had come. They thought the race problem had at last been solved through Art plus Gladys Bentley. . . .

I don't know what made any Negroes think that—except that they were mostly intellectuals doing the thinking. *The ordinary Negroes hadn't heard of the Negro Renaissance. And if they had, it hadn't raised their wages any* [italics added].[25]

Perhaps black women writers are only "in vogue," and perhaps when the national mood changes they will once again be ignored as artists. But we cannot impose the past on the present or see with certainty into the future. We know only that, for the first time in the literary history of this nation, black women writers are receiving the attention and applause they deserve as artists. Gwendolyn Brooks, Ann Petry, Dorothy West, Carolyn Rodgers, Paule Marshall, Toni Cade Bambara, Mari Evans, Alice Walker, Toni Morrison, Gayl Jones, and other gifted black women writers are finding their way into anthologies, national magazines, learned journals, and, most of all, into a community of readers celebrating the discovery of a rich tradition of black women's literature which gives voice to the black woman as artist and as subject.

A dominant theme in this literature, writes Claudia Tate in *Black Women Writers at Work*, "is the quest theme—a character's personal search for a meaningful identity and for self-sustaining dignity in a world of growing isolation, meaninglessness, and moral decay."[26] Tate continues:

> Black women writers project their vision of the world, society, community, family, their lovers, even themselves, most often through the eyes of black female characters and poetic personae. Their angle of vision allows them to see what white people, especially males, seldom see. With one penetrating glance they cut through layers of institutionalized racism and sexism and uncover a core of social contradictions and intimate dilemmas which plague all of us, regardless of race or gender. Through their art they share their vision of possible resolution with those who cannot see.[27]

Of the twenty-six major novels written by black women between 1946 and 1976, twelve cut most brilliantly "through layers of institutionalized racism and sexism" and take us to the core of black women's humanity. Listed chronologically, they are as follows:

1946: Ann Petry, *The Street*
1948: Dorothy West, *The Living Is Easy*
1953: Gwendolyn Brooks, *Maud Martha*
1959: Paule Marshall, *Brown Girl, Brownstones*

1969: Sarah Wright, *This Child's Gonna Live*
1970: Louise Meriwether, *Daddy Was a Number Runner*
       Toni Morrison, *The Bluest Eye*
       Alice Walker, *The Third Life of Grange Copeland*
1973: Toni Morrison, *Sula*
1975: Gayl Jones, *Corregidora*
1976: Gayl Jones, *Eva's Man*
       Alice Walker, *Meridian*

All these novels have been well received by the general reading public and by critics, and many have been excerpted in reputable anthologies of American literature in general and black American literature in particular. They are not novellas or novelettes, and they are not adolescent fiction. It is necessary to underscore this point because much of the fiction written by black (and white) women is often placed in either or both of these categories.

The twelve novels draw portraits of black women who accept their racial identity as distinct from black women who "pass." Our understanding of this painful decision is limited, for we have fixed in our minds the image of Pinky in the film *Pinky* (1946), who passes for white with the assistance of her black mother, who, ironically, serves as Pinky's maid. The reality is much more complex than Hollywood suggests. It can be argued that black women characters who "pass" should be included in this book because they are responding to the impact of race and sex on their lives. However, their existence in a white environment makes it inappropriate to include them. To understand the complexity of black womanhood, we must first understand the lives of black women who function in black situations; we cannot understand black women who "pass" until we fully understand the reality they choose to reject. Black women in black situations, then, are the subject of this book. They come from different regions, family sizes and structures, and economic conditions. They are southern/rural women and northern/urban women; married women and divorced women; women with one child and women with many; poor women and middle-class women; churchgoing women and whorish women—black women with individual frustrations, needs, and dreams.

With the exception of two minor characters, the women are heterosexuals. This sexual homogeneity does not mean that lesbianism is not a theme in black women's literature. To the contrary, there are significant black lesbian novels that are on the cutting edge of sensitivity to human sexuality. However, as a distinct group in black women's literary history, they were not written between 1946 and 1976.

For historical integrity, I begin with an overview of black women in real life from 1946 to 1976. In addition to considering the political and economic developments that shaped the lives of black women in these decades, chapter 2 discusses interpretations of black women in the popular media and in scholarship, and demonstrates how these interpretations are corroborated, qualified, extended, or seriously undermined by black women's novels.

Chapters 3–6 sketch the four levels of consciousness that so sharply define the postures of the women toward race and sex that they serve the aims of the book more effectively than would a chronological scheme. In chapter 3, "The Halo and the Hardships: Black Women as Mothers and Sometimes as Wives," I look carefully at the experiences of women characters who are either wives or mothers or both. These roles dominate the visions of the novels discussed, but they are important for another reason: they are the roles in which women are always defined as women and often limited as persons. According to traditional myth, women who are married are "more woman" than women who are single, and mothers are the very epitome of womanhood, even if they are not married. In approaching the women from these perspectives, I am not suggesting that sexual roles define them and racial experiences are only minor points in those definitions. I focus on sexual roles quite simply as an effective way of locating the women where they are as women, and proceeding from there to examine their total reality.

Chapter 4, " 'Going Nowhere Immediate': Black Women of Hopelessness," concentrates on women who are so burdened by their race, sex, and class that they resign themselves to their "place," wishing only to survive with as few problems as possible.

Chapter 5, " 'Journeying from Can't to Can' and Sometimes Back to 'Can't': Black Women of Challenge and Contradiction," deals with women who wrestle with the ambiguities of their dilemma, articulating strong objections without ever finding the courage to sustain a struggle for change.

Chapter 6, "Giving Birth to Self: The Quests for Wholeness of Meridian Hill and Sula Mae Peace," examines the lives of two women who spit in the eye of the Furies and demand to define themselves and name their reality.

The concluding chapter, "The Space and the Enclosure: Analysis of the Collective Vision," moves in and out of the different novels to illumine further the narrow space of race and the dark enclosure of sex in which the imaginative women are confined and in which many of them struggle to give birth to self.

The period of the study—World War II to the present—is a fertile one, mainly because the war had a tremendous impact on the reality of blacks and women in this country. In the case of blacks, the war precipitated a large-scale migration from the rural South to the industrial North, laying the foundation of today's black urban culture. And because the war was a struggle for "freedom and democracy" abroad, it intensified the impatience of blacks with the absence of freedom and democracy at home, giving rise to organized resistance to segregation. For women, the war opened doors to employment in munitions plants and other factories, temporarily suspending assumptions about the female role. By the time the war ended, the die had been cast, for many women refused to return to their "place" and even went on to explore wider options. The war so raised the level of consciousness of blacks and women that it seeded the national soil for the civil rights movement of the fifties and sixties and the black power movement of the seventies, as well as the women's liberation movement of the sixties and seventies.

Individually and collectively, the novels take us into the narrow space of race and the dark enclosure of sex where black women characters speak for themselves, and to us. They tell a story we are familiar with. It is our grandmothers' story; our mothers' story; the story of black women we live with and work with; the story of others we know only from the annals of history or the back pages of our nation's newspapers; and it is our own story. It is a poignant story in which race and gender are engaged in a *danse macabre* for control, and the women, seeing the dance, respond in various ways.

chapter 2

A HISTORICAL OVERVIEW

Black Women in White America, 1946–1976

> I
> am a black woman . . .
> strong . . .
>   impervious
> indestructible . . .
>   —Mari Evans, 1964

World War II forced the American tradition of sexual and racial discrimination to give way to the crisis of national survival. As soon as the war was in progress, Robert Brisbane explains, it was clear that victory was dependent on the country's willingness to make concessions to its minority groups. For blacks, these concessions were reflected dramatically in unprecedented gains in the labor market. Although early in the war years there was resistance to the employment of blacks in war factories, by the middle of the war, under pressure from the Fair Employment Practices Commission and other government agencies, blacks were visible in defense plants throughout the nation. In significant numbers they were employed in aircraft, shipping, iron, steel, and other industries that thrived in the wartime economy. Employment gains were not limited to defense plants, however. Blacks worked in various war-service agencies, in hospitals, in retail stores, and in civil service positions, doubling their number in the last category.[1]

The need for labor had an equally weighty impact on employment patterns for women. Indeed, there was such a drastic change in
the nation's attitude toward "woman's place" that the "war marked a
watershed in the history of women at work, and, temporarily at least,
caused a greater change in woman's economic status than half a century of feminist rhetoric and agitation had been able to achieve."[2] Six
million female workers were employed during the war years in jobs
that had previously been identified as too strenuous for the "weaker
sex"—hard labor in munitions plants, aircraft factories, the auto and
steel industries, and other industries that met the needs of the war.
"In eight of ten war-impacted cities surveyed by the Women's Bureau, the number of women workers doubled from 1940 to 1945."[3]
Over a period of fourteen months, women made up 80 percent of
new workers, and in many cities the number of women employed in
factories by 1944 exceeded the number of women in the entire labor
force in 1940.

Black women were well represented in these statistics, a major
departure from the American tradition that had excluded them from
gains extended to black men and white women. Involvement in the
labor market, however, was not a new experience for black women.
They were "twice as likely to be employed as [white women] but their
economic horizons were severely limited. Over seventy percent
worked as domestics in white private homes, and another twenty
percent toiled in the fields, picking crops and hoeing gardens on small
farms."[4]

During the war, however, more than four hundred thousand black
women left their jobs as domestics to work alongside white women
in defense plants throughout the nation. "Rosie the Riveter," the national symbol of female strength and patriotism, though depicted in
the media as a white woman, was often black. As the percentage of
black females who worked as domestics dropped from 72 to 48, and
the percentage who labored on farms dropped from 20 to 7, the percentage of black women who worked outside those areas increased
from 7.2 to 18.6.[5] Sociologist Delores Aldridge writes that the gains
were not confined to factories. The number of "black women employed in clerical and sales positions quadrupled . . . and the number

of black women in federal service positions also increased significantly."[6] No longer confined to domestic and farm work, black women experienced during the war what perhaps amounted to "economic liberation."[7]

These gains for blacks and for women did not mean that racial and sexual discrimination disappeared from American life. When discrimination could be practiced without directly jeopardizing America's success in the war, it was practiced. Many of the jobs held by blacks in war factories, for example, were the traditional ones of janitor and scrubwoman; for white women, clerical and sales jobs remained high on the list of possibilities. Moreover, as John Hope Franklin documents, there were major differentials between the wages paid to whites and the wages paid to blacks. In *Women and Equality*, historian William Chafe, writing of the plight of women, makes the same point: men were paid more than women for the same jobs. And as visible as the two groups became in the labor market, they were not seen in upper-management positions.[8] They were the workers, not the policymakers. Since black women belonged to both minority groups, they were at the bottom of the labor hierarchy, and they earned the least.

This high visibility of women in the labor market—for white women a new experience and for black women an old experience slightly upgraded—did not create a raised sexual consciousness or new cultural definitions of "woman's place." White women worked because war needs left vacuums in the manpower pool that, out of patriotism, they had to fill. And they worked because they realized, as did their husbands, that one income was hardly sufficient for a comfortable standard of living. After the war, when white female workers "were asked why they wished to continue on the job, a total of 84 percent cited 'economic need,' or the desire to assist with family support. Only 8 percent, in contrast, gave the need for self-expression or dissatisfaction with the traditional role of women in the home."[9] This new reason for white female participation in the labor market was the old reason that had always forced black women into the role of helpmate for their struggling families. In one sense, then, the war and subsequent inflationary trends narrowed the gap between the reality of black women and the reality of white women. But the gap remained cavernous because black women, even in their so-called economic liberation, were discriminated against in the labor market, both in positions offered and in salaries earned. Barriers that had held them back for centuries had been only momentarily lifted and had then fallen back in place. It is not surprising, therefore, that at the end of the war "black women were the first to be fired . . . and through economic need were forced back into domestic and other service jobs."[10]

The late forties was a period of well-considered and carefully executed plans for racial progress as gains made during the war intensified the efforts of blacks to achieve complete integration in the nation. In fact, as Robert Brisbane documents, there was an aggressive black posture toward change even during the war. Black organizations, notably the National Association for the Advancement of Colored People (NAACP), pushed for desegregation in the armed forces, in employment, in housing, and in education. As early as 1946 President Harry Truman appointed a committee of nationally known black and white leaders (the majority of them men) to study ways to improve the status of blacks in the nation; and in 1948 he endorsed the committee's report, *To Secure These Rights*, and engineered its inclusions in the Democratic party platform of that year.[11]

Acting often without support from established organizations, black women and men took their case for freedom to the nation. Though they did not brandish the Black Power fist that would become popular in the late sixties, they were no less insistent on power and change. In 1946 a black woman named Irene Morgan challenged segregation in interstate travel when she refused to move to the back of a bus on a trip from Gloucester County, Virginia, to Baltimore. Her challenge led to the Supreme Court decision of *Morgan* v. *Virginia* in June 1946, which prohibited segregation in interstate bus travel. A year later the Congress of Racial Equality (CORE) tested the strength of the decision by sending the first group of "freedom riders" in history into the South. In 1946 the Supreme Court ruled that "a state must provide legal education for blacks at the same time it is offered to whites." This ruling, like CORE's famous freedom rides, resulted from the courage of a black woman, Ada Sipuel, who in 1946 filed to attend the University of Oklahoma Law School.[12] There were other major rulings in the late forties, but what is often missed in the recitation of these landmark cases is the presence of black women as "movers and shakers."

While blacks and liberal whites sought to disrobe Jim Crow, Jane Crow was bedecked in pearls. For several reasons the pearls could not be removed, or even dulled in their shine. First of all, as discussed earlier, there had been no major challenge to sexual discrimination during the eventful years of "accomplishment" for women during the war. Second, the resurgence of racism after the war, as evidenced in race riots and demonstrations, minimized the significance of the woman's question for black Americans—indeed, for the entire nation. Any discussion of the woman's question by black women could easily have been perceived as "bitching" during a time when black men, still in uniform, were being brutally attacked in cities across the nation and, when not attacked, discriminated against in housing, employment, and public accommodations. And third, the exigencies of life in northern ghettos pushed the issue of sexual liberation into a holding pattern.

Lured by jobs in the war industry, blacks left small southern farms to migrate in sizable numbers to cities in the South and, most especially, in the North, increasing the size and aggravating the problems of the ghettos that had come into existence at the turn of the century. Overcrowding, exploitation, poverty, crime, and violence were pervasive and unchecked in black communities in Chicago, Detroit, Cleveland, Newark, Philadelphia, and, of course, Harlem. But the existence of these large black communities gave blacks more political power than they had known since Reconstruction. In several northern cities they held the balance of power in close elections. Their votes were sought by politicians and, recognizing this, blacks established their own mini-machines and made demands on the white political machines. It did not seem to matter to black women, who carried more than their share of burdens in the ghetto,[13] that black political leaders and black newly elected officials were male. Like the men of their race, they believed that political success for a few blacks would aid in ameliorating the plight of all blacks.

The wartime gains for women were short-lived, for "almost immediately after the war ended, a concerted campaign developed among political leaders, the media and employers to persuade women to return to the home."[14] In 1947, the same year that President Truman set up the Civil Rights Commission, a special issue of *Life*, then a barometer of national opinion, called woman's confusion about her role a national crisis. As Chafe explains, "There was no middle ground, no way to combine marriage and a career, a job and motherhood. A woman became either a well-adjusted homemaker or a feminist neurotic."[15]

Just as white women such as Phyllis Schlafly and Anita Bryant would oppose women's liberation in the seventies, so white women opposed new roles for women in the fifties. Helene Deutsch, a Freudian psychoanalyst, argued that women and men are "polar opposites whose spheres . . . ordained them to remain permanently separate."[16] Her work had a greater impact on the nation than did the profound scholarship and insight of Simone de Beauvoir's brilliant *The Second Sex* (1953), which was poorly received by critics and by the reading public. Two well-known critics "called the work paranoiac," and Margaret Mead, though impressed with "its basic soundness, expressed annoyance with de Beauvoir's denigration of the role of mother."[17] Everywhere the signs were clear and the bell's tolling was resonant. The "feminine mystique," about which Betty Friedan would later write, muted the cry for women's liberation for more than a decade.

The postwar climate was symbolized by Adlai Stevenson's remarks to white women college graduates. This pillar of the liberal establishment advised young women that their task was to push their men into the seat of success by serving effectively in the "humble role of housewife."[18] Moreover, the issue of women's rights was not one to which black women were likely to be attracted. They were aware of the racism that had always marked feminist movements in America. Rosalyn Terborg-Penn writes that from 1830 to 1920, key years in the history of feminism, racism was an unhealing sore on the suffrage and feminist movements. "Discrimination against Afro-American women reformers was the rule," she emphasizes, "rather than the exception."[19] Women of the stature of Frances Harper, Mary Church Terrell, Sarah Remond, Ida Wells-Barnette, and Josephine Pierre Ruffin spoke candidly of their experiences with racist white women reformers, even the legendary Susan B. Anthony, who discriminated against black male and female reformers because it was expedient to put aside racial equality in order to win the support of southern white women. In the late forties and early fifties this attitude, printed indelibly on the psyches of black women, put white women and black women into separate and warring camps. Finally, the aggressive demands of blacks for racial equality militated against the creation of any large-scale organization involving black women and white women as equal partners in a common struggle.

A cursory examination of images of black women in the media during the late forties and early fifties furnishes another explanation for black women's muted interest in women's rights. For when we look beyond employment statistics and political gains to media images, we realize that World War II only scratched the surface of this nation's racist and sexist psyche. This was the era of the "scatterbrained maid or superstitious comic servant"[20] who added color and humor to insipid films about plastic people in plastic situations. This was the era when white America's fascination with the myth of Aunt Jemima made Hattie McDaniel and Butterfly McQueen[21] archetypal black domestics loved by white and black audiences alike. The Aunt Jemima myth had its origin in the South's need to create "passive, long-suffering and submissive" black mammies whose devotion would prove that slavery was not all bad. The myth persists in spite of the fact that, as historians have documented, the typical black mammy was a "young and attached" woman rather than "an aged mammy who remained in her antebellum place out of loyalty to a white family or because whites had a special concern for such women."[22] But overweight, submissive, devoted, older black domestics were the norm in American films of the era, such as *Song of the South* (1946) and *Pinky* (1946).

In the fifties Sidney Poitier began what later became a monopoly on nonstereotypical roles for blacks in the movies. In *No Way Out* (1950) he was a medical intern. In *Blackboard Jungle* (1952) he was a schoolteacher. For black women, however, the old stereotypes held on. In *Imitation of Life* (1951) a black woman appeared as the overweight, apron-wearing, self-sacrificing mother of a tragic mulatto. *Show Boat* (1951) also had its tragic mulatto, but the film was best known as a musical extravaganza that idealized the Old South: William Warfield sang "Ol' Man River," and black women in long skirts and red bandannas swayed, sang, and served white people. To the traditional images of Aunt Jemima and the tragic mulatto, Hollywood added the image of the black woman of sensuality and questionable morals. *Carmen Jones* (1954) and *Porgy and Bess* (1954) were laudable attempts to depict with sensitivity the complexity of black life, but both were variations on the old theme of the juice being sweeter when the berry is blacker.

It was in the fifties that "television became the most popular new form of entertainment. Whereas in 1947 there were 10,000 television sets in American homes, ten years later the figure was 40 million. Television had such a major impact on the 'leisure-time habits' of people in this nation that, in 1954, the 'TV dinner' was invented."[23] The effect for blacks was that larger numbers of Americans were indoctrinated with the old images on a regular basis. It was a television series, *Amos 'n Andy*, that presented the most negative images of blacks. The black man in the series is a head-scratching, shiftless, henpecked husband. His wife is a "Sapphire"—loud-mouthed, strong-willed, and practical. Barbara Christian writes:

> Sapphire's most salient quality is her ability to make black men look like fools, partly because she is unfeminine, that is, strong and independent, and partly because she is, by nature, emasculating. Although similar to the mammy, Sapphire is not so much maternal toward white folks as she is unfeminine in relation to black men. To them, she is, cold, hard and evil.[24]

According to bell hooks, "Sapphire's shrewish personality was used primarily to create sympathy in viewers for the black male lot" and in the present day "is projected onto any black woman who overtly expresses bitterness, anger and rage against her lot." Indeed, it is such a dominant image, hooks writes, that it has caused many black women "to repress these feelings for fear of being regarded as shrewish Sapphires."[25]

Given these pervasive negative images of black women, a national black agenda that ignored the reality of sexism, and American preference for the "feminine mystique," it is not surprising that Frances

Harper's nineteenth-century assessment of the respective importance of race and sex in the reality of black women of that day was equally applicable in the late 1940s and early 1950s. When it came to choosing between sex and race, Harper said, "the lesser question of sex [had to] go."[26]

It "had to go" in the fifties for yet other reasons. The outbreak of the Korean War in 1950 fashioned new priorities for the nation, but, more important, the acceleration of court cases, demonstrations, and racial violence heightened the black community's commitment to change. Thus when we study the historic civil rights movement of the sixties and the black power movement of the seventies, we must begin with a careful examination of the fifties.

In 1950 Ralph Bunche became the first black American to win the Nobel Peace Prize, and a year later Mary Church Terrell took her place in history alongside other black women activists when she won a case against segregation in restaurants in the nation's capital. In 1951 the worst northern race riot since the infamous one of 1919 took place in Cicero, Illinois, when a black family attempted to move into an all-white neighborhood. A year later, in 1952, racist bombings increased significantly in the South. In 1954 the landmark Supreme Court decision in *Brown* v. *Board of Education* outlawed "separate but equal" educational facilities, thereby overruling the Court's earlier decision in *Plessy* v. *Ferguson* (1896). In that same year, with the death of Terrell, the nation lost one of its most valiant and persistent black women reformers. In 1955 a wave of lynchings swept the South after the brutal murder of Emmett Till, and Mary McLeod Bethune, a creative black woman educator and shrewd political leader, died in Daytona Beach, Florida. It was also in 1955 that Rosa Parks, a black seamstress in Montgomery, Alabama, refused to give up her seat at the front of a city bus.[27] Her courage was the seed of the Montgomery bus boycott, which catapulted Dr. Martin Luther King Jr. into national prominence.

By the beginning of the sixties the Montgomery movement had given birth to a nationwide civil rights movement that would have far-reaching effects on blacks and women in this nation. In 1960 four students "sat in" at a segregated lunch counter in Greensboro, North

Carolina. After that first sit-in, others followed, and soon there were wade-ins, kneel-ins, and freedom rides—successful nonviolent protests against segregation all across the South. On May 6, 1965, with the signing of the Voting Rights Act, the hopes of the movement for a new society were bolstered. Blacks and whites, committed to the philosophy of nonviolence eloquently articulated by King, came together for a common cause in greater numbers than at any other period in history. Students, Hollywood and Broadway stars, ministers, musicians, Ivy League professors, and professional athletes gave their time, talent, and, in some instances, their lives to the realization of the dream King immortalized in his "I Have a Dream" speech, delivered at the March on Washington in August 1963.

It was an exciting decade characterized by visibility for black male leaders: Andrew Hatcher, Robert Weaver, James Pearson, Thurgood Marshall, Edward Brook, Leroy Johnson, Carl Rowan, and Walter Washington, to name only a few. They took their places in history as the first blacks in various prominent offices or positions. Black male leaders were also impressively visible in the movement. The roll call included Julian Bond, Eldridge Cleaver and Huey Newton, Elijah Muhammad and Malcolm X, Stokely Carmichael and H. Rap Brown, Wyatt T. Walker, Ralph David Abernathy, Jesse Jackson, Floyd McKissick, and, of course, Dr. Martin Luther King, who received the Nobel Peace Prize on December 10, 1964. To this list we can add the names of Constance Baker Motley, only the second black woman in history to be appointed a federal judge, and Shirley Chisholm, the first black woman elected to Congress.

If the roll of black leaders was predominantly male, so, too, was the obituary page of American history in the sixties. In a wave of violence—lynchings, brutal beatings, and assassinations—black men were victims: Mack Parker, Medgar Evers, James Chaney, Malcolm X, and King. Violence also claimed the lives of activists Viola Liuzzo, Andrew Goodman, and Michael Schwerner, and President John F. Kennedy, all of whom were white. The "river of blood" that flooded the nation not only in assassinations but also in race riots (Watts in 1965, Cleveland in 1966, and Newark in 1967) explains why Dr. W. E. B. DuBois before his death on August 17, 1963, in Accra, Ghana, relinquished his citizenship in a nation that was unwilling to make a commitment to justice. He gave up on America because he saw

> more clearly than yesterday that back of the problem of race and color lies a greater problem which both obscures and implements it: and that is the fact that so many civilized persons are willing to live in comfort even if the price of this is poverty, ignorance and disease of the majority of their fellowmen.[28]

The sixties was a decade as complex as it was violent. It was a time when students agitated for free speech on university campuses across the nation, forging into existence a new academe that would bear the scars of the students' rights movement well into the eighties. It was a time when revisionist sexologists such as William H. Masters and Virginia Johnson called the nation's attention to the need to redefine the sexuality of both men and women. And it was a time when the nation's image at home and abroad was marred by an irrational war in Southeast Asia.

These upheavals were, in large part, catalyzed by the civil rights movement that had begun in 1955 with the courage of a black woman, but the movement's agenda was too simple to deal with "the problem of the color line." In retrospect, participants decry their emphasis on integration, which did little to alleviate the lot of the masses of black people in America and much to advance middle-class blacks, who would, in the seventies and eighties, become entrenched in the system. The ghetto, it seems, had become a permanent part of the reality of urban black people, and a culture of poverty limited the horizons of blacks on small farms. "Almost four out of ten . . . black families were living in poverty in 1965. This compares with a poverty ratio of about one out of ten in white families." Further, poverty was more likely in black families headed by women: "In 1965, sixty-two percent of the 1,132,000 [black] families headed by a woman were poor. Of the 3,860,000 white families headed by a woman [only] thirty percent were poor."[29]

In 1964, 32.5 percent of black female workers were employed in private households as domestics, compared to 4.9 percent of white women; and 23.4 percent were employed in service work (hotels and restaurants), compared to 14.5 percent of white women. Whereas 34.1 percent of white women were employed in clerical jobs, only 11.3 percent of black women were in this line of work.[30] After eight years of vigorous civil rights protests, the black thrust for integration and voting rights had not altered the position of black women in the labor market.

In the study "Family Roles, Occupational Statuses and Achievement Orientation among Black Women in the United States," Walter Allen corrects certain fallacies about black women workers. In 1964 black women, in spite of the era's myth of full employment, were "the most frequently unemployed and had the highest rates of unemployment *regardless* of occupational category." Also, black women earned significantly less than white men, white women, and black men in that order—again, Allen emphasizes, "*regardless* of occupation."[31] In the same year that the civil rights movement began, the statistical profile of the black woman was that "she has a harder time finding a mate, remains single more often, bears more children, is in the labor market longer, has less education, earns less, is widowed earlier, and carries a heavier economic burden as a family head than her white sister."[32]

While it has been historically true that most (though not all) black women tended to identify all discrimination against them as racial in origin, in the late sixties more of them began to examine the burdens that were directly traceable to their sex. Ironically, they did so in Student Nonviolent Coordinating Committees (SNCC), the most militant of the civil rights organizations in the sixties. SNCC was a good starting place for black women's articulation of their dissatisfaction with sexual limitations because it was so blatantly sexist. Though black women were a majority of the membership, the leadership of the organization lay firmly in the hands of black males. One black worker complained that SNCC relegated women, and especially black women, to simpleminded, nonpolicymaking tasks. She wrote that "we run errands, lick stamps, mail letters and do the door-to-door."[33] SNCC's sexist attitudes toward its women members were manifested, but largely ignored by the nation, in the historic March on Washington in August 1963. All the speakers were men. All the delegates who met with the president were men. "This omission was deliberate," writes Pauli Murray. "A group of women had asked for recognition in advance of the march, but their request had been denied because the male leaders of SNCC doubted that women could agree on a delegate—a typical response from an entrenched power group."[34] A year later, in 1964, black women in SNCC staged a sit-in against sexist definitions of responsibilities. They made their point, but they had no intention of insisting on change.

Obviously, there were major problems in the relationship between black males and black females in SNCC, problems that could have generated a women's caucus in the organization. But no such caucus was formed, because black women were not willing to jeopardize progress for their people by insisting on rights for their sex. Nor were they willing to embrace an issue that had always been dominated by white women, especially since relationships between black men and white women in the movement had destroyed the sense of sisterhood that black women and white women thought they shared at the beginning of the struggle. It was only a short time before they came to admit that there were two problems: one was "the man" and the other was the white woman, or more specifically her interest in, if not pursuit of, black men. In "I Have Been Hungry," a poem palpable with anger, Carolyn Rodgers, rejecting the "fancy fierce platitudes" of white women, writes that sisterhood with "you white girl" positions the black woman as "a road/you would travel to my man."[35]

Before they camped as a family of dreamers on Mississippi soil, black women and white women had already been positioned as antagonists by capitalism, which divides and therefore controls and conquers. The dream of the movement and, no less, the historic bitterness between black women and white women genuinely interested in bonding became catalysts for the white feminist movement of the sixties, just as the abolitionist movement was a catalyst for the suffrage movement of the nineteenth century.

When we discuss the cause-and-effect relationship between the civil rights movement and the birth of the women's movement in the late sixties, we cannot ignore the historical animosity between black

women and white women in SNCC, an animosity that had been temporarily mollified by belief in the dream and a genuine commitment
to the creation of a humane society. Many black women activists were
later to admit that their fires of anger burned silently even as they
marched arm in arm with white female volunteers. They wanted
bonding with white women activists, but as black women they had
internalized the assumption that "being feminine meant being
white."[36] Still, the difficulties of living in Mississippi during a summer of violence and fear made *any* definition of "feminine" seem
irrelevant, for the experience was not, at least on the surface, about
male–female relationships; it was a struggle that pulled together into
one family poor black farmers (male and female) and college students (male and female, black and white). Black women and white
women were equals—sisters—in the struggle. Even the old specter
of the white woman's beauty as symbolized by straight hair was not a
problem for black women activists, who walked tall and dignified in
their Afros, a sign of self-acceptance and black pride.

The history of the synergistic relationship between race and sex,
however, was stronger than the workers' commitment to the dream.
There is never a time in this nation, Calvin Hernton explains, when
the "sexualization of racism" can be ignored. It is a "unique phenomenon in the history of mankind," Hernton writes,

> an anomaly of the first order. In fact, there is a sexual involvement,
> at once real and vicarious, connecting white and black people in
> America that spans the history of this country from the era of
> slavery to the present, an involvement so immaculate and yet so
> perverse, so ethereal and yet so concrete, that *all race relations tend
> to be, however subtle, sex relations.* [italics added][37]

It was the "sexualization of racism" that made Mississippi during the
summer of 1963 a veritable playground for many black men and many
white women. As the black "buck" of phallic superiority and the white
woman of beauty, femininity, and chastity played out their historic
attraction for each other, black women were reminded that the nation and black men believed that "being feminine meant being white."

They were participants in the freedom struggle and spectators of interracial sex relations. Their pain was real, intense, and shattering—all the more so since black men and white women were coming together in the very region that had made black women mammies, mistresses, and breeders and white women "the center and circumference, diameter and periphery, sine, tangent, and sextant of all our affections."[38]

In the many articles and books published after the civil rights movement was replaced by the black power movement, black women wrote that they were angered by the menial assignments they were given and by the "extreme insensitivity" of white women, but their deepest anger was directed at the devaluation of black womanhood. This anger permeates Ruby Davis Smith Robinson's paper delivered at a SNCC conference, in which she attacked black men "for their failure to do justice to black women." The counterpart paper, written by two white women, Mary King and Casey Hayden, was one of the opening statements of the women's liberation movement.[39]

As white women were laying the foundations of a major women's movement, many black women were seeking security and an alternative to devaluation in organizations that idealized traditional definitions of "woman's place." In the Nation of Islam, Black Muslim women were required "to accept their men as 'first among equal' and in theory, at least, regard the man as the breadwinner and head of the family."[40] In an analysis of the devaluation of black women, bell hooks discusses the ideology and rituals that made the Nation of Islam one of the narrowest of enclosures for women members. Arguing that throughout history women have been viewed as evil, she sees the persistence of the idea of the purification of women in the Muslim requirement that they wrap their heads in cloth and cover their bodies in long skirts and dresses.[41]

The Republic of New Africa (RNA) went a step further—it required women literally to walk behind their men. Submission to black manhood, wrote founder Amiri Baraka, was a reflection of "the closeness, the completeness we are for each other, the expansion we provide for each other." "Expansion" was hardly what women experienced in RNA. Baraka preached that the salvation of the race could be realized if black men and black women together embraced "a value system that knows of no separation but only of the divine complement the black woman is for her man." He did not cloak in flattering rhetoric his belief that women should be men's helpmates rather than their own persons. His sexist arrogance, albeit in the interest of building a strong black nation, is unmistakable. He wrote:

> We do not believe in the equality of men and women. We cannot understand what the devil and the devilishly influenced mean when they say equality for women. We could never be equals . . . nature has not provided thus.[42]

Many black women were willing to walk behind their men because the women were hungry for the respect and attention they believed whole black men could or would give them. Also, they were sensitive to black men's hardships in the narrow space. But these were not the only reasons for their rejection of feminism. As Michele Wallace explains, "The most popular justification Black women had for not becoming feminists was their hatred of white women."[43] They were obviously caught in the historic dilemma of double jeopardy. As females in a culture that placed white women on pedestals, they wanted a "crystal stair," a reality in which there were no "tacks" or "splinters, and boards torn up." As blacks, they wanted the movement for freedom to improve the lot of their people. Thus they brandished fists at white feminists and invoked the mercy of our ancestral gods for those of us who were feminists and therefore traitors to the race. They stroked the egos of black men whose chauvinism they tolerated as a necessary display of manhood for the time being, and they accepted (and even advanced) the argument that black women would be free as blacks and as women only when black men were in full possession of their manhood. This was the theme of "BLACKWOMAN," one of the most-recited poems of the Black Arts movement. The poet, Don L. Lee (now Haki Madhubuti), wrote that the black woman can be "together/if/he/bes."[44]

At the beginning of the seventies much of the rhetoric of the civil rights movement had grown tired, if not irrelevant to the building of "the nation." Stokely Carmichael's cry for "Black Power" had replaced the movement's hymn "We Shall Overcome," and the glorious, media-supported image of blacks and whites working together in a nonviolent struggle gave way to the threatening image of blacks arming themselves and ousting "whitey" and "honky" from the movement. In "Farewell to Liberals" Loren Miller wrote bitterly of the crisis within the movement: Having brought the movement to a position of power, white liberals received "a fond farewell with thanks for services rendered."[45] Charles Silberman, writing from a different perspective, contended that the breakup of the "friendship" was predictable: "Besides resenting their dependency [blacks] have never really trusted white allies; they have always had a nagging suspicion that . . . they could gain more . . . if they were only free to act on their own."[46] The decade of the seventies, then, like the decade following the abolitionist movement, was a period of tension between blacks and white liberals.

The seventies was also the decade that saw black mayors elected in cities such as Atlanta, Newark, Cleveland, Gary, and the District of Columbia. All the new black mayors were men. Some black women did enter national politics—Shirley Chisholm, Barbara Jordan, and Patricia Harris, for instance—but they were a decidedly small minority. When black men were not going into politics, they were finding their way into upper-management positions in federal, state, and local programs. As one black woman scholar has observed, "When translated into actual opportunities . . . the Movement really meant rights for black men."[47]

The statistical profile of black women in the sixties, given earlier in this chapter, had not changed much. "Black women were still paid lower salaries than white men, white women, and black men, in that order—in the high paying positions . . . in the middle paying jobs, or the low paying jobs." Also, "there [was] proportionately more unemployment among black women than [among] black men . . . at each level of attainment."[48] Although black women had closed the gap between their educational attainments and those of white women, they were held to undergraduate degrees, whereas black men were encouraged to attain graduate and professional degrees. "Two

surveys in all fields from all institutions in 1969 and 1970 show that
black women hold roughly 21 percent of these degrees."[49] These statistics relate to middle-class black women, and they show that middle-
class status did not alter black women's positions at the bottom of
the wage ladder and the power structure. And for poor black women,
who were the majority, the statistical profile Pauli Murray drew of
them in the sixties was just as applicable in the seventies. They still
had a "harder time finding a mate," stayed "single more often," received lower wages, bore more children, stayed "in the labor market
longer," were "widowed earlier," and carried "a heavier economic burden as a family head than [their] white sister(s)."[50]

The seventies was also the decade when black women in greater
numbers than ever before expressed explicitly and publicly an interest in their reality as women. *The Black Woman*, the first book in history that pulled together black women's views on black womanhood,
was published at the beginning of the decade. Significantly, the anthology was edited by a black woman, Toni Cade Bambara. In her
powerful preface to the book, addressed to black women, Bambara
speaks of the need "to unify" and "to get basic with each other." This
requires, she explains, that black women "find out what liberation
for ourselves means, what work it entails, what benefits it will yield."
It also requires that black women turn away from their traditional
role of entertaining "the enemy: white people, whiteness, or racism;
men, maleness, or *chauvinism* . . . [italics added]."[51]

Other important books or articles on black women followed. Gerda
Lerner's *Black Women in White America: A Documentary History* was
the first major work on black America to deal exclusively with women.
Collected works edited by white feminists included landmark essays
by black women on black women. Pauli Murray's "The Liberation of
Black Women," for example, appeared in *Voices of the New Feminism*
(1970), as did Shirley Chisholm's "Women Must Rebel." The 1973 issue of *Black Scholar* was devoted exclusively to the black woman and
contained, among other major essays, provocative contributions by
Barbara Sizemore and Mae King. The most controversial and courageous book on black women published in the 1970s was Michele
Wallace's *Black Macho and the Myth of the Superwoman* (1978), which

galvanized black women into discussing black men's sexism openly and fearlessly. It remains in a class by itself.

Other significant works written by black women in the seventies were *Beautiful, Also, Are the Souls of My Black Sisters* (1978), the first history of black women in America written by a black woman, and *Sturdy Black Bridges* (1979), the first study of black women as writers and as fictional subjects written from a positive perspective and edited by black women. Major black feminist scholars included Michele Wallace, Gloria Joseph, Toni Cade Bambara, Barbara Smith, Pat Scott, Gloria Hull, Beverly Guy-Sheftall, Bonnie Dill, Miriam Willis, Roseann Bell, and bell hooks.

Given such impressive scholarship on and by black women, it is not surprising that it was in the seventies that black women began to organize as feminists and not exclusively as blacks. As yet, no history has been written of the black feminist movement, for it is but an infant in the story of change in this nation. Therefore one can only speculate, but in an informed way, on the direct and indirect stimuli of the movement. Certainly high on the list of stimuli in this speculative investigation are the blatant sexism of SNCC, the impressive gains made by black women in the sixties, and the high visibility of the white feminist movement.

Less obvious stimuli are the courage, tenacity, and strength of several black women figures during the late sixties. Surely if black women could serve as role models for white women who were hampered by race, class, and culture in achieving total identification with black women, they could be real role models for black women. Angela Davis was such a model. She did not espouse the cause of the women's movement. Her involvement with the Black Panther Party, and especially her struggle to free the nationally recognized Panther George Jackson from prison, left her little time for a cause that would not alter the plight of her brothers. However, she did see black women as a separate group within the race. Her courage in becoming a fugitive from America's capitalistic system of injustice afforded a renewing experience to black women, and her charge to her "sisters" to step forth as leaders and fighters is often seen as a call for black women to assert their personhood:

We, the black women of today, must accept the full weight of a legacy wrought in blood by our mothers in chains. As heirs to a tradition of supreme perseverance and heroic resistance, we must hasten to take our place, wherever our people are forging on towards freedom.[52]

The late Barbara Jordan, the brilliant and politically astute congresswoman from Texas, fearlessly pushed for truth in the Watergate proceedings until Richard Nixon was forced to resign. She did not speak about women's rights. Her behavior was her statement, and it carried a strong message about female independence, self-confidence, and assertiveness.

The statement of Shirley Chisholm, on the other hand, was explicit—perhaps too explicit for the times. A congresswoman from New York, she had the audacity as a black woman to run for the presidency in 1972 and, in her campaign speeches, the boldness to challenge the sexism of all men, regardless of color or class. Before there were any formal organizations of black feminists, Shirley Chisholm exhorted black women to put aside their loyalty to black men—a loyalty that demanded the postponement of women's rights until black men had won "black rights"—and recognize that racism and sexism are inseparable battles of equal urgency: "I say there is no need to fight two battles; we should fight [racism and sexism] at the same time."[53] She was the first black woman to break publicly with the tradition of rating sexual inequality as "the lesser question." In her autobiography, *Unbought and Unbossed* (1970), she wrote, "Of my two 'handicaps,' being female put many more obstacles in my path than being black."[54] It is worth noting here that the male members of the Congressional Black Caucus were hostilely opposed to Representative Chisholm's bid for the presidency.

A fourth stimulus for black feminism was Fannie Lou Hamer. Uneducated, one of twenty children born into a Mississippi sharecropper family, the mother of two, Hamer was a rare woman. Race, sex, and class she pushed aside, asserting in magnificent ways her personhood, her humanity. She was a speaker at the 1964 Democratic Party Convention and a candidate for Congress from her state. As an older woman in SNCC and a leader in Sunflower County, she was not affected by the sexism of the young black men in the organization. Already a leader before she joined SNCC, she was therefore useful in pushing the Mississippi platform of the organization. She was "not hung up on this thing about liberating myself from the black man," however.[55] She was committed to working on behalf of poor black farmers, regardless of their sex. She had great disdain for white women, for they had abused black women domestics for generations; and she had great disrespect for middle-class black women because they disavowed any identity with lower-class blacks.

Hamer's disclaimer of interest in women's rights aside, she was one of the most liberated and forceful women leaders in the sixties and seventies. She did not wait for black men to assign her tasks in the struggle. On her own, like so many black women of courage in history, she put her shoulders to the plow and pushed where pushing was needed, refusing to take a back seat to anyone. She founded the Freedom Farm Cooperative, which grew from 40 acres of land in 1969 to 680 in 1971; which fed 1,500 people in 1969; and which owned 168 houses in 1971. Until her death, she was the head of the Coop. When Fannie Lou Hamer spoke of the kinds of roles black women should play in the racial struggle, she referred explicitly to leadership roles.

The growing body of major sociological studies of the black family, notable among them the work of Andrew Billingsley, should receive credit for the raised consciousness of black women in the seventies, for it provided significant scholarship on black women as wives, mothers, and workers. Daniel Patrick Moynihan's *The Negro Family: The Case for National Action* (1965) inadvertently created a new school of sociological thought with its thesis that most of the socioeconomic problems blacks encounter in white America are created by the matriarchal structure of the black family rather than by racism. The countless articles and books written in opposition to Moynihan's thesis sounded the death knell for the theory of black female control and castration that had dominated sociology since the thirties. To be sure, some sociologists wrote, there are black matriarchs, for myth is never totally unrelated to truth. "Culture creates a mystique and real women fill its roles."[56] But the new studies of the black family went inside the myth and documented that the black matriarchy was not a deviant structure, did not explain the so-called deterioration of the black family, and did not reflect a penchant on the part of black women to castrate their men. Other studies disavowed the existence of a black matriarchy altogether and documented black women's powerlessness within the family, along with their response to burdens unique to their reality as wives and mothers.

And finally, the success of the white feminist movement contributed immeasurably to the formation of black feminist organizations. For if the sixties was the decade of black protest, the seventies was most assuredly the decade of women's liberation. The feminine mystique had been stripped of its apron, petticoat, pearls, and bra, and its mascara was conspicuously smeared. White women marched and petitioned, as black people had done in the sixties. They organized caucuses for the Equal Rights Amendment (ERA) in states across the nation, supported the right to abortion, agitated for a fuller understanding of rape, founded magazines, and wrote books on sexual oppression in America. History made room for "herstory." The dialogue on women's issues was intense, full of energy and conflict, but often so abstract that critics of the movement called feminists Ivy League intellectuals who could not translate theory into concrete, realizable goals. Marxists, socialists, liberals, radicals, lesbians, or simply women activists—the groups were many, and their disagreements on priorities and perspectives resulted in brilliant books and articles that would guide the movement in the eighties to what Betty Friedan calls the "second stage." Friedan's own book *The Feminine Mystique* was popular among "laywomen"; the new books found an audience mainly among women scholars. They demonstrated that Friedan had raised only peripheral questions about sexual oppression in America and had failed to address head-on the issues that were at the core of a vision of a new society for all people, regardless of race or sex. Works by Zillah Eisenstein, Kate Millett, Shulamith Firestone, Susan Brownmiller, Sheila Rowbotham, and Adrienne Rich raised tougher questions for white women in the movement.

Still, herstory was essentially white. This, according to bell hooks, was in keeping with a tradition among white women: "Every woman's movement in America from its earliest origin to the present day has been built on a racist foundation."[57] Angela Davis underscored the racism of the suffrage movement by printing in its entirety a letter to the *New York Times* from Elizabeth Cady Stanton, the preeminent suffragette:

> The representative women of the nation have done their uttermost for the last thirty years to secure freedom for the negro; and as long as he was the lowest in the scale of being, we were willing to press his claims; but now, as the celestial gate to civil rights is slowly moving on its hinges, it becomes a serious question whether we had better stand aside and see "Sambo" walk into the kingdom first.[58]

Such blatant racism was not present in the women's movement of the seventies, but white feminists, like nineteenth-century suffragettes, were "the representative women of the nation," and they were known to recite the "uttermost" they had done for blacks in the struggle for liberation. And they *had* struggled for black people in courageous ways, but black feminists were not impressed enough to ignore what they considered a tradition of racism in the women's movement. They insisted that white women own up to their racism, be held accountable for it, and exorcise it from their attitudes, platforms, and ideology. They did not accept Adrienne Rich's argument that charging white women with racism "impedes any real discussion of women's instrumentality in a system which oppresses all women and in which hatred of women is also embedded in myth, folklore, and language."[59] They would work toward bonding with white women only if white women dealt honestly with their conditioning as whites in a racist society. For bell hooks, feminists must be

> willing to examine woman's relationship to society, to race and to American culture as it is and not as we would ideally have it be. That means confronting the reality of white female racism.[60]

The case against white feminists was not helped by the fact that they owned the printing presses, that they had the "right" connections, that they were writing the books (and getting them published), and that they held positions of influence at white eastern universities. It did not matter that this edge, so to speak, was created by a racist system rather than by individual white feminists themselves. What mattered was their inability, or failure, to understand black women as women. What mattered, too, was the history of black women as devalued persons in the dark enclosure of sex and the narrow space of race. Black women owned no printing presses, had no power to affect media images, had few "right" connections, and were in only a few rare instances in positions of power and influence in predominantly white eastern universities. Most black women were struggling with survival issues at historically black colleges and were so overextended by the workload at those institutions that they could not spare time for extensive research and scholarship. It is easy to understand why black feminists were reluctant to join a movement that was predominantly white in origin, leadership, attitudes, and ideology.

Moreover, black feminists could see little evidence that the gains of the civil rights movement and those of the women's movement had improved national understanding of black womanhood. Ironically, while white women were educating the nation on sexist images of women in the media, the media were thriving on negative images of black women. Some of the most popular shows during this period were ugly reminders that black women were still devalued in American society. In *Sanford and Son* (Aunt Esther) and *The Flip Wilson Show* (Geraldine), the black woman was depicted as oppressive and disagreeable. In *Saturday Night Live* she turned up in various comical guises, impersonated by the token black male in the cast. In movies, black women were pitiful creatures hungering for the attention of a macho man (*Superfly*) or religious fanatics falling for transparently devious games played by men, and even sensuous women, powdered down, rouged, and/or nude (*Cotton Comes to Harlem*). Melvin Van Peebles's *Sweet Sweetback*, a highly popular movie made during the sixties, used black women as minor characters without complexity and humanity, which was all the more painful since the film deals with a black man's obsessive desire for white women.

For all the reasons speculated on here (and many others as well), more than three hundred black women met in San Francisco in January 1973 and founded Black Women Organized for Action (BWOA). In December of that year four hundred black women founded the National Black Feminist Organization (NBFO) in New York. Both organizations acknowledged the relevance of many of the issues addressed by white feminists, but they rejected the idea that their reality was the same as that of white women. The Combahee River Collective articulated the new ideology with compelling clarity. Black women, they wrote, live

> in structural opposition with a dominant racial and a dominant sexual group. In each subordinate group they share potential common interests with group co-members, black men on the one hand and white women on the other. Ironically, each of these is a member of the dominant group: black men as men, white women as whites.[61]

This was such a radical departure from the ideology of the sixties, which had left the anchor of black male dominance undisturbed and unchallenged, that, understandably, it drew vociferous charges of disloyalty from many black men. The best defense against black feminism, they seemed to believe, was a reminder that in the narrow space of race black men and black women share a collective history of oppression. From this vantage point, they argued, it was clear that black women were pawns in a national conspiracy against black men. Without data to support their claim, they were convinced that black women, used to meet racial and sexual quotas in the world of work, were robbing black men of jobs. In all their critiques of black feminism, black men disclosed how narrowly they read liberation. When Robert Staples wrote that a "movement that augments sex-role antagonism extant in the black community will only sow the seed of disunity and hinder the liberation struggle,"[62] he was, in essence, recognizing the existence of only the male gender and only the racial liberation struggle. His response was not unlike Imamu Baraka's declaration in *Muanamke Mwananchi* that women were created to be submissive to men, or the unwritten slogan of SNCC which held that "the only position for women in [the organization] was prone."[63] Having been in the prone position, literally and figuratively, throughout history, black feminists in the seventies were determined to stand tall and give birth to themselves as whole persons.

Barbara Sizemore spoke for black feminists when she put an end to black women's silence on sexism, writing in italics and caps about the suffering of black women, especially poor black women, in the dark enclosure. We have suffered, Sizemore explained, because black men "have been socialized into male superiority."[64] Her essay "Sexism and the Black Male," published in 1973, was the precursor of a body of black feminist writings on sexism in the black community that would appear in the seventies. Alice Walker's poem "He said come/Let me exploit you"[65] was the most poignant. In prose, Michele Wallace's *Black Macho and the Myth of the Superwoman* was the most courageous.

Unlike Sizemore's essay and other black feminist studies that focused on the black community in general, Wallace's book focused on the movement in particular. It was the needed response to the SNCC "slogan" about the prone position of women in the organization. The "brother" with his "baaad" Afro whom Nikki Giovanni in the sixties had described as "the same ol danger/but a brand new pleasure"[66] was, in Wallace's view, a "narcissistic macho" who expected "a big Afro, a rifle, and a penis in good working order" to be all the weapons he needed "to lick the white man's world."[67] She writes that he

> has become a martyr . . . not because of the dependency inflicted
> upon him in slavery, but because his black perspective, like the
> white perspective, supported the notion that manhood is more
> valuable than anything else.[68]

With anger moving her pen, Wallace asks for the courage that change requires when she writes: "Can we afford to sit by and allow [sexist black *men*] to orchestrate *our* future?"[69] For black feminists in the seventies, the answer to this question was a resounding "No." In "A Black Feminist's Search for Sisterhood," published three years before *Black Macho and the Myth of the Superwoman*, Wallace drew clearly the lines of our new battleground:

> We exist as women who are *Black* [italics added] who are *feminists*
> [italics added], each stranded for the moment, working indepen-

dently because there is not yet an environment in this society remotely congenial to our struggle—because being on the bottom, we would have to do what no one else has done: *we would have to fight the world* [italics added].[70]

The fight for black feminists who were lesbians was particularly challenging, for not only were they black and women in a nation that meted out power to men and to whites, but they were also lesbian in a nation that privileged and empowered heterosexuals. Women in the Combahee Collective who, in 1977, wrote "A Black Feminist Statement" identify themselves as lesbians, but they focus on the struggle of all black women, regardless of sexual orientation, rather than on their struggle as lesbians. An incisive and insightful analysis of the interlocking of race, gender, and class in white America, their "Statement" was the clearest and most compelling manifesto for black feminist organizations and action published in the seventies. That women in the Combahee Collective called for unity in the black community around all race, gender, and class underscores the extent to which black men's resistance to feminism was an expression of their refusal to give up power. In contrast to Robert Staples's contention that black feminism exacerbates male–female conflict in the black community, there are these poignant words from Combahee:

Although we are feminists and lesbians, we feel solidarity with progressive Black men and do not advocate the fractionalization that white women who are separatists demand. Our situation as *Black people* [italics added] necessitates that we have solidarity around the fact of race, which white women of course do not need to have with white men, unless it is then negative solidarity as racial oppressors. We struggle together with Black men against racism, while we also struggle with Black men about sexism.[71]

In the nineteenth century, Sojourner Truth stood tall before a gathering of white women, exposed scars that slavery had inflicted on her, and, in an unwavering voice, identified herself as *woman*. Any plans the women were making for women's liberation, then, Sojourner explained, could *not* exclude her and others like her. In the seventies, we black feminists stood tall before the entire nation, exposed scars unique to us as black women, and, in an unwavering voice, named ourselves *feminists*. As *feminists*, we charged ourselves to struggle against oppression in the narrow space of race and also, if not especially, in the dark enclosure of sex. Doing so would position us as warriors in all the places where oppression brutalizes people, for we believed then, and believe now, that "if Black women [are] free, it would mean that everyone else would have to be free since our freedom would necessitate the destruction of all systems of oppression."[72]

Having seen in this historical overview the impact of race, gender, and class on the lives of real black women between 1946 and 1976 and the various responses women made to the impact, we turn informed and sensitive to the visions of black women in the twenty-six novels written during those three decades. While we must avoid the unforgivable mistake of seeing literature as sociology artistically rendered, we must at the same time acknowledge the fact that fiction often mirrors reality; and in that it *particularizes* reality, fiction can reveal aspects of the human experience that our conditioning, our prejudices, and our imprisonment in space and time conceal from us. In the novels under study, black women live in a fictive world that is both similar to and different from our own, and they function in that world in ways that are both similar to and different from our own. We hear the women breathe and sigh.

We enter their thoughts, their dreams, their fantasies. In a word, we enter their world and come to *know* them as individuals uniquely themselves. It is in this knowing of their lives that we are made more sensitive to the lives of real black women in white America.

chapter 3

THE HALO AND
THE HARDSHIPS

Black Women as Mothers
and Sometimes as Wives

"I didn't mean that, Mamma. I know you fed us and all. I was talkin'
'bout something else. Like. Like. Playing with us. Did you ever, you
know, play with us?"

"No time. They wasn't no time. Not none. Soon as I got one day
done here comes a night. With you all coughin' and me watchin' so
TB wouldn't take you off and if you was sleepin' quiet, I thought, O
Lord, they dead and put my hand over your mouth to feel if the
breath was comin' what you talkin' 'bout did I love you girl I stayed
alive for you."

—Toni Morrison, *Sula*, 1973

Because women are biologically capable of bearing children, it is assumed that all women look to motherhood for fulfillment in life.
Nine months of discomfort, hours of painful labor, years of physical
and emotional exhaustion—all this women endure and welcome because motherhood, they are told, more than any other experience
they can have, makes them "beneficent, sacred, pure [and] . . . nour-
ishing."[1] It is "a sacred calling"[2] that confers upon women an untarn-
ishable halo. And once is not enough, for "what is more precious in
all this wide world/than a baby—unless it is two?"[3]

The myth of the "sacred calling" was one of many sexist assumptions that Simone de Beauvoir challenged in *The Second Sex* (1953).

Writing of the cultural conditioning of women for an "inward, passive, and simply present existence,"[4] de Beauvoir posited that the institution of motherhood assists in the conditioning. She was well ahead of her times, for it was not until the late sixties that her ideas struck a responsive chord among women scholars. By the decade of the seventies, these ideas were dominant themes in many works of "herstory." Adrienne Rich's *Of Woman Born: Motherhood as Experience and Institution* (1970) is one of the most provocative of these works. It examines "cracks in [the cultural mask] of motherhood"[5] and makes mockery of the myth of the "sacred calling." Distinguishing between the "institution" of motherhood and the "experience," Rich argues that there are profound differences between what women are programmed to expect in motherhood and what they often experience. The institution of motherhood is a "system which recorded civilization has never actively challenged, and which has been so universal as to seem a law of nature."[6] The institution confers on men the titles of father, breadwinner, and protector, but it demands of them few of the responsibilities associated with parenting. The care of children and the home is assigned mainly to females—either mothers, grandmothers, neighborhood women, or female children. The work entailed is neither recognized nor recompensed, for "what a woman does as wife or mother in her own home is considered a labor of love, is not defined as work by the society, and is not done for direct wages."[7] This is as it should be, according to the myth, for why should one be paid for responding to one's "sacred calling"?

Moreover, the institution of motherhood paints a picture of "Sistine tranquillity" and creates images of mothers as "Madonnas who are . . . calm in their fulfillment."[8] When we look beyond these myths into the reality, Rich writes, we often find the opposite of tranquillity and fulfillment. For in the experience of motherhood many women are besieged by supreme boredom, frequent depression, recurring rage, and an unsettling feeling that their intellectual powers are atrophying. The institution of motherhood is based on the sexist assumption that women have "maternal instinct rather than intelligence, selflessness rather than self-realization, relation to others rather than interest in self."[9] While the experience necessitates maternal care, understanding, and service to others, it does not quiet the stirrings in women's souls for self-actualization and for personal accomplishments outside the role of mother. Indeed, it often pushes women from the center of their dreams.

The theory of motherhood as both institution and experience is applicable to the reality of black women, but in the alembic of race, sex, and class, it is altered significantly and enmeshed in complexity: black women are "mammies," but they are no less imbued with "maternal instinct rather than intelligence, selflessness rather than self-realization, relation to others rather than interest in self."[10] Indeed, racist interpretations of the black experience, undergirded by sexist interpretations of motherhood, place the myth of the "sacred calling" in high relief in national images of black mothers. Just as "all black people can dance," so can all black women become superhuman mothers, not only for their own people, but for white people as well. More than white women, the assumption goes, black women look to motherhood as their chief justification in life; and more than white women, they are physically and emotionally capable of handling the responsibilities associated with it.

In *Tomorrow's Tomorrow* (1971) Joyce Ladner writes that black women are "legendary figure(s) in American thought, . . . stronger than other women and certainly stronger than black men."[11] In many sociological studies of the black family, the legend seems to be a documented fact of life for a large majority of black women. Robert Staples argues this point in "The Myth of Black Matriarchy" when he states that giving birth to a child is "the high point" of a black woman's life and that "motherhood represents maturity and the fulfillment of one's function as a woman."[12] Daniel Thompson makes a similar assertion. In a sociological study of women in a New Orleans ghetto in the seventies, he found that almost all his subjects were self-sacrificing women who saw motherhood "as the only honorable, creative role in which they can reasonably hope to participate."[13] Because of the exigencies of black life in white America, black women have been forced to function heroically in the role, and their heroic functioning is often perceived as fulfillment.

In literature, as in sociology, the strength of the black mother is a dominant theme. Maya Angelou writes of a

> kind of strength that is most frightening in Black women. It's as if a steel rod runs right through their heads down to the feet. And I believe that we have to thank Black women . . . for keeping the Black family alive.[14]

Andrea Benton Rushing, in a study of images of black mothers in poetry, refers repeatedly to a long tradition celebrating "poor and pious women whose outstanding characteristics are self-sacrifice, hard work, and fierce maternal love."[15] To this tradition belongs Langston Hughes's well-known "Mother to Son," written in the twenties and quoted in the title of this book. "Well, son, I'll tell you: Life for me ain't been no crystal stair." And to it also belongs Carolyn Rodgers's frequently anthologized "It Is Deep," written in the seventies:

> . . . she pushed into my kitchen so she could open my refrigerator to see what I had to eat, and pressed fifty bills in my hand saying, "Pay the talk bill and buy some food; you got folks who care about you." . . .
> My mother, religious-negro, proud of having waded through a storm is very obviously, a sturdy Black bridge I crossed over, on.[16]

Daryl Dance, in a similar study of images of mothers in black American fiction, examines "two antithetical views" rather than "a tradition." Using mainly works by black male writers such as Richard Wright, James Baldwin, Leroi Jones, and John Oliver Killens, she discusses the black mother who "brings death and destruction" and the black mother who "brings life and salvation." The former, whom Dance calls Eve, was created by the racist culture of white America. She represses

> the spirit and vitality of her Black men, whether as a result of her blind acceptance of the dictates of white America or her subservience to them. [In the] emasculation of the Black male . . . the Black mother has been unwillingly forced into the role of accomplice.[17]

Having written of the black mother's emasculation of black males, Dance immediately defends the mother's repressive spirit by arguing that it is an expression of her maternal devotion and love. In Dance's description of the black mother, whether she is depicted as an Eve or as a Madonna, we see similarities with the self-sacrificing mother on whom civilization throughout history has bestowed a halo. A more truthful rendering of black mothers, Dance writes, should balance their repressive spirit with their magnitude of character. Speaking almost in monolithic terms, she writes that the black mother

> is unquestionably a Madonna, both in the context of being a savior and in terms in giving birth and sustenance to positive growth and advancement among her people. It is she who has given birth to a new race; it is she who played a major role in bringing a race from slavery and submission to manhood. It is largely because of her that we can look back on the past with pride and look forward to the future with courage.[18]

When we turn our attention to black women's novels written between 1946 and 1976, we find that the writers as a group pay tribute to black mothers who are committed to their families and who are remarkable for their strength, endurance, and achievement. There is no question that black women writers value motherhood in the same way that real black women do—that is, in Thompson's words, as "the only honorable creative role in which they can reasonably hope to participate."[19] We will see this point developed in the novels I discuss in this chapter. We will also see that black women novelists are familiar with the legendary, self-sacrificing, monolithic black woman of history and sociology.

Given these similarities, the contribution of black women novelists to our understanding of black motherhood must lie elsewhere. It lies unmistakably in the fine details of the portraits of mothers rather than in the captions that label them. Able to create fully developed characters in a way that poets are not, the novelists examine the tension that exists between the institution of motherhood and black women's experience of it, keeping central to their vision the interdependence of race, sex, and class. Imbued with an inside understanding of the tension, black women novelists are able, as their male counterparts are not, to distinguish between the mothers' feelings about the role and their functioning in it. They question whether devoted mothers are pleased with their realities, and they search for hidden explanations of the posture of an Eve as well as that of a Madonna. In essence, they are concerned with black women not only as they function in the role of motherhood but also as they dream for themselves outside the role, reject the role, or carry it like an iron-heavy cross.

We see these fine details in the portraits of Mrs. Hill in Alice Walker's *Meridian* (1976), Pauline Breedlove in Toni Morrison's *The Bluest Eye* (1970), Eva Peace in Morrison's *Sula* (1973), Mem Copeland in Walker's *The Third Life of Grange Copeland* (1970), Maud Martha in Gwendolyn Brooks's *Maud Martha* (1953), Silla Boyce in Paule Marshall's *Brown Girl, Brownstones* (1959), and Henrietta Coffin in Louise Meriwether's *Daddy Was a Number Runner* (1970). The complexity of black motherhood becomes apparent as we listen to these women speak for themselves.

In their praise for Alice Walker's *Meridian*, critics understandably focus on the heroine Meridian Hill, for it is in her "quest for wholeness"[20] that Walker examines "the nature of social change and its relationship to the past and the future, a question that [was] at the crux of the Civil Rights Movement."[21] But early in the novel, Walker established that the sense of emptiness that engulfs her mother is a major stimulus for Meridian's quest. She writes, "[Mrs. Hill] was not a woman who should have had children.[22]

As a single woman and a schoolteacher in a small Mississippi town, Mrs. Hill enjoys the "freedom of thinking out the possibilities of her life" (p. 39). It does not matter that these possibilities are rather limited: she can stay in this small town and teach, or she can move to another town and teach. They are her possibilities, and they represent her independence and her personhood. However, the patterns of the lives of the other women in the town raise unsettling questions for Mrs. Hill about her own life as a woman without a husband or children. It is a selfish life, she feels, devoted entirely to sleeping late on the weekends, teaching during the week, and enjoying the material things her life as a professional woman makes possible. The lives of the other women, by contrast, are devoted to the daily tasks associated with the nurturing of children and husbands, and perhaps this devotion gives them that glow of excitement her life lacks. In the glances of other women and of men, Mrs. Hill believes she sees respect, but not approval, and the unalterable judgment that a woman does not have the right to live for herself. Although she is not eager to marry and has no genuine interest in rearing children, she is conditioned to the cultural expectation that makes the role of mother a necessity in the life of a woman. Unable to live outside the culture, she marries. Within the space of a few years, she conceives her first child. The transformation of her life from one of independence to imprisonment is almost immediate. As her body changes during the pregnancy, Mrs. Hill feels "distracted from who she is" (p. 40) and laments that "her personal life is over" (p. 39). Even before she experiences motherhood, she is certain that the "mysterious inner life . . . she had imagined gave women a secret joy was simply a full knowledge of the fact that they were dead, living just enough for their children" (p. 41).

This view of motherhood is not an uncommon theme in black women's fiction, as subsequent discussions will show, but it often operates as a comment on the dynamics of race and class, not of sex. It is also present in sociological studies of real black mothers that are at odds with the stereotypical picture of black women basking in the joys of motherhood. When Camille Jeffers, for example, writes in *Living Poor* (1966) of the frustrations of mothers in a Washington, D.C., housing project, she documents the impact that racism and economics have on the women's aspirations both in the role and outside it.[23] Walker's statement is a departure from this thesis, however, for Mrs. Hill is not poor by the standards of her small Mississippi town. She is, in fact, a privileged woman in her training, speech, manner, and possession of "things" and leisure.

Comparative security, Walker suggests, does not save Mrs. Hill from the fate of her poorer sisters, however, for she is as limited as they are in what she can do with her life once she becomes a mother. Certain fundamentals about the institution cut across class lines:

> The primary role to which black women have been assigned and for which they are perpetually praised is also, paradoxically, the means by which they are cut off from life. Since, in principle, society places motherhood on a pedestal, while, in reality, it rejects individual mothers as human beings with needs and desires, mothers must ... love their role as they are penalized for it. True for all mothers, this double-edged dilemma is heightened for black women.[24]

It is particularly heightened for Mrs. Hill, who reasoned herself into motherhood only because she heard the "praise" and traced the lines of the "pedestal" with hungry eyes. She could not have known the truth hidden from her—that being a mother is like "being buried alive, walled away from her own life, brick by brick" (p. 41). She could

> never forgive her community, her family ... the whole world, for not warning her against children. ... Her frail independence gave way to the pressures of motherhood and she learned—much to her horror and amazement—that she was not even given the right to be resentful that she was "caught." ... There was no one she could cry out to and say, "It's not fair!" (p. 40)

That Walker writes only about Meridian and never informs the reader of other "children" Mrs. Hill births not only emphasizes the mother–daughter relationship that is the stimulus for Meridian's quest for wholeness, but also, and significantly, underscores Mrs. Hill's view of herself as a woman engaged in "a war" against those who did not warn her against children. She rebels by refusing to learn "to cook well ... to braid hair prettily or to be in any other way creative in her home" (p. 51). She rebels by refusing to embrace her children with affection. Walker writes that "in the ironing of [their clothes] ... [Mrs. Hill] expended all the energy she should have put into openly loving them.... In their stiff, almost inflexible garments, they were enclosed in starch of her anger" (p. 73).

The mother's anger is visited upon the daughter, for when Meridian becomes a mother, she echoes Mrs. Hill: "So this . . . is what slavery is like." She dreams of murdering the infant and "to suppress the thought," she "conceived, quite consciously, methods of killing herself" (p. 59). When the novel begins, Meridian has given up the child to join the movement, aborted a second child, had her tubes tied, and, finally, experiencing the wholeness for which she has been searching, becomes a spiritual mother to her people. It is in flashbacks that we see Meridian carrying the weight of her mother's anger. When she "was not preoccupied with the Movement," Walker writes, Meridian's "thoughts turned with regularity and necessity" to her mother who was responsible for the "wave . . . of an almost primeval guilt" (p. 71). Instead of removing the guilt, Mrs. Hill intensified it. "When she tried to express her feelings to her mother, [Mrs. Hill] would only ask: 'Have you stolen anything?'" (p. 49). Without fully understanding why or how, Meridian knows that by being born and remaining alive, she stole "her mother's serenity . . . her mother's emerging self" (p. 51), her mother's life.

Alice Walker's vision challenges the assumption that black women are a monolithic group with the same needs, the same strengths, the same weaknesses, and the same dreams. They are, instead, variegated flowers in a garden of humanity. Some of them have the personality makeup to handle well the experience of motherhood in a sexist culture. Others, like Mrs. Hill, need to be "unfettered by the needs of dependents, or the demands, requirements of a husband. Their spirit is of such fragility that the slightest impact on it [could] cause a shattering beyond restoration" (p. 39). Walker is clear and emphatic in her thesis that for such women there should be alternatives to motherhood.

In *Meridian*, we hear a mother's rageful cry of unfairness. In *The Bluest Eye* (1970), Toni Morrison's first novel, we hear a mother's hymn of resignation. Pauline Breedlove, the mother of two children, copes with emptiness and a sense of unworthiness by believing that her real life will begin in heaven, where God will reward her for carrying the crosses of wifehood and motherhood.

The novel is really the story of Pauline's daughter, Pecola, who covets blue eyes as a symbol of beauty and worth, but, as Barbara Christian writes, "How Pecola comes to want blue eyes demands more than just telling Pecola's story." It demands telling the story of "three hundred years of unsuccessful interface between black and white culture in a small Ohio town."[25] It also demands telling the story of Pauline Breedlove's life as it is shaped not only by this interface but also by sexist assumptions about black women and by class and racial restrictions that undergird those assumptions. As we cannot understand Meridian Hill's guilt without understanding Mrs. Hill's feeling that she has been buried alive by motherhood, neither can we understand Pecola's desire for blue eyes without understanding the equally insane fantasies of Pauline Breedlove.

The novel begins with Claudia McTeer, Pecola's friend, telling us that the story "takes place in the year 1940–41, from fall to fall, in the year when the baby Pecola had by her own father is born dead, in the year when the marigolds did not sprout."[26] "The seeds shriveled up and died," Claudia says; "her baby too."[27] It is Claudia's voice as an adult woman remembering the past that guides us through the incidents in the small Ohio town that tell Pecola's story—how she was raped by her father, how she desired blue eyes, and how she eventually plunged into insanity. In the telling of this story, Morrison uses nature images as headings for the four chapters in the novel. Within each chapter she devotes sections to characters who in some way participated in Pecola's tragedy. Each section begins with familiar lines from Dick and Jane primers that were used in schools throughout the nation in the forties, but Morrison runs the familiar lines together to emphasize how far this all-American fantasy is from the reality of Pecola Breedlove. The section that introduces the Breedlove family distorts the Dick and Jane picture of a very pretty green and white house with a red door:

HEREISTHEHOUSEITISGREENANDWHITEIT
HASAREDDOORITISVERYPRETTYITISVERY
PRETTYPRETTYPRETTY (p. 30)

Immediately after these lines, Morrison describes the "abandoned store" that is the home of the Breedlove family. Like its occupants, the house is "irritating and melancholy" (p. 30) and ugly. It is in this house that Pauline Breedlove fights with her husband Cholly, beats her daughter Pecola and her son Sammy, and sings her hymns of resignation.

Morrison travels back in time and place to Pauline Breedlove's childhood. As the ninth of eleven children in a poor Alabama sharecropper's family that lived seven miles from the nearest neighbor and the nearest road, Pauline Williams knows "only separateness and unworthiness."[28] Her parents, consumed by the responsibilities of rearing a large family on meager earnings, have no time for parental embraces. It is Pauline's lot to be virtually ignored. Unable to understand her parents' lives, she believes her predicament stems from a slight limp in her right foot, the result of a wound she suffered at the age of four. Slight as it is, this "deformity" becomes Pauline's crutch, explaining "many things that would have been incomprehensible" (p. 88).

Because her mother has to work outside the home to help support the family, Pauline is taken out of school to care for the younger children. Thus prematurely initiated into the reality that will define her in adulthood, she performs interminable "woman's work" with efficiency. The quick rhythm of Morrison's description of this work heightens the reader's appreciation for the extent to which Pauline's life is consumed by housework:

> She kept the fence in repair, pulling the pointed stakes erect, securing them with bits of wire, collected eggs, swept, cooked, washed, and minded the younger children. (pp. 89–90)

Entering puberty at fifteen produces a change in Pauline's desires and interests. Instead of the pleasure she once derived from keeping house, she feels an unsettling emptiness. Something is missing, she thinks, and as she responds to her sexuality, she names that "something" in fantasies about "men and love and touching." In all of these fantasies she is a passive, solitary figure waiting for a man to complete her—to validate her existence. When Cholly Breedlove comes into her life, her deformity becomes an asset: "instead of ignoring [Pauline's] infirmity . . . he made it something special and endearing" (p. 90). His touch, his interest in her, his presence in her life, salve her damaged psyche. Pauline remembers her first meeting with Cholly as the day of her salvation:

> "When I first seed Cholly, I want you to know it was like all the bits of color from that time down home when all us children went berry picking after a funeral and I put some in the pocket of my Sunday dress, and they mashed up and stained my hips. My whole dress was messed with purple, and it never did wash out. . . . I could feel that purple deep inside me. And that lemonade Mama used to make when Pap come in out the fields. It be cool and yellowish, with seeds floating near the bottom. And that streak of green them june bugs made on the trees the night we left from down home. All of them colors was in me. Just sitting there. So when Cholly came and tickled my foot, it was like them berries, that lemonade, them streaks of green the june bugs made all come together." (pp. 91–92)

Morrison's moist and colorful images of "down home" call our attention to Pauline's alienation in the steel-mill town of Lorain, Ohio, to which she and Cholly move shortly after their marriage. Cholly is able to find work in the mills and, fully employed, he should be able to keep the "bits of color" in Pauline's life vivid. But there are no colors in the cold Midwest. Once she leaves Alabama with its warm springs, its "berry picking," and its "streak of green them june bugs made on the trees," Pauline experiences again the separateness she had known as a child. Cholly begins to drink heavily. He leaves for work every day; she stays home in isolation. Their life together, once filled with pleasure and companionship, is perforated with quarrels and fights. She fights Cholly and calls on Jesus to "strike the bastard down from his pea-knuckle of pride" before she kills him, but she looks forward to the fights. They "gave substance to the minutes and hours otherwise dim and unrecalled. They relieved the tiresomeness of poverty, gave grandeur to the dead rooms" (p. 36).

In much the same way, Cholly needs Pauline and their marriage of conflict. When he was "four days old, his mother wrapped him in two blankets and one newspaper and placed him on a junk heap by the railroad" (p. 105). He was reared by Aunt Jimmy, a poor woman who belonged to the group of women Morrison describes as "edging into life from the back door. Becoming. Everybody in the world was in a position to give them orders" (p. 109). When Aunt Jimmy dies, Cholly, then only a teenager, goes in search of his father, Samson Fuller. The experience is traumatic. Cholly's attempts to claim his father cannot compete with Samson Fuller's interest in a crap game.

> He bent down to toss a bill on the ground, and waited for a throw. When it was gone, he stood up and in a vexed and whiny voice shouted at Cholly, "Tell that bitch she get her money. Now, get the fuck outta my face!" (p. 123)

Morrison writes sympathetically of Cholly's boyhood: "Abandoned in a junk heap by his mother, rejected for a crap game by his father, there was nothing more to lose" (p. 126). But she writes most movingly of Cholly's psychological castration by two white men who come upon Cholly in his first sexual act with a young girl.

> When he was still very young, Cholly had been surprised in some bushes by two white men while he was newly but earnestly engaged in eliciting sexual pleasure from a little country girl. The men had shone a flashlight right on his behind. He had stopped, terrified. They chuckled. The beam of the light did not move. "Go on," they said. "Go on and finish. And, nigger, make it good." (p. 37)

Cholly does not struggle against the men, for he had long ago learned from "myriad other humiliations, defeats and emasculations" (p. 37) that he could not win against their power and their predilection for violence. So he mounts the girl and makes "it good" in the beam of the flashlight. Morrison writes, "Cholly had not hated the white men; he hated, despised the girl" (p. 37). It is the taste of this remembered humiliation that shapes Cholly's attitude toward Pauline. "He poured out on her the sum of all his inarticulate fury and aborted desires.

Hating her, he could leave himself intact" (p. 37). And so they fight with a "darkly brutal formalism that was paralleled only by their lovemaking. Tacitly they agreed not to kill each other" (p. 37), but they knew that they must fight as if they would. During this difficult period in their marriage, Pauline discovers that she is carrying Cholly's child.

The consummate maternal joy that Staples and Thompson document in sociological studies is not present in Pauline's expectations and feelings. The notion of motherhood as a sacred calling lived out in Sistine tranquillity is a rhetorical lie in Pauline's culture. Pauline had seen no gratifying maternal experiences in her mother's life, since each new birth—and there were eleven—meant more work for a woman already exhausted by her responsibilities as farmer, wife, and mother many times over. The only joy the unplanned pregnancy brings Pauline, ironically, comes from Cholly, who treats her with more tenderness because his male ego is enlarged by this proof of his virility. "They eased back into a relationship more like the early days of their marriage," Pauline recalls (p. 97). This fictive picture connects with the cultural pattern of escorting women "with child" into "an atmosphere of approval."[29] It was this atmosphere that pulled Meridian's mother into marriage and then into motherhood, and it is this atmosphere that gives Pauline her only joy as an expectant mother.

Like Mrs. Hill, however, Pauline Breedlove quickly discovers the difference between what she expects and what she experiences. She is not ushered into bliss but thrust into loneliness. All day she keeps house and hears the sounds of life outside. She returns, out of desperation, to her earlier dreams of escape from melancholy into bliss, and she escapes by experiencing vicariously the lives of white men and women on America's silver screen. At the movies, she sees beautiful white women and servile black women. The polarities never change—white luxury and black powerlessness, white beauty and black ugliness. It is at the movies, Morrison writes, that Pauline Breedlove is introduced to "the idea of physical beauty." This idea, and that of "romantic love," which has long shaped Pauline's fantasies, are "the most destructive ideas in the history of human thought.

Both originated in envy, thrived in insecurity, and ended in disillu-
sionment" (p. 97). Together they convince Pauline that she is irredeemably ugly. As she watches a Clark Gable–Jean Harlow film, she
loses a tooth—a front tooth at that—and the loss plunges her into
self-hatred. Her telling of the incident, written with Morrison's
brilliance for creating mood, is one of the most moving moments in
the novel. I reproduce it here at length, for it is such a compelling
statement on the impact that images of black women in America's
white media have on Pauline Breedlove's dreams and frustrations:

> "The onliest time I be happy seem like was when I was in the
> picture show. Every time I got, I went. I'd go early, before the show
> started. They'd cut off the lights, and everything be black. Then the
> screen would light up, and I'd move right on in them pictures.
> White men taking such good care of they women, and they all
> dressed up in big clean houses with the bathtubs right in the same
> room with the toilet. Them pictures gave me a lot of pleasure, but it
> made coming home hard, and looking at Cholly hard. I don't know.
> I 'member one time I went to see Clark Gable and Jean Harlow. I
> fixes my hair up like I'd seen hers on a magazine. A part on the side,
> with one little curl on my forehead. It looked just like her. Well,
> almost just like. Anyway, I sat in that show with my hair done up
> that way and had a good time. I thought I'd see it through to the
> end again, and I got up to get me some candy. I was sitting back in
> my seat, and I taken a big bite of that candy, and it pulled a tooth
> right out of my mouth. I could of cried. . . . I don't believe I ever did
> get over that. There I was, five months pregnant, trying to look like
> Jean Harlow, and a front tooth gone. Everything went then. Look
> like I just didn't care no more after that. I let my hair go back,
> plaited it up, and settled down to just being ugly." (p. 98)

The tragedy of the incident is not Pauline Breedlove's loss of a
front tooth but her use of fantasies to help her cope with reality. These
fantasies, which can never become realities, remove her from the healing memories of the Kentucky spring. Tragically, she resigns herself
to being an ugly women whose only hope for a better life lies in serv-

ing God. She serves by carrying two crosses—her children and her husband.

For Pauline, the experience of motherhood is a mixture of maternal rage and maternal regret. Thus she beats her children, feels guilty that she has beaten them, but then beats them again. She understands why she does this, and her understanding echoes Camille Jeffers's observation that poor black women's functioning in the maternal role is shaped "by the lack of sufficient money and its irregular flow."[30] Pauline puts it lucidly: "Perhaps it was having no money or maybe it was Cholly, but [the children] sure worried the life out of me" (p. 98). The daily needs of her children are like lighted matches to the fuse of her disappointment as a black woman denied beauty and romantic love. Like Pauline, Cholly is frustrated, for he is a black man in a white-controlled society that keeps his sense of self turning in the wind. But he is free from having to care for the children, a privilege conferred on men by the laws of the institution of motherhood.

An interesting dimension of Morrison's portrait of Pauline Breedlove is the character's desire for a second child despite the bitter disappointment of her first experience with motherhood. Pauline does not know why she "actually tried to get pregnant" (p. 98), but she believes it was because she knew what to expect this second time and therefore was not afraid. Morrison offers a different explanation. In a culture that limits woman's creativity to the single act of childbirth, Pauline naturally chooses to become pregnant in a moment of deep depression. She experiences a sense of power and possession in this second pregnancy because *she* made it happen and because, unlike the first child, this one of her making will be her special friend. The myth of maternal service is reversed here. Instead of taking up a "sacred calling" to which she will give a lifetime of unselfish devotion, Pauline sees her second venture into motherhood as a retrieval from the pits of loneliness. Her attitude is touching and pathetic. She sees the child within her womb as the "other self" who understands her, as Cholly does not, and who makes her happy, as her reality does not:

> "I used to talk to it whilst it be still in the womb. Like good friends we was. You know. I be hanging wash and I knowed lifting weren't good for it. I'd say to it holt on now I gone hang up these few rags,

don't get froggy; it be over soon. It wouldn't leap or nothing. Or I be
mixing something in a bowl for the other chile and I'd talk to it
then too." (p. 98)

Because this special child deserves more than the hands of a mid-
wife and the ugliness of the Breedloves' house, Pauline plans her first
hospital delivery. To suggest the ironic contrast between her expectations and reality, Morrison first describes the comfort Pauline antici-
pates—she is "eased" back into her earlier bliss, her pregnancy is a
"state of ease"—and then moves immediately into the horror of
Pauline's labor in the sterile, insensitive white-run hospital. As a
woman in this world, Pauline feels life breaking forth from her with
urgency and force, but she cannot communicate what she feels to the
team of white male doctors who are sexually outside her experience.
As a poor woman, Paulines lies defenseless, her nakedness exposed
to a group of interns who callously treat the nameless patients in the
charity ward. And as a black woman, she is humiliated and debased
by the racist assumptions these doctors make about her. She observes
them using gentle hands on the white women, conveying concern
with their "nice friendly talk," and she is outraged and deeply wounded
when they push her legs open and jam rough hands inside her body.
But it is their talk that cuts with deep sharpness into her soul: "Now
these here women, you don't have any trouble with. They deliver right
away and with no pain. Just like horses" (p. 99).

Pauline is wrenched by the experience because it is so radically
different from her expectations, but she does not comprehend why it
is different. She understands, of course, that financial need placed
her in a charity ward, but the presence of white charity patients makes
the matter of class insignificant. Since the medical profession then
systematically excluded blacks and women, she expected the doctors
to be white men. She believes she suffers not because she is female
and poor, but only because she is black. She reasons that if the ability
to endure pain in silence distinguishes her from white women, she
should scream out in excruciating pain:

"I moaned something awful. The pains wasn't as bad as I let on, but
I had to let them people know having a baby was more than a bowel

movement. I hurt just like them white women. . . . What'd they think/ That jus' cause I knowed how to have a baby with no fuss that my behind wasn't pulling and aching like theirs." (p. 99)

Pauline *is* stronger than the white women because she can endure pain in silence. She knows "how to have a baby with no fuss," but she is too overwhelmed by racism in the delivery experience to understand that her quiet endurance of pain is an expression of her dignity, not an indictment of her as a lesser woman (p. 99). Seeing herself through the eyes of others, however, she attempts to express her humanity by imitating the very women whose behavior calls her humanity into question. She "moaned something awful."

Myths spawned by the institution of motherhood suggest that women, because of their experience with "creative pain,"[31] immediately approve of their newborn child. The experience of motherhood sometimes teaches us differently. If beauty is in the eye of the beholder, there is sometimes a direct relationship between the mother's image of herself and her image of her child. Thus Pauline Breedlove sees her newborn as "a cross between a puppy and a dying man" (p. 98). Nevertheless, she makes a commitment to the child, and in that is unlike the hundreds of black mothers in real life who, according to Jesse Bernard, "disappear once they have delivered."[32] Commitment does not translate into affection and nurturing, however. Out of a deep well of self-hatred and psychic pain, Pauline gives Pecola the fullest measure of her own misery. She beats the child, teaching her

fear of being clumsy, fear of being like [her] father, fear of not being loved by God, fear of madness like Cholly's mother . . . fear of growing up, fear of other people, fear of life. (p. 102)

Cholly also loves Pecola, but he, too, responds to the child out of the fullest measure of his misery. When he sees her bending over the sink washing dishes, "The sequence of his emotions was revulsion, guilt, pity, then love. His revulsion was a reaction to her young, helpless, hopeless presence."

Why did she have to look so whipped? She was a child—unbur-
dened—why wasn't she happy? The clear statement of her misery
was an accusation. . . . Guilt and impotence rose in a bilious duet.
What could he do for her—ever? What give her? What say to her?
What could a burned-out black man say to the hunched back of his
eleven-year-old daughter? . . . What could his calloused hands
produce to make her smile? (p. 127)

He "loves" her physically, but his "hatred of her slimed in his stomach and threatened to become vomit" (p. 127). He rapes her, breaking
into her virginal tightness, and when he finishes, his "hatred would
not let him pick her up, the tenderness forced him to cover her" (p.
129).

Pauline's beatings, Cholly's rape, and daily reminders that *white*
girls are beautiful reinforce Pecola's belief that she has been assigned
to the "bottom category in the scale of absolute beauty."[33] She wishes
to disappear.

"Please God," she whispered into the palm of her hand. "Please
make me disappear." She squeezed her eyes shut. Little parts of her
body faded away. Now slowly, now with a rush. Slowly again. Her
fingers went, one by one; then her arms disappeared all the way to
the elbow. Her feet now. Yes, that was good. The legs all at once. It
was the hardest above the thighs. She had to be real still and pull.
Her stomach would not go. But finally it, too, went away. Then her
chest, her neck. The face was hard, too. Almost done, almost. Only
her tight, tight eyes were left. They were always left. (p. 39)

But she wishes most intensely for blue eyes. She is a "little black girl
who wanted to rise up out of the pit of her blackness and see the
world with blue eyes" (p. 137). Pecola is her mother's child, for in a
real sense Pecola's desire for blue eyes is not unlike Pauline's desire to
be Jean Harlow with a "little curl" on her forehead, but Pecola suffers
from self-rejection more tragically than Pauline because she has never
seen the "bits of color" in a Kentucky spring, tasted the sweetness of

lemonade prepared by a mother who greets her husband at the end of the day, or felt the "deep purple of berry picking" within. She has not been "down home." She has never known "home" in the Breedlove house. Alone in her pain, she goes to a community recluse known for his strangeness, his madness, his rejection of the traditional ordering principles of the community: "I'd like a pair of new blue eyes" (p. 142). His understanding of her pain makes him an accomplice to her insanity:

> I, I have caused a miracle. I gave her the eyes. I gave her the blue, blue, two blue eyes. Cobalt blue. A streak of it right out of your own blue heaven. No one else will see her blue eyes. But she will. And she will live happily ever after. (p. 143)

White America's definition of beauty and its effect on black women's self-images are handled differently in Gwendolyn Brooks's *Maud Martha*, which was published two decades before *The Bluest Eye*. Set in Southside Chicago, the novel is a "series of lyrical, perhaps auto-biographical, vignettes of life"[34] in small kitchenettes during the late thirties and early forties as it is experienced by Maud Martha and those with whom she interacts. "We hear through her mind's voice the sounds of her family, her community and the unknown white world," and we see Maud Martha receiving love and guidance from a strong, cohesive black family and support from the nurturing "communal rituals" that make the black community a large extended family. "Her world is a cocoon in which she has protection and nourishment to find herself."[35]

The self she finds is decidedly different from Pauline Breedlove's self, for Maud Martha never knows the separateness Pauline feels so acutely. Whereas Pauline is one of eleven children in a sharecropper's family that lives miles from the nearest neighbor, Maud Martha is one of two children in an urban family that shares doors, walls, steps, stoops, schools, and churches with other people in like circumstances. This explains why Pauline Breedlove's reality is suffocating and Maud Martha's is a warm cocoon. One woman is the product of a southern/rural experience, the other of a northern/urban experience. One woman is uneducated, isolated, and afraid of life; the other is educated, involved in a world of activity, and eager to embrace life. Pauline escapes at the movies. Maud Martha finds pleasure and beauty in "candy buttons, and books, and painted music . . . and dandelions."[36]

> She would have liked a lotus, or China asters or the Japanese iris, or meadow lilies—yes, she would have liked meadow lilies, because the very word meadow made her breathe more deeply, and either fling her arms or want to fling her arms, depending on who was by, rapturously, up to whatever was watching in the sky. But dandelions was what she chiefly saw. (p. 6)

Brooks's image of dandelions as "yellow jackets for everyday, studding the patched green of the back yard," reflects Maud Martha's picture of herself as an ordinary woman. She prefers dandelions to more exotic flowers because of their "demure prettiness" and everydayness, proving that "what was common could also be a flower" (p. 5). The theme of "everydayness" is related to Morrison's theme of blue eyes for Pauline. While Pauline Breedlove, after comparing herself to white images of beauty, decides that she is irredeemably ugly, Maud Martha, less damaged by the comparison, considers herself "sweet . . . but certainly not what one would call pretty" (p. 41).

Other comparisons between Pauline Breedlove and Maud Martha alert us to the different ways the problem of color has been treated by black women writers. Even on this issue—almost a given in the reality of black women—there is no monolithic statement. For Pauline Breedlove, white women are the symbols of beauty. For Maud Martha, "high-yellow" (light-skinned) black women with straight or curly hair serve the purpose. Of course, it can be argued that what is involved here is only the flipside of the same coin because admiration for high-yellow black women is a reflection of the black community's acceptance of the white ideal. But intraracial color prejudice is a different dynamic. This is not to say that the preference for light skin within the race does not pierce the souls of black women. It does. Brooks describes the deep injury Maud Martha suffers because she is darker than her sister, Helen, and, for this reason, teased by her peers and disregarded by her father:

> It does not please [Maud Martha] ... to watch her father ... think ... how daintily [Helen] ate, how gracefully she sat in her chair, how pure was her robe and unwrinkled, how neatly she had arranged her hair. (p. 29)

Brooks even seems to suggest that Maud Martha's interest in "candy buttons," and certainly her interest in books, is created by her status in her family and among her peers as an unattractive girl. However, admiration for high-yellow black women produces less intense rage than admiration for white women. The latter are always outside the culture. The former are often biological sisters, as in Maud Martha's case, and always racial sisters. This fact, along with sustaining family love, explains why Maud Martha's sensitivity to her everydayness is an irritant in her soul rather than an Achilles' heel in her life.

As an irritant, it shapes Maud Martha's attitude toward her relationship with Paul, a gentle man and a fairly sensitive husband. Here again, there are similarities and differences between Pauline Breedlove and Maud Martha. Pauline waits for a man to touch her and make her whole because she is lacking in self-esteem. She is, therefore, grateful for Cholly's love. Similarly, Maud Martha is grateful for Paul's love because she is convinced she is not a prize catch. Therefore she promises to give in love and understanding what she cannot give in beauty. She will be like the women of old who were

> strong women, bold; praiseworthy, faithful, stout-minded; with a stout light beating in the eyes. . . . Women who would toil eminently to improve the lot of their men. Women who cooked. She thought of herself, dying for her man. It was a beautiful thought. (p. 146)

Neither Pauline nor Maud Martha considers the possibility of giving birth to herself without a man in her life. Pauline waits by the roadside for that someone special. Maud Martha "hooks" (p. 43) Paul into marriage. Just as dandelions prove that "what was common could also be a flower," so does Paul's troth prove that a woman who is not what a man "would call pretty" can also be desired. Still, Maud Martha is never free from the feeling that Paul thinks he "can do better than this black girl." Since a man wants more than everydayness in his woman, Maud Martha is convinced that

> even with all this hair . . . even with whatever I have that puts a dimple in his heart, even with these nice ears, I am still definitely not what he can call pretty if he remains true to what his idea of pretty has always been. Pretty would be a little curly-haired thing the color of cocoa with a lot of milk in it. Whereas, I am the color of cocoa straight, if you can be even that *kind* to me. (p. 41)

Brooks's portrayal of Maud Martha's life is, on one level, a sensitive picture of problems in the lives of black people in an urban ghetto. On another level, it is a hymn to the beauty of everydayness and the beauty and character of ordinary black people. Maud Martha is perhaps the only one among the characters analyzed in this book who is neither a heroine nor a victim. She has her share of problems, however. She lives with the knowledge that she is an unattractive woman. She faces the cutting superiority of upper-class Negroes. And she copes with the condescension of the white woman who employs her as a maid when Paul cannot find a job. Her life is not all candy buttons, but it is a life of flowers because Maud Martha plants them in her vision of possibilities. Her knowledge that white America circumscribes her reality as a black woman does not deprive her of her ordinary joys or lessen her pride in the unique beauty of the kitchenette culture of black people. Her knowledge that marriage and parenthood demand more of her than of Paul because she is a woman does not diminish the joy she receives in bathing her child, cooking baking powder biscuits for her man, washing, ironing, and cleaning. These responsibilities incorporate her into a community of women she admires and respects. In her "everydayness" she is a tribute to her own dreams of life.

Brooks imbues her portrait of Maud Martha with genuine admiration for the character's humanity, humility, intelligence, and ability to see the beauty in small things. Indeed, she depicts Maud Martha as a "spiritually pretty" woman. Predictably, Maud Martha's response to motherhood is one of warmth, enthusiasm, and joy. The child-birth scene is wrapped in all three emotions. Maud Martha screams out in pain, but she sees the pain as an experience that is creative in the fullest sense of the word. She would have everyone in the building know that she, Maud Martha, is giving birth to a child. Her screams, then, are not like the screams of Pauline Breedlove. They come from her sense of her own worth. Whereas Pauline Breedlove is surrounded by white male doctors, Maud Martha is surrounded by supportive black women—her mother and a neighbor—and she is aware that Paul has rushed to find the doctor. Whereas Pauline gives birth in the hostile environment of a white-run charity hospital, Maud Martha gives birth in the warmth of her home. These differences in the two experiences explain why Pauline Breedlove screams to prove her humanity, and Maud Martha screams to announce her joy in being a woman. She feels as if

> her whole body were having a bowel movement. The head came. Then, with a little difficulty, the wide shoulders. Then easily, with soft and slippery smoothness, out slipped the rest of the body and the baby was born. (pp. 71–72)

The painful labor gives Maud Martha a "handsome child" (p. 73) and a feeling of triumph. Brooks does not romanticize motherhood, for she writes that Maud Martha does not dwell long on "the fact of the baby." Responsibilities for this "fact" would "be [hers] all her life long" (p. 73). Rather, Maud Martha prefers to enjoy "the bright delight that had flooded through her upon hearing that part of Maud Martha Brown Phillips expressing itself with a voice of its own" (p. 73). It is significant that Maud Martha's triumph, as her long name for the child indicates, is an expression of her own achievement as a woman. It is a triumph that never diminishes, for throughout the novel, Maud Martha is the most marvelous of dandelions.

Henrietta Coffin in *Daddy Was a Number Runner* (1970) is also an "ordinary woman," but she rarely feels good or triumphant about it.

Set in Harlem during the difficult years of the Depression, her story is one of frustration, fear, and unrelenting struggle. She and her husband struggle to rear three children into wholeness in a community that is "nothing but one big garbage heap."[37] They have no way out of Harlem. Mrs. Coffin has no skills and has been prevented from getting a job by her husband's wish to be the acknowledged head of the family. Mr. Coffin is a number runner who barely earns enough to keep his family. All around, in the streets outside and in the various apartments within their tenement, the Coffins see devastation and, most frighteningly, the victimization of black teenagers in a world of drugs, violence, and crime. In this world there are no dandelions or candy buttons.

The novel is told from the point of view of fourteen-year-old Francie Coffin, who is too young to understand the complexity of her mother's life. In Francie's eyes, only "Daddy" truly loves her. She compares him to the "knots of men" who sit on Harlem stoops or stand "wide-legged in front of . . . storefronts, with their black ribs shining through shirts limp with sweat. They spend most of their time playing the single action," and Daddy is the one to whom they give their bets. She is glad "Daddy [is] a number runner" because people come to her for tips as if she were "somebody special" (p. 15). Her description of her father is a touching tribute of love:

> Mother was always telling me that men were handsome, not
> beautiful, but she just didn't understand. Handsome meant one
> thing, and beautiful something else and I knew for sure what Daddy
> was. Beautiful. (p. 20)

Mrs. Coffin is not "beautiful." She is an unattractive woman, "short and dumpty dumpty" with "long breasts and wide hips" that run together, hair that is "short and thin," and teeth that are "rotting yellow" (p. 18). Consumed by motherhood and poverty, she has "let herself go." Indeed, Francie's description of her mother would fit any number of poor black women in black American novels—and in real life as well—on whom the exigencies of black life in the ghetto have taken their toll. But for Francie, the problem with "Mother" is not simply that she is unattractive. Rather, it is that she is unaffectionate, and, in personality, stern and sour: Mrs. Coffin "seldom" smiles. "Daddy shouted and cursed when he was mad and danced around and hugged you when he was feeling good," but Mother does not show her feelings at all. "It was hard to know what Mother was sensitive about. . . . She didn't curse you but she didn't kiss you either" (p. 18).

Instead of the stereotypical image of the strong black mother who pulls children to her all-embracing bosom, Louise Meriwether develops the image of the distant mother who has no time for embracing. Mrs. Hill in Walker's *Meridian* is also a distant mother, but her distance is not to be confused with that of Henrietta Coffin. Mrs. Hill is distant because she is sensitive to the unfairness of motherhood, its theft of her "emerging self." Mrs. Coffin, on the other hand, is distant because she is sensitive to the unfairness of a racist system that divides society into blacks and white, have-nots and haves, respectively. In Meriwether's portrait of Mrs. Coffin, references to sexual consciousness are singularly absent. Although the novel was written in 1970 and is a rather obvious response to the sociological controversy over the black matriarchy, it does not reflect the concurrent controversy over women's rights. All the details of the portrait are racial and class details, drawn boldly to dramatize the impact that poverty and racism have on intact black families that are spiritually strong. The key to Meriwether's interpretation of such a family is her emphasis on Mrs. Coffin's posture as a supportive wife. She walks behind "Daddy" because she loves him and also because, sharing with him a history and, more acutely, a present experience of oppression, she supports his right to be a man. She therefore submerges herself in the roles of wife and mother and sacrifices her life for her children's future.

It is her commitment to maternal sacrifice that explains Mrs. Coffin's distance, a fact that Francie comes to understand only later in the novel. As the mother of three children, Mrs. Coffin is engaged in the miracles of "making a way out of no way"—altering cast-off clothes so that they fit her children, shopping for bargains of "cardboard" shoes, planning menus on a shoestring budget, and cleaning the apartment so that the bedbugs do not take over. Repeatedly, Meriwether pushes Mrs. Coffin's maternal aspirations to the center of the novel. The children will get a college education. Even when the Depression and the welfare system succeed in pushing Mr. Coffin out of the family, even when potted meat can no longer be "stretched from here to yonder with mayonnaise" (p. 89), Mrs. Coffin remains committed to her maternal aspirations. Even when her sons drop out of school, she is confident that her daughter will succeed. And so she preaches to the girl the only sermon she knows: "You don't be no fool, you hear? You finish school and go on to college. . . . You hear?" (p. 173).

It is appropriate to follow a discussion of Meriwether's *Daddy Was a Number Runner* with Paule Marshall's *Brown Girl, Brownstones* (1959), since both novels deal with the experience of growing up black and female in a black community in New York. Interestingly, the female adolescents in both works love their fathers and must struggle to understand their mothers. These are only surface similarities, however, for Marshall writes about a West Indian family living in Brooklyn during the forties and fifties, and Meriwether about a black American family living in Harlem during the thirties. The differences in time and location are of less importance than the cultural differences. As Marshall's novel teaches us, West Indians are black, but they are not to be confused with black Americans. They have their own values, lifestyles, rituals, dreams, and problems, and they have a different history. In her story of the Boyce family, Marshall translates the proverbs, interprets the conversations, and renders the poetic language and rhythm of Barbadian culture. She writes specifically about Silla and Deighton Boyce and their two daughters, Selina and Ina, and generally about a people who have a strong sense of themselves as a distinct group and a passion to acquire things, especially property. The controlling symbol in the novel is the brownstone. To be Barbadian and to own a brownstone is to possess status and security—to have arrived in "this mahn's land."

Marshall begins her book with a poetic description of the "unbroken line of brownstone houses down the long Brooklyn street" on which the Boyce family lives. The brownstones resemble "an army massed at attention" with their "uniform red-brown stone" and "high massive stone stoops and black iron-grille fences staving off the sun." They are "formidable" structures "draped in ivy as though mourning. Within their larger rooms, yawning endlessly one into the other,"[38] is a history of migration or white flight common to this nation. Whites built the brownstones and lived in them for a century, but slowly abandoned them as new immigrants—black immigrants—"edged" themselves into the community. "Like a dark sea nudging its way onto a white beach and staining the sand, they came" (p. 4). In 1939 the last of the whites were "discreetly dying" (p. 4), or simply running as their tradition had taught them to, and Bajans were replacing them as landlords and tenants, loving the brownstones with "the same fierce idolatry as they had the land on their obscure island" (p. 4).

Just as they claimed the land as theirs but had no power on their "obscure island," so do they claim the brownstones as theirs but have no security in white America. They share with black Americans the peculiar reality of acquiring things while remaining outside the circle of power and influence in this country. The brownstones the Bajans work hard to own are for Selina Boyce, who is wise beyond her ten years, museums "of all the lives that had ever lived there" (p. 5). We see her alone at the beginning of the novel, interpreting the "aged and inviolate silence" of the brownstone her parents are renting. She imagines the white family who had once served tea in this house and rustled long dresses across the parquet floor imploring "her to give them a little life" (p. 5). She imagines, too, that she is "no longer a dark girl alone and dreaming at the top of an old house, but one of them, invested with their beauty and gentility" (p. 5). This child's fantasy is like Pauline Breedlove's desire to be Jean Harlow and Pecola's obsession with blue eyes: born of the psychological conditioning that makes many blacks think white, act white, or desire to be white.

Living in her family's museum, where a "floor-to-ceiling mirror retained their faces as the silence did their voices," Selina feels that she is "something vulgar in a holy place" (pp. 5–6). Possessed of more understanding than the Bajan men and women who idolize the brownstones, she realizes that her "heavy silver bangles which had come from 'home'" conflict with the clutter of a white past. She decides that "she did not belong here":

> The room was theirs, she knew, glancing up at the frieze of cherubs and angels on the ceiling; it belonged to the ghost shapes hovering in the shadows. But not to her. (p. 6)

In the description of the family portrait, Marshall symbolically presents the theme of Selina's need to find or create her own place beyond the brownstones that do not belong to her. Selina mutters "contemptuously" that her deceased brother looks "like a girl with all that hair":

> He had been frail and dying with a bad heart while she had been stirring into life. She had lain curled in the mother's stomach, waiting for his dying to be complete, she knew, peering through the pores as the box containing his body was lowered into the ground. Then she had come, strong and well-made, to take his place. *But they had taken no photographs.* (p. 8; italics added)

The novel is Selina's story of self-discovery, a journey that takes her from Brooklyn to Barbados and teaches her to reject capital and material things as the ordering principles of her life.

Selina's attitude toward the brownstones is in direct contrast to the attitude of her mother. Silla Boyce is obsessed with owning a brownstone, and she will do anything in this man's country to achieve that goal. The American emphasis on materialism and power has claimed Silla to the extent that she is willing to jettison values that interfere with her ambition:

> "If you let a little noise and dirt 'pon your hand keep you from making a dollar you should starve. I tell yuh, to make your way in this world you got to dirty more than yuh hands sometime."

Deighton Boyce, on the other hand, is content with leasing a brownstone. When his friend Seifert advises him to buy—"You might not get the chance again to own such a swell house"—Deighton answers, "Yearwood, what's the rush. I don' owe tiger nothing that I got to break loose my inside buying these old houses" (p. 39). His nonchalance hampers Silla's dream, and Silla, Selina realizes, is capable of destroying Deighton if owning a brownstone requires his destruction.

Silla and Deighton are two contrasting forces in Selina's life, each adding to her self-discovery. Silla is strong, fearless, and, like the brownstones she idolizes, "formidable." In a park where sunshine lies down with lounging women and runs with laughing children, Silla Boyce brings "the theme of winter . . . with her dark dress amid the summer green":

> Not only that, every line of her strong-made body seemed to
> reprimand the women for their idleness and the park for its
> senseless summer display. Her lips, set in a permanent protest
> against life, implied that there was no time for gaiety. And the park,
> the women, the sun even gave way to her dark force; the flushed
> summer colors ran together and faded as she passed. (p. 16)

Deighton, on the other hand, is warm, and Marshall uses the sun as the controlling image in her pictures of him. When Selina complains about missing a movie, Deighton responds, "I don' know what wunna New York children does find in a movie. . . . Sitting up in a dark place when the sun shining bright-bright outside" (p. 9). He was the only one in the family photograph Selina believed:

> For her, he was the one constant in the flux and unreality of life.
> The day was suddenly bright with the thought of him upstairs in
> the sun parlor. (p. 8)

Selina is torn between respect and awe for her mother and sympathy and affection for her father. She understands the truths of the family: Silla works hard to buy a brownstone; Deighton tries one get-rich-quick scheme after another. Silla plans for the future; Deighton dresses in silk shirts and promenades down Fulton Street to the apartment of his concubine. Deighton wishes for the old days when they were lovers in the sun parlor and "could see the sky with its low stars from the bed"; Silla holds herself from him, beating him with guilt for the death of their son and trying to blackmail him into buying a brownstone in exchange for absolution. When Deighton acquires property in Barbados, Silla insists that he sell the land and use the money on the brownstone. His refusal to do so plunges the family into tragedy. Silla plots against Deighton and sells the land, but Deighton, ironically, spends the money on things. Outraged by his betrayal and his continued visits to his concubine, Silla becomes a woman possessed by vengeance.

In fiction, as in real life, the tragic dimensions of black men's reality often obscure the harsh realities of black women. This is the case in *Brown Girl, Brownstones*. It is not easy to admire and respect Silla Boyce, so cruel is her attack on Deighton, whom racism and poverty in Barbados had turned into a broken man. In conversations with Selina he speaks romantically of his childhood in Bimshire, where racism and class oppression created island sport for rich white men:

> We would pick up weself and go seabathing all down Christ Church where the rich white people live. Stay in the water all day shooting the waves, mahn, playing cricket on the sand, playing lick-cork. . . .
> And when a tourist ship come into Carlisle Bay we would swim out to it and the rich white people from America would throw money in the water just to see we dive for it. (p. 10)

But inside, where the wounds have never healed, he remembers "things thrust deep into forgetfulness":

> . . . those white English faces mottled red by the sun in the big stores in Bridgetown and himself as a young man facing them in his first pair of long pants and his coarse hair brushed flat, asking them for a job as a clerk—the incredulity, the disdain and indignation that flushed their faces as they said no. (p. 39)

Deighton's attempts to leave his narrow cot in the sun parlor—first through unrealistic get-rich-quick schemes and finally in a bona fide job at the factory—sap what little strength he has, but he was destroyed long before he came to this "mahn's land," long before the machine crushes his arm, and long before he surrenders to a religion where allegiance to "Father" robs him of the last vestiges of his manhood and his desire to live. Silla's rage is like a strong wind that topples trees fierce storms have already uprooted: "It was his wish to suffer that suddenly spurred in her the need to make that suffering full" (p. 175). She swears out a warrant for his "arrest and deportation for illegal entry into the United States" (p. 181). Deighton jumps overboard and commits suicide before the ship reaches Bimshire. Rage against the mother consumes Selina:

> "Hitler!" She spat the name in the mother's face and brought her small fist down on Silla's shoulder. "Hitler!" she cried and struck again. This time her bangles glanced sharply across the mother's chin. (p. 184)

Like Selina, we curse Silla Boyce and weep for Deighton. And yet, like Selina, we are in awe of the formidable beauty of Silla. The child's reaction to the contrasts of Silla's severity and Deighton's nonchalance are brought together in Marshall's description of the parents' tales of Barbados. Selina is fascinated by Deighton's stories of his childhood in Carlisle Bay, but "thoughts of the mother intruded":

> What had she and the others who had lived down in gullies and up on the hills behind God's back done on Saturdays? She could never think of the mother alone. It was always the mother and others. (p. 10)

The others are the community of black women who share a collective history of oppression in the West Indies and in America. Silla epitomizes the awesome strength of this community of "watchful, wrathful women whose eyes seared and searched and laid bare, whose tongues lashed the world in unremitting distrust" (p. 11). They remind us of the many unnamed black women whose lives provide the data on domestics presented in the historical overview in chapter 2:

> Each morning they took the train to Flatbush and Sheepshead Bay to scrub floors. The lucky ones had their steady madams while the

others wandered those neat blocks or waited on the corners—each with her apron and working shoes in a bag under her arm until someone offered her a day's work.

When white children laugh at their blackness and call them "niggers,"

the Barbadian women sucked their teeth, dismissing them. Their only thought was of the "few raw-mout' pennies" at the end of the day which would eventually "buy house." (p.11)

Silla and the other women are accustomed to hard work and humiliation, having known both in Bimshire, where, though they were in the majority, they were subjected to racism and starvation. Silla's memories of her years in Bimshire are evocative of sharecropping experiences of poor blacks in the deep south. With a "sardonic laugh," she talks about hard work and deprivation, remembering herself among

a set of little children picking grass in a cane field from the time God sun rise in his heavens till it set. With some woman called a Driver to wash yuh tail in licks if yuh dare look. Yes, working harder than a man at the age of ten. (p. 45)

She remembers putting "a basket of mangoes 'pon muh head and go selling early 'pon a morning when still *only a child* [italics added] (pp. 45–46). And she remembers the

image of her father swaggering through the town as a boy and bounding on the waves in some rough game slanted across that of the small girl hurrying from the dawn ghosts with the basket on her head. (p. 46)

Marshall keeps the victimization of black men in focus throughout the novel as she paints the details of racism and poverty in the Bajan community. But she makes the women in the community towering figures in the picture, whose caption reads: "Of all things upon the earth that bleed and grow, a herb most braised is woman" (p. 29). The picture is similar in Brooklyn, where Bajan women board the train to Flatbush. Bajan women cook the meals, rear the children, and work like men in factories. Bajan women carry several burdens on hips stretched wide by bearing children for Bajan men. Their perseverance, strength, and tenacity of will are the life forces for the children, the men, and other women.

Miss Thompson is not a Bajan woman, but she is no less strong and no less admirable. She is a maid, hairdresser, and mother. Her workday began

> at nine o'clock that night in the office building where she worked as a cleaning woman. At dawn she had eaten in an all-night diner, dozing over her coffee, then as the morning cleared, she had come to the beauty parlor. (p. 28)

There, for only a stolen moment, she dressed

> the ugly unhealed ulcer, yawning like a small crater on the instep of her foot. . . . This done, she leaned back and, for the first time in twenty-four hours since she had been up, *permitted herself to feel tired.* (p. 28; italics added)

When her long workday ends, she returns to her small tenement apartment to care for three small girls. Marshall writes with admiration of Miss Thompson's warm flowing of love and compassionately of "the eyes shrouded with a profound sadness" (p. 41). She writes with tenderness of the friendship between Selina and Miss Thompson. Unlike Silla Boyce, whose conversations with Selina are battles for control, Miss Thompson listens with patience to the young girl's frustrations. Significantly, when Selina is confronted with the racism of a white woman, she remembers Miss Thompson's resistance to racial humiliation. In no small way Miss Thompson's racial pride helps shape Selina's racial consciousness. Perhaps her portrait is a criticism of Bajan dismissal of black American pride. Surely Miss

Thompson in her strength can keep company with the community of Bajan women.

But no black woman in the novel is equal to Silla Boyce in strength, fierce tenacity of will, and dogged determination. In the factory scene, Marshall compares Silla's strength to the pistons of large and formidable machines. The scene is engrossing and rich in the concrete images that make Marshall's prose so brilliantly poetic. Selina goes to the factory to "intimidate" Silla, hoping that the mother's plans to sell her father's land in Barbados will not be realized:

> Timidly she pushed open a heavy metal door and almost slammed it back in fright as an enraged bellow tore past her. She was suddenly drowned in a deluge of noise: belts slapping on giant pulleys, long shafts rearing and plunging, whirling parts plying the air, the metal whine of steel being cut, steam hissing from a twisting network of pipes on the ceilings and walls, the nervous, high-strung hum of the smaller machines and finally the relentless frightening stamp of the larger ones, which made the floor shudder. It was a controlled, mechanical hysteria, welling up like a seething volcano to the point of eruption, only to veer off at the climax and start again.

Selina sees her mother matching her strength against the force of the machines:

> She fitted the lump of metal over the lathe center and, with a deft motion, secured it into the headstock and moved the tailstock into position. The whine of her lathe lifted thinly above the roar as the metal whirled into shape. Then she released the tailstock and held the shell up for a swift scrutinizing glance before placing it with the other finished shells. (pp. 99–100)

Silla Boyce is the "collective voice of all the Bajan women" (p. 45). It is a voice of sadness, but never resignation; of pain, but never despair; of struggle, but never defeat. This is the voice Selina has heard all her life, the voice that names her, that circumscribes her, that mutes her own. In her adolescence, she begins to speak in her own voice, challenging the power and influence of the women, of the community, of the culture so anchored in the past and so hungry for security in the world of Brooklyn brownstones. She wants to choose the self she will become, but this is not an easy task, for in addition to Silla, there is the Barbadian society, "persistently reaching out to claim her, not only as her mother's daughter but as an adult member of the tribe."[39]

Selina rebels, striking out at Silla with both anger and love. She continues an affair with Clive, an artist whom the Bajan community does not approve of and whom Selina eventually leaves, and she feigns devotion to the Association of Barbadian Homeowners and Businessmen only to win the association's annual scholarship and use the money for a trip to the islands for herself and Clive. But she is too anchored in the culture and too connected to Silla to follow through with her plans. When she receives the scholarship, she refuses it and in a public confession gives voice to herself as a woman of understanding and character.

Silla is outraged:

> Lies! Getting up in front people talking a lot of who-struk-John about how much you like them and then throwing their money back at them. Talking in parables! Using a lot of big words and still not saying why you refuse good money. Disgracing me before the world! (p. 304)

As a young girl, Selina was in awe of such rages. As a woman she faces Silla without fear. She confesses that she has fought Silla with "spitework," blaming her for Deighton's tragedy, but she accepts what she has not wanted to believe: she is Silla's child: "Remember how you used to talk about how you left home and came here alone as a girl of eighteen and was your own woman? I used to love hearing that. And that's what I want. *I want it!* [italics added]" (p. 304). She no longer fears Silla; she appreciates fully the mother's "awesome beauty" and strength:

The world would collapse [without Silla], for wasn't the mother, despite all, *its only prop?* [italics added] (p. 46)

Selina books passage on a ship to the island. She will retrace her mother's steps and, like Silla, stand "at the ship's rail, watching the city rise glittering with promise from the sea" (p. 307). But the community to which she will return will be different from the old community of brownstones that "resembled an army massed at attention" (p. 3). At the end of the novel, Selina walks through the park she had known as a child, where Bajan women had once sat gossiping in the summer heat. It now belongs to dope addicts, winos, and hot-blooded young men. She wanders past rows of brownstones from which Bajan music and talk had once emanated. "Now, the roomers' tangled lives spilled out the open windows and the staccato beat of Spanish voices, the frenzied sensuous music joined the warm canorous Negro sounds to glut the air" (p. 309). The Bajan community of her childhood is making way for new immigrants. The brownstones are being razed to make room for housing projects. Selina feels that the "bodies of all the people she had known were broken, the familiar voices . . . shattered." She wants to leave something for them, for the past. She removes one of her silver bracelets and throws it high over her shoulder. The bracelet, which connects all Bajan girls with their ancestry, "strikes stone. A frail sound in that utter silence" (p. 310). By symbolically giving up one bracelet and holding on to the other, Selina expresses her awareness that she "is part of this immigrant community forever. But she must leave it; she must go backward and forward in time, in her own personal revolution." Barbara Christian's explanation is insightful: "We feel, because of [Selina's] self-knowledge, that she may be able to sustain what the mother could not— her own independence and wholeness."⁴⁰

In black American culture, grandmothers are sometimes the only prop in a child's life. Functioning as surrogate mothers in the black extended family, they are the bridge between the generations, the perpetuators of black culture, the griots (reciters) of family history, the disciplinarians, housekeepers, cooks, and repositories of wisdom and strength. Sociologists and historians alike extol the grandmother's contributions to the survival of black families. But there is no monolithic black grandmother either in real life or in fiction. Like black mothers, they are individuals with their own dreams and aspirations and problems. This is a dominant theme in Toni Morrison's story of Eva Peace in *Sula* (1973), the only grandmother in our gallery of black women. In a small Ohio community singularly impressive for its poverty, Eva Peace struggles alone for the survival of her family. When the youngest of her three children is only five months old, she is deserted by her husband, Boy-Boy, without warning and without explanation. Believing that the survival of her children is contingent on her temporary abandonment of them, Eva leaves them with a neighbor, who expects her to claim them the next day. Her desertion lasts eighteen months. Maternal abandonment is, of course, a cardinal sin in a society that perceives motherhood as a sacred calling, but Morrison shows clearly that Eva's decision represents courage and vision. For in her absence from her children, Eva prepares herself for a lifetime of service to their survival. When she claims them, she has only one leg, and the community rumor is that she sold the leg or put it under a moving train for insurance money—for her children. In this strange story Morrison gives us a black mother's desperate response to destitution.

The rest of the portrait of Eva as mother is less positive, revealing a desire to manipulate her children's lives and the lives of others as well. When she returns from her mysterious trip as a cripple, she begins building a "house of many rooms," of which she is "creator and sovereign."[41] On the second-floor balcony she sits in a wagon— her throne, really—"directing the lives of her children, friends, strays, and a constant stream of boarders" (p. 26). She is "godlike," Morrison said of Eva in an interview, seeking to rule the lives of others as would a "king."[42] Especially in her response to her son's wasted life does Eva "play god." Because he is an empty shell, his body emaciated by drug addiction, Eva pours kerosene on him as he sleeps off a "fix" and then sets a match to the mattress. She takes her son's life, not because it was "a worthless life," but because "it was too painful to her."[43]

The portrait of Eva as a manipulative woman is important because it is shaped more by sexism than by racial and economic pressures. Eva's character is profoundly the result of her five years of marriage to Boy-Boy. In her marriage she was not the "creator and sovereign" of anyone's life, least of all her own. She was a typical woman, standing in the background as the man used all of life as his playground. Symbolically named, "Boy-Boy" is twice over a boy and not a man, immature and irresponsible. He likes "womanizing best . . . drinking second, and abusing Eva third" (p. 27). Michele Wallace's observation in *Black Macho and the Myth of the Superwoman* (1978) that the macho man believes "his sexuality and the physical fact of his penis were the major evidence of his manhood and the purpose of it"[44] is an apt description of Boy-Boy. When he leaves Eva with three children, without warning or explanation, she is so consumed by poverty that she has little understanding of her dilemma as a woman used and betrayed by a man. Her identity as mother directs both her emotions and her decisions.

Two years later, Boy-Boy returns, unscarred and unafraid, and Eva wonders if she will "cry, cut his throat [or] beg him to make love to her" (p. 30). Morrison here catches woman's need for love and for male attention, as well as her training in passivity and understanding—training that has led to the cultural assumption that woman has an innate propensity for forgiveness. It is inconceivable that Boy-Boy would return, in laughter, to the scene of his sins if the person he had sinned against were another man, just as it is inconceivable that a wronged man would only "imagine" what he might do to an enemy. For one of the manifestations of sexism, Ashley Montagu explains, is the socialization of men as warriors who have the right, if not the masculine obligation, to take "an eye for an eye and a tooth for a tooth." Women, on the other hand, are socialized "to be nurses who bathe the warrior's wounds," who live to forgive and "preserve others." Man is the "eagle on the wing" and woman is "the cricket on the hearth."[45] It is out of this cultural conditioning that Boy-Boy, unafraid and boastful, returns, and that Eva equivocates between loving him and killing him.

She prepares lemonade (a woman's task) and engages in polite conversation with Boy-Boy, observing that he is the "picture of prosperity and good will" in shiny orange shoes, a light-colored suit, a garish stickpin in his tie, and an ostentatious straw hat. But "underneath all that shine" there is "defeat," for in the big and fast cities of the Midwest Boy-Boy exchanged his soul for a glittering emptiness (p. 31). Morrison does not linger on Boy-Boy's destruction, for the scene is clearly Eva's existential moment and Morrison's answer to a question rarely raised by one-dimensional and traditional images of the self-sacrificing and devoted mother: How does a woman handle deep and devastating hurt? She can turn to religion, as Pauline Breedlove does in *The Bluest Eye*; she can busy her hands making feminine artifacts, as Mrs. Hill does in *Meridian*; or, like Eva Peace, she can descend into a pit of hatred. When Boy-Boy courts the citified woman he brings with him—when he ignores Eva's existence as a *woman*—the descent begins. Within seconds Eva has cast her life in a mold of hatred. The woman's laugh, Morrison writes,

> hit [Eva] like a sledge hammer, and it was then she knew what to feel. A liquid trail of hate flooded her chest. Hating Boy-Boy, she could get on with it, and have the safety, the thrill, the consistency of that hatred as long as she wanted or needed it to define and strengthen her from routine vulnerabilities. (p. 31)

The direction of her life from that moment on is traceable to disappointment in love. "Happy or not," Morrison writes, "after Boy-Boy's visit [Eva] began her retreat to her bedroom" (p. 32). She began her existence as a manipulator and as a cold and domineering mother.

Morrison handles the theme of romantic love in a new way that, according to Barbara Lounsberry and Grace Honet, "offers us new perspectives of feminine reality."[46] Like other "traditional ordering principles—the family and the church, to name two—romantic love is a "limited and limiting vision" that promises the constricting view that women become fulfilled individuals only as wives and mothers. Also new in Morrison's treatment of romantic love is her definition of men. She "upturns and jangles our traditional view" so that, "far from heroic and powerful, men are diminished, literally and figuratively, in *Sula*. The male characters' names themselves [Boy-Boy, Tar Baby, Chicken Little, Jude Greene] suggest their immaturity." Lounsberry and Honet go on to observe that "this new perspective of men stunted in growth and development is conveyed most graphically through the Deweys [Eva's boarders] who will never grow taller than four feet and who, in their three-in-oneness, telegraph the horrifying homogeneity of the male experience."[47] This new view of men makes us reexamine the cultural assumption that all women need men and that men are necessarily dominating presences in the reality of women. Further, Eva's decision to keep herself invulnerable to pain impels us to reexamine the vaunted magical powers of motherhood to turn a bitter life into a sweet reality. In her cause–effect treatment of Eva's desertion by Boy-Boy and her maternal stance, Morrison suggests that what women experience in their relationships with the fathers of their children has a major effect on both their maternal postures and their vision of life.

Alice Walker writes brilliantly on the interrelatedness of the roles of wife and mother in *The Third Life of Grange Copeland* (1970). It is, in fact, the thread with which she sews "bits and pieces of used material rescued from oblivion"[48] into a profound and terrifying picture of black suffering in the South. The novel is an appropriate culmination to our discussion of black motherhood because it tells the story of generations of black women within one family; the action of the novel begins with the Grange Copeland family in 1900 and ends with the Grange Copeland family in the 1960s. More than any other work in this chapter, Walker's novel, a reflection of her search for our mothers' gardens, shows how tragically the lives of black women can be shaped by racial violence, sexual abuse, and class oppression—problems that are festering sores in the South. The vision is a feminist vision, as Barbara Christian points out:

> Walker describes a legacy from which the creativity of the contemporary black woman can flower. To develop further, the black women of her generation must garner wholeness from the bits and

pieces of the past and recreate them in their own image. Walker then uses the unheralded heritage of black women, the creative sparks as well as the history of restrictions, as the foundation of her artistic vision. A feminist, she explores the relationship between this tradition and societal change as crucial to the search for freedom—not only for woman, but for man, the child, the society, the culture, the land.[49]

The novel is a southern work of art—southern in that it is set in a black rural community in Mississippi, southern in that its characters have not ventured far from the insular environment of this community, and southern in that Alice Walker's artistic vision bears the imprint of the South she knew as a child, a young woman, and a civil rights worker. It is not essentially a catalogue of the crimes committed by white people against black people of the soil, though such crimes explode in the foreground and the background of the lives of the characters. Rather, it is Walker's vision of the cruelty that often exists in black male–black female relationships when racism and sexism work together as deterrents to joy and wholeness. More specifically, the novel is about the peculiar burdens of black women in white America. As Walker herself admits, she is "preoccupied with the spiritual survival, the survival whole of black people, and beyond that committed to exploring the oppressions, the insanities, the loyalties, and the triumphs of black women."[50] They are Walker's "revolutionary petunias" growing into beauty in a resistant soil. Such a woman is Mem Copeland.

Young, gentle, and pure, Mem is immunized, it seems, against the pollution of soul and body that claims Josie, an aunt with whom she lives during the summers in a house of prostitution. Josie is a "ruined" woman, a crass and crude prostitute, a slattern who brandishes a razor expertly and hurls at anyone who offends her the low-life language of Poontang Street. Mem is a "walking proper . . . talking proper" lady whose character is reflected in her "cherry brown face and demure slant eyes."[51] Josie "turns tricks" and Mem turns dreams into possibilities by teaching people in the backwoods community to read and write. "Mem put some attention to what she was [teaching], and some warmth from her own self, and . . . concern for the person she was speaking to" (p. 47).

When Brownfield Copeland, who is Josie's "kept man," meets Mem, he experiences a profound sense of shame and, for the first time in his easy life with Josie, wishes for a way out of the sordid entanglement. "Ain't no need for you looking," Josie informs him; "she ain't got no real itch in her pussy" (p. 45). Josie does not understand that a woman can be appreciated for gifts that are not physical or sexual. She has so prostituted herself in every way that she cannot comprehend Brownfield's hunger for something more substantive, more spiritually filling and lasting than the now-monotonous "balling" he engages in with Josie and her daughter. In her "quiet strangeness," Walker writes, Mem awakens in Brownfield these other needs. However, Walker quickly establishes that Brownfield's awakening is not an entry into liberating definitions of male–female relationships. Like all too many men, Walker implies, Brownfield has two missions for a woman in his life. He wants her to be his wife, loving him physically, and his mother, caring for him as if he were a child. Walker writes, "He thought of [Mem] as of another mother" (p. 45).

We do not understand why Mem decides to marry Brownfield, an illiterate man whose character, she knows, has been compromised by his sordid affair with Josie, for Walker does not convincingly show the two characters in courtship. In a few brief scenes we see Brownfield awkwardly attempting to win Mem's love, and then we read that Brownfield, out of fear that he was losing Mem to another man, "caught her in his arms [one night] . . . and vowed in words and kisses never to let her go" (p. 48). One could argue that Mem loves Brownfield because he is, like a child, in need of instruction and love. Or one could even argue that Mem's decision to marry Brownfield turns on the myth of women liking to be swept off their feet by men. Walker's emphasis is not on the *why* of Mem's love for Brownfield; it is, instead, on the *beauty* of their love. For three years they enjoy a relationship of physical joy, surpassing in intensity and passion the lovemaking Brownfield had known with Josie. Mem, like Josie, is a "devouring cat," but she has no claws and no sly intentions. Walker describes the lovemaking of Mem and Brownfield lyrically:

> They were passionate and careless . . . making love in the woods after the first leaves fell, making love high in the corncrib to the clucking of hens and the blasting of cocks, making love and babies urgently and with purest fire at the shady ends of cotton rows. (p. 49)

Mem Copeland is a woman of song who completes her woman's work to the rhythm of a joyful melody: "[Mem] sang while she cooked breakfast in the morning and sang when getting ready for bed at night. And sang when she nursed her babies [three in three years], and sang to [Brownfield] when he crawled in weariness and dejection into the warm life-giving circle of her breast" (p. 49). Walker revives her earlier image of woman as mother for her husband when she writes that Brownfield, like the babies, "sucked and nursed at [Mem's] bosom . . . and grew big and grew firm with love, and grew strong" (p. 49).

The love relationship betweeen Mem and Brownfield is equaled in beauty and intensity only by the relationship of Janie and Teacake in Zora Neale Hurston's classic novel *Their Eyes Were Watching God* (1937). After two unfulfilled marriages, Janie is enveloped by joy in her relationship with Teacake because he treats her as an equal. She is liberated from the curse of black womanhood, which her grandmother preached when Janie was a young girl:

> Honey, de white man is de ruler of everything as fur as Ah been able tuh find out. Maybe it's some place way off in de ocean where de black man is in power, but we don't know nothin' but what we see. So de white man throw down de load and tell de nigger man tuh pick it up. He pick it up because he have to, but he don't tote it. He hand it to his womenfolks. De nigger woman is de mule uh de world so fur as Ah can see.[52]

The load to which the grandmother refers is carried equally by Janie and Teacake, for there is no place for sexual politics in their relationship.

To some extent, the load is also carried equally by Brownfield and Mem early in their marriage, but it is divided according to sexual definitions of labor. He tills the fields. She keeps the house. But their mutual respect for each other's jobs eases the line between "man's duty" and "woman's work," making them communicants in a ritual of love. Walker seems to suggest that when a woman's love for a man is returned in kind and intensity, sexual definitions of work and power pale in significance.

If racism and poverty were not the burdens they are in the black experience, Mem's song as woman fulfilled might have been an unbroken chord in her life. But in the small Georgia town where black men's dreams are shattered in the pernicious institution of sharecropping, Brownfield falls victim to the powerlessness and humiliation of a life of "endless sunup to sundown work on fifty acres of cotton" that brings him nothing more than "two diseased goats for winter meat, some dried potatoes and apples from the boss's cellar, and some cast-off clothes for his children from his boss's family" (p. 53). His manhood is devastated by the sight of his five-year-old daughter "hand-mopping the cotton bushes with arsenic to keep off boll weevils" and by the recurring nightmare that his own life is becoming a repetition of his father's. "He could not save his children from slavery; they did not even belong to him" (pp. 53–54). He is a tragic figure whose emasculation at the hands of a cruel system robs him of his dreams, vitiates his humanity, and leaves in his soul a taste of bitter bile. Walker's sympathy for Brownfield is genuine and deep: "he was never able to do more than exist on air" (p. 55). His destruction as a man becomes, in time, Mem's suffering as a woman: "he determined . . . to treat her like a nigger and a whore" (p. 54).

Conflict between black men and black women is a common theme in black American fiction, and it is more often than not engendered by racism and poverty. In "Father May Bring Home the Bacon, but He Don't Cut No Ice: The Economic Plight of the Father Figure in Black American Literature" (1975), Daryl Dance shows how the system's emasculation of black men often makes them abusive to their wives. The American economic system, she writes, "conspires to make it impossible for the black man to acquire anything more than a mere biscuit, no matter how he plays the economic man. Unable to protect

and provide for his family," the black man "is inevitably . . . psychologically castrated." Men who suffer this fate, Dance writes, "yield the
reins of power to their wives, abandon their families, or often take
out their frustrations [on their wives] and become cruel tyrants in
their home."[53] The last response to victimization is Brownfield
Copeland's.

Abusive fathers in fiction have their counterparts in real life. Indeed, when black writers, male or female, hold up their artistic mirrors to life, they find reflected therein a history of black male–female
conflict. "Historically," writes black activist Ron Karenga, "we black
men and black women have been unkind to each other. . . . We have
sent each other to hospitals, graves and prison." This has been our
history, he continues, because "the systematic destruction of our culture and families threw us into chaos, often confused and misdirected
our loyalties and called into question our love."[54]

Another school of thought traces the conflict to the mesmerizing
effect the symbol of white feminine beauty and power has had on
black men for centuries. This argument was the bone and sinew of
the work of Eldridge Cleaver, which captured national attention during the same period that Alice Walker's novel was receiving literary
accolades. Confessing that he perfected his rape techniques on black
women before he attacked prized white women, Cleaver calls the black
man's desire for white women "a sickness [that] must be brought out
into the open, dealt with and resolved."[55] Until it is, black men will
continue to revere white women and abuse black women, Cleaver
believes. Shulamith Firestone expands this thesis and offers another
unconvincing and excessively Freudian interpretation of the triangle
of black women, black men, and white women. One must recognize,
she says, that racism and sexism together have created "an Oedipus/
Electra Complex, which is not easily neutralized in the psyches of the
three victims."[56]

Walker's vision is not consonant with Shulamith Firestone's thesis of the "Oedipus/Electra Complex" or with Cleaver's notion of the
"sickness" that generates the psyche of black men, for white women
are not central to the story Walker tells so brilliantly, and white men
are present only because they represent the injustice that cripples

Brownfield. Walker's vision of black womanhood, then, belies the assumption that at the root of the black woman's problems with her man are the omnipresence and omnipotence of the specter of white female beauty. This is not to suggest that the specter is not present in the small black community; there is no place in this country where it has not made its way into the culture of the people. Indeed, Brownfield attempts to belittle Mem with the reminder that "you ain't white" (p. 58). But Walker quickly explains that Brownfield hates white women and "did not want his wife to imitate [them]." He means that Mem's "color was something she could not change and as his own colored skin annoyed him, he meant for hers to humble her." However, he does not succeed in making Mem "ashamed of being black," because she believes that "color was something the ground did to flowers, and that was an end to it" (p. 58). Her agony lies elsewhere.

Karenga's thesis that the "systematic destruction of our culture" is the cause of black male–female conflict is, to be sure, similar to the explanation Walker gives for Brownfield's abuse of Mem, but it is Calvin Herton's analysis that best shows Walker's imaginative picture of the problem as an unblurred reflection of real life. In *Sex and Racism in America* (1965) Hernton writes that the historical chaos results from the black man's need to blame someone for his failures in a racist society. It is a common saying among black men, Hernton explains, that "when anything goes wrong," the black woman is at fault. A retrenched "depreciatory concept of Negro females" explains why "the black man asserts, halfheartedly, but significantly, that black women are hell to get along with."[57] This attitude becomes, in Walker's portrayal of the Copelands, a disease that is passed down through generations. Destroyed by the same cruel sharecropping system that gnaws at Brownfield's soul, his father, Grange, beat his wife, accused her of sleeping with white men (an egregious sin in the community), abandoned her and the children for weeks on end, and literally drove her to suicide.

While Walker's picture of the relationship of Brownfield and Mem mirrors the facts presented in sociology and history, it does so in a way that makes the imaginative statement more powerful than any scholarly documentation. Walker produces a tour de force of black male–female tension. Her characters are powerful; her pictures are worth hundreds of documents. The shadow of eternal bondage in which Brownfield lives is not an abstract concept; it is as real as life and rich in particulars:

> His heart had actually started to hurt him, like an ache in the bones, when he watched his five-year-old daughter swinging the mop, stumbling over the lumps of hard clay, the hot tin bucket full of arsenic making a bloodied scrape against her small legs. (p. 53)

The color of the scene is the bright red of fury. The odor is the stench of arsenic and human vomit. The sound is Brownfield's heart splintering as he sees his daughter breathing with difficulty and carrying the "beaten down" look of a "tiny asthmatic old lady" (p. 54). The power of Walker's images and metaphors leaves us as moved by Brownfield's tragic decline into self-hatred as we are angered by his abuse of Mem. Punctuated with italics and exclamations, Walker's paragraph on the "new" Brownfield is a eulogy for a dead man:

> His crushed pride, his battered ego, made him drag Mem away from school teaching. . . . It was his great ignorance that sent her into white homes as a domestic, his need to bring her down to his level! It was his rage at himself, and his life and his world that made him beat her for an imaginary attraction she aroused in other men, crackers, although she was no party to any of it. His rage could and did blame everything, *everything* on her. (p. 55)

An appropriate analogy for Brownfield's treatment of Mem is the wife as nigger. She is Brownfield's inferior simply because she is a woman and he is a man. In her woman's world of servitude there is no need for education, so she must burn her books or use their pages to stuff large rat holes in their shack. She saves her earnings to purchase a house; he steals the money and buys a pig. She saves again; he steals to buy a little red car. He should have the "things" and the power, even if they come from her work. Their living conditions are appropriate to her status as "nigger." Outhouses, rat holes, manure-filled cowsheds turned into living quarters—all these she should accept in gratitude. And like a "nigger," she must serve him even as she is abused by him. Her role is clearly and narrowly defined. She is woman. He is lord. She must please him. He is free to please only himself. He succeeds in fulfilling his promise to himself: "he determined . . . to treat her like a nigger" (p. 54).

Mem's identity as a woman means, first, that she cannot adequately defend herself against the beatings Brownfield gives with his plough-heavy hands and his field-large body. After the birth of three children in three years, Mem is truly the "weaker sex." It means, secondly, that she is powerless against a culture locked into the pathology of masculine dominance, which gives Brownfield justification, in his own thinking, for his mistreatment of her. Thirdly, and most tragically, it means that she is vulnerable to physical abuse in intercourse. Brownfield takes her "in his drunkenness," Walker writes, and boasts to his friends of both his sexual power and his fist power. "Give this old blacksnake to her," he says, showing his penis and rubbing it suggestively, "and then I beats her ass. Only way to treat a nigger woman" (p. 54). Mem's response to this abuse makes Brownfield's cruelty an egregious crime: she is "a submissive, accepting wife" (p. 59). She is too weak physically to resist his beatings. And she has no refuge to which she can escape. Her mother is dead, her father has disowned her, and Josie does not want her. She is too gentle and too afraid to challenge, even in words, the fierceness of her husband's control. And yet, there are times in her conversations with herself when her woman's rage desires revenge:

> If I was a man, she thought, frowning later, scrubbing the dishes, if I was a man I'd give every man in sight and that I ever met up with a beating, maybe even chop up a few with my knife. (p. 84)

Loneliness is a dominant feature of Walker's portrait of Mem, for she is a woman without a past, without fond memories, without life-giving myths, without self-reinforcing stories related by a grandmother, without ties to a warmly hysterical black church that beckons the disconsolate to its bosom, and without neighbors who give advice and lend support. Mary Helen Washington, writing of black women in real life, captures the loneliness of Mem Copeland. Black women have been alone, she writes, "because the damage done to our men has prevented their closeness and protection; and alone because we have had no one to tell us stories ourselves."[58] But it is Toni Morrison's definition of loneliness that is the most incisive caption for Alice Walker's moving portrait of Mem Copeland: "the loneliest woman in the world is a woman without a woman friend."[59]

In spite of her aloneness and her misery, Mem Copeland functions as a devoted mother. In this role she *is* the superhuman woman of strength, endurance, and compassion to whom a tradition of black American poetry has paid tribute since the nineteenth century. Her every goal, every wish, every struggle, is born of her identity as a mother. She cleans cow manure out of sheds to make them "habitable for her children" (p. 78). She fights Brownfield with words, though never with blows, "always for the children (p. 95). "She slogged alone, ploddingly, like a cow herself" (p. 99), for the sake of her children. And it is for the sake of her children that she begins to run, to gallop, to race like a stallion bent on freedom.

Risking Brownfield's rage, Mem rents a house in the city and returns to the shack in the country to take control of her life—for the sake of her children. As Brownfield sleeps off his drunkenness, she wakes him by pushing a loaded gun barrel into his "balls," a symbolic statement that her liberation is sexual in nature. She analyzes Brownfield. She understands what "the man" has done to him, but she also understands, more painfully, what Brownfield has done to himself and to his family. Further, she understands, and would have him understand, that a real man should "quit wailing like a seedy jackass" (p. 59). Race cannot be ignored, but neither can it be used as an excuse for all one's weaknesses and sins. This is Mem's message to Brownfield, and one of the major themes of the novel (as well as many of Alice Walker's poems). Walker indicts Brownfield for his failures as a man when she writes that he "did not have the courage to imagine life without the existence of white people as a prop" (p. 47).

Mem invites Brownfield to join her in her new life with the understanding that "it's going to be my house and in my house what the

white man expects us to act like ain't going to git no consideration"
(p. 96). She lays down nine rules he must follow, all of which can be
summed up in one: he will treat her and her children with respect
and dignity. In "her house" Brownfield finds respect and dignity for
himself. There is heat at all times. There is electricity for reading and
looking through catalogues. And there is a toilet where Brownfield
can "shit . . . without much odor or rain, and much like a gentleman"
(p. 96). Walker puts the metamorphosis of Brownfield's life well: he
is living "like a white man" (p. 102). But he is a bird of prey that bides
its time, circling ominously above those who will be its victims. He
plants "a seed . . . that would bring Mem down in weakness and dependence" (p. 103), the seed of procreation. Two pregnancies that do
not bear fruit dissipate Mem's energies, rendering her helpless against
Brownfield's criminal designs on her destruction. Unable to work,
she cannot keep up the payments on the house. Like a vulture, in one
fell swoop Brownfield descends on her weakened body and returns
her to the manure-filled shack, where she becomes, once again, a
"plodding cow."

In spite of her own destruction, Mem holds fast to her sanity and
dignity. For the sake of her children, she works as a domestic and
returns home to tend house and cook; and she manages, also for the
sake of her children, to stretch her face of defeat into a smile. Finally,
carrying packages for her children, she faces Brownfield's gun. Seconds later, she lies "faceless in a pool of blood," her still body decorated by a "halo of [the] dozen bright yellow oranges" she had carried in her arms for her children (p. 122). Like the women Walker
pays tribute to in "In Search of Our Mothers' Gardens," Mem had
worked "for a day when the unknown thing" inside her, pushing her
to plant flowers and to dream of different alternatives, "would be made
known; but [she] guessed, somehow, in [her] darkness, that on the
day of . . . revelation [she] would be long dead."[59]

The story of Mem Copeland carries much of Alice Walker's own
rage against black men who abuse black women in real life. In an
interview published in *Encore* Walker said that she gets very angry
with black women for taking all the stuff they take, "simply because
they have a perverted sense of loyalty to black men."[61] However, to

suggest that Walker does not respect black men would be far from the truth. Her moving poetry is replete with positive images of black men. To suggest, further, that she sees black men as "the enemy" would be an insult to an artist whose work is rooted in love, understanding, and forgiveness. The largeness of Alice Walker's soul makes her a sensitive and embracing poet. But her largeness of soul does not stand in the way of her artist's search for truth, just as the black woman's belief in what Carrie McCray calls our unquestionable "special set of humanistic values"[62] must not stand in the way of an honest examination of black motherhood. Walker, then, writes of the tragedy, abuse, loneliness, and desperation she finds present in black reality. Like her colleague and friend Barbara Smith, she believes that "sexual politics are as real in black women's lives as racial politics, and are as real as the politics of class."[63] She does not argue, as does Jessie Bernard, that sexism is the greater burden for black women and racism the greater burden for black men.[64] Rather, she argues that the American reality alienates one economic group from another, one race from another, and the male from the female. And it is in the experience of motherhood, and in wifehood as well, that the sound of the destruction is most profound.

chapter 4

"GOING NOWHERE IMMEDIATE"

Black Women of Hopelessness

> Edging into life from the back door. Becoming. Everybody in the world was in a position to give them orders. White women said, "Do this." White children said, "Give me that." White men said, "Come here." Black men said, "Lay down." The only people they need not take orders from were black children and each other.
>
> —Toni Morrison, *The Bluest Eye*, 1970

Poor and unskilled black women have historically been ghettoized in the labor market of white America. They are domestics in white homes, service workers in white-owned hospitals and hotels, field hands on white-owned farms, and operatives in white-owned factories. In large urban areas they are often number runners, prostitutes, and procurers. Of all these categories, that of domestic is the job slot most often associated in the national thinking with black women, and for obvious reasons: black women are disproportionately represented in the labor market in this category.

Jeanne Noble analyzes this labor picture within the context of history, and within that context she emphasizes race, gender, and class. Explaining that racial and class patterns are stubborn and unyielding in white America, Noble writes that black women have been systematically programmed for the last hundred and twenty years to do what was essentially theirs to do during slavery—to serve as maids and mammies for white Americans:

> The long shadow of slavery may be fading for some, but over one fourth of all black sisters are still marketing the skills of our ancestors who washed, scrubbed, and hoed in the mansion yards and cotton fields of Southern plantations, and whose daughters entered the census page of the twentieth century with little choice except to do the same.[1]

As late as 1973, "25.5 percent of [black women in the labor market] worked in the service occupations, and among this group 17.9 percent worked exclusively in private households—in other words, as domestics." Of a total of 1.5 million domestics in the nation, 69 percent were black women.[2]

Domestic work is emotionally charged for black women for several reasons. First of all, it has been viewed by the nation, and by black women themselves, as demeaning. "Reflecting the feelings of their society, black women domestics look upon their jobs as requiring little skill, and they believe that nobody would do this work if they could do anything else. . . . They have little sense of their beauty and rarely realize their worth."[3] Second, the job brings home in concrete ways the magnitude of the injustice they suffer because they are poor, black, and female. They leave apartments of poverty to spend the day working in homes of comfort and luxury, and they return to those apartments with meager earnings and injured pride. They see the stark contrast between the world of the have-nots and the world of the haves they labor in to alleviate their families' suffering.

Such work is emotionally charged also because it reinforces for many black women their status in American culture as unattractive women of superior strength. Because they are strong women, they are capable, it is assumed, of performing tasks that white women are not expected to do—such as washing windows, mopping and waxing floors, and carrying heavy bags of groceries. And because they are unattractive by white America's standards, they are expected to receive pleasure from caring for wardrobes, polishing trays on which cosmetics and fragrances are placed, and keeping clear of streaks and blurs the mirrors that reflect white beauty. In Hollywood movies, black domestics prepared baths for their female employers and even brushed the hundred strokes thought needed for healthy hair. It was her resentment of these demeaning roles that caused Hattie McDaniel to refuse to be "ghettoized" in the movie industry.[4] In the real world, working as a domestic in white homes has been for some black women like working in the lioness's den. The lioness does not roar; she condescends and humiliates. She does not devour with claws and superior strength; she demeans with expressions of her idealized fragility and beauty.

Added to these problems is the unending list of responsibilities black domestics are required to take on, for the job is never simply a housecleaning job; it includes almost all of the tasks identified by American culture as "woman's work." Black women cook family meals, often preparing favorite dishes for the children and unplanned snacks for the husbands of white women. They launder shirts, polish shoes, and carry and pick up cleaning. And they often serve as the large bosom of humanity on which members of the white family lay their individual burdens of white children, for whom they are surrogate mothers. This last role is emphasized in William Faulkner's portrait of Dilsey in *The Sound and the Fury*. Dilsey "endures" through various crises in the Compson family, and out of her great humanity salves their deepest hurts. She is seen by the nation as the epitome of the black domestic in white America.

The contributions of black domestics to the lives of white women and men are exceeded only by their contributions to the lives of white children. The point being made here is that black domestics throughout history have not been just maids; they have been the great earth mother of this nation.

When we look carefully at all that the job of domestic entails, we understand why it is not simply a job. It is an institution in American culture. The tragedy is that for all this institution asks of black women and for all it receives from them, it gives little in return. Black domestics understand this imbalance. A character in Douglas Turner Ward's play *Happy Ending* describes her life as a domestic with controlled anger:

". . . from top to bottom, I cook the food, scrub the floor, open the
door, serve the tables, answer the phones, raise the children, lay out
the clothes, greet the guests, fix the drinks and dump the garbage—
all for bad pay. . . . The money I git in my envelope ain't worth the
time 'n' the headache."[5]

Black women understand the polarization of white women and
black women into two distinct groups. They know, too, that this polarization is rooted at least as much in race as in class, for black women,
regardless of their class, looks, and skills, are never "ladies":

There are two kinds of females in this country—colored women
and white ladies. Colored women are maids, cooks, taxi drivers,
crossing guards, schoolteachers, welfare recipients, bar maids and
the only time they become ladies is when they are cleaning ladies.[6]

Denied respect and admiration, "cleaning ladies" in American culture "grow old fast . . . watching white women stay young."[7]

Not all the characters discussed in this chapter are "cleaning ladies," but all are overworked in menial jobs, underpaid, humiliated,
used, abused, and ignored. They are sensitive women who understand why they are suffering, and they respond with submission, bitterness, religious rationalizing, clever game playing, or anger. Though
they are not always aware of all the factors that affect their lives, they
do know that their lives are hostage to forces over which they have
little control. Min and Mrs. Hedges in Ann Petry's *The Street* (1946),
Josie in Alice Walker's *The Third Life of Grange Copeland* (1970), and
Pauline Breedlove in Toni Morrison's *The Bluest Eye* (1970) are on a
treadmill, "going nowhere immediate."[8]

Set in Harlem during the thirties and forties, *The Street* is a tour-de-
force protest novel that blames American capitalism for the tragic
interlocking of race, class, and gender in the lives of working-class
women. The tragedy of black life, Petry writes, is that "the women
have to work until they become drudges and the men stand by idle."[9]
Young and old, the faces of the women on 116th Street "have a look of

resignation, of complete acceptance" that reveals their inability to "protest against anything—even death" (p. 125). The heroine of the novel is a young woman who struggles to save herself and her young son from the destructive clutches of the street, but Petry opens the lens of her protest to reveal a group of women responding in different ways to the harshness of life on 116th Street in Harlem.

Min is the most resigned among them. She has spent her life as a domestic in white homes, never challenging the racial assumptions her employers make about her and never asking for more than what they consider her due. Though her outward response is one of total submission, Min is acutely aware of her exploitation by the white "madams" she works for. When a job is described by the employment agency as "a little cleaning," she knows the white women will add "heavy jobs like washing windows and walls and waxing floors," and "the care of innumerable children whose existence was never indicated on the employment contract." They will ignore her right to "days off" and "increase the work week to include Saturday and often even Sunday" (pp. 82–83).

In sentimental portrayals of the black domestic in white American fiction, praise and affection from white employers serve as palliatives, but for Petry's Min, there are no palliatives. Without exception, Min observes, her madams are "openly contemptuous women who laughed at her even as they piled on more work; acting as though she were like a deaf, dumb, blind thing completely devoid of understanding" (p. 82). The sexual identity she shares with them is vitiated by race and by class. Indeed, Min sees white women as more her enemy than white men, because they overwork her one moment and humiliate her the next. The only white women Min knows are her cold and insensitive madams and the beautiful creatures whose faces appear in the conspicuous billboards that decorate the train that carries her from Harlem to suburbia.

Her life experience has destroyed Min's sense of self-worth. All she has ever known, Petry writes, is the polarity of black women as subjects of hard work and abuse and white women as madams of affluence and hostility. Nothing in her experience—or in the experiences of the other blacks she knows in Harlem—suggests that change is even remotely possible. Thus Min is resigned to things as they have always been. She looks closely at her life and sees "years and years like that": working as "a seven-day-a-week domestic serf who must do any job ordered by the white employer," burying herself under "great mounds of dirty clothes . . . getting no extra pay for the extra time involved," and remaining on a job "no matter how much work there was or how badly people treated her." Through it all, she has accepted whatever happened to her without making any effort to avoid or change a situation. By her own admission, she has "permitted herself to be used and mistreated" (p. 82).

From the houses of white women, where she is exploited because of her race and class, Min returns to a small basement apartment, where she is exploited because of her sex. This is the point Petry makes as she fits the jagged pieces of Min's relationships with men into a picture of horror. In her experiences with white madams, Min at least receives something in return for her submission to hard work and humiliation; there are, after all, her meager earnings. But from black men, to whose control and hostility she also submits, Min receives nothing. What is worse, she must devise ways to keep what she has earned from being stolen from her. Three husbands always managed to find her money, "as though they could smell it out . . . where it was put in coffee pots, under plates, in the icebox, under mattresses, between the sheets or rugs" (p. 76). And when they were not robbing her, they were physically abusing her. All of them "had taught her" the techniques of brutality:

> First, the grip around the neck that pressed the windpipe out of position, so that the screams were choked off and no sound could emerge from her throat, and then a whole series of blows, and after that, after falling to the ground under the weight of the blows, the most painful part would come—landing with force, sinking deep into the soft, fleshy parts of her body, her stomach, her behind. (p. 221)

Wife beating and rape are sanctioned by the cultural notion that man has the right to dominate woman. Susan Brownmiller writes that a woman is vulnerable to rape because "forcible intercourse" is possible, and she is likewise vulnerable to beatings because she is, in most instances, physically weaker than a man. In Petry's imaginative re-creation of the reality of poor black women in Harlem, we find the suggestion that black women are distinguishable from black men as "victims" by their peculiar vulnerability to "man's basic weapon of force." Force, whether as rape or as a physical beating, is "the ultimate test of [man's] superior strength," or a conscious "act of intimidation by which . . . men keep . . . women in a state of fear."[10]

Petry's depiction of the dynamics of race and sex in Min's life is complex, shifting back and forth in emphasis. She does not pit race against sex, for every observation she makes about sexual oppression is clearly tied to "the street," her compelling metaphor for racial and class oppression. But in the structure of her novel, especially in the chapters dealing with Min, she reflects the ideas of Susan Brownmiller and other contemporary feminist scholars. In that male intimidation is physically and ruthlessly brutal, in that it takes place in the sanctity of Min's home, in that it is committed by a member of her own race, and in that it is offered in response to a caring that approaches maternal tenderness, it is indisputably the greater personal burden. This is Petry's imaginative depiction of the point Abbey Lincoln makes in her essay "Who Will Revere the Black Woman?" In a list of abuses the black woman suffers, Lincoln includes the following observation: "her head is more regularly beaten than any other's woman's, and *by her own man*."[11] By including this suffering in her portrait of Min, Petry debunks the idea of the black woman as emasculator.

Min's self-destructive submission to male abuse is credible and in character. Her powerlessness and humiliation in the world of white madams has convinced her that there can be no comfort, peace, security, or respect for "colored women" and programmed her to accept abuse at the hands of black men. Lacking any awareness of the interplay between sexual oppression and racial oppression, and having no will for a struggle of any kind, Min places her life in the hands of white women and black men, two "others" whose reality is very different from hers.

In her common-law marriage with the superintendent of the apartment, Min is "spineless and ... limp ... like a soggy dishrag," a "whis-
pering woman" whose "shrinking withdrawal in her way of sitting"
suggests a "profound sense of self-denial" and a desire to take up "the
least possible amount of space" (p. 21). When she opens the door to
the apartment in the evenings, she seems to question her right to
enter: "Min's key was inserted in the lock timidly, with a vague grop-
ing movement, and when the lock finally clicked back, she stood there
for a second as though overwhelmed by the sound it made" (p. 90).
Once inside the damp, narrow basement apartment, Min serves the
superintendent as dutifully and unquestionably as she serves her
madams: she washes his clothes, darns his socks, cooks his meals. In
her own home she is an unpaid maid who keeps the place tidy for his
comfort, without any assistance from him. She does not think or speak
or ask questions. She simply moves through her "woman's work" as
one who has internalized the most fundamental assumptions about
woman's place and man's role. She has told herself repeatedly, and
always with conviction, that "a woman by herself didn't stand much
chance" (p. 86).

Until the superintendent is distracted by the presence of a new
tenant, Lutie Johnson, Min accepts her posture of "shrinking withdrawal from life." However, when she learns that her home is threatened by the super's insane and aberrant desire to possess Lutie
Johnson, Min makes what she believes is the first "defiant gesture" in
her life: she goes to a prophet to have the super "fixed" (p. 82). Be-
neath the surface, this gesture is not a challenge to things as they are,
for the "fixing" of the super is meant only to assure that Min's place
in the apartment as servant is not disturbed. But the "fixing" achieves
the opposite of what Min expected: instead of changing the super, it
changes her. She gains confidence from the magic of the bright green
powder and the candles that she burns surreptitiously each day, and
she becomes aware of a part of herself that she had hidden under the
mask of submission. She now puts her key in the door with a thrust
of "assurance," and the sound is "decisive and loud" (p. 90). For the
first time in her life she has power over someone, though she doesn't
realize that this "magic" power is at every moment threatened by her

acceptance of assumptions about her basic powerlessness. These assumptions have blinded her to a fundamental fact about power that Marilyn French expresses simply and forcefully in *The Woman's Room* (1977): "power is not something you possess, but is something granted to you by those you have power over."[12]

When Min forgets to observe the rituals suggested by the prophet, she is seized by a profound sense of dread. Every movement of the super

> made her heart jump. . . . Every sound he made was magnified. His muttering to himself was like thunder . . . and . . . set her eyes blinking so that she couldn't stop them. When he beat the dog, it made her sick, because as each blow landed the dog cried out sharply and her stomach would suck in against itself. [And when he was quiet], she felt impelled to locate him . . . for there was no telling what awful thing he might be doing. (p. 225)

This seizure of fear, heightened by her belief that she cannot win in a struggle of any kind, precipitates Min's decision to leave 116th Street. She speaks of "having room to breathe," and realizes at last that "she'd been running, running, running, and hadn't been able to stop long enough to get a nose full of air" (p. 224). She comes close to self-realization, but a lifetime of racial and sexual oppression prevents her from coming close enough. Once out on 116th Street, away from the superintendent, Min searches again for the "security" that the presence of a man offers. She speaks coquettishly to a pushcart man, who assists her with her few belongings. Min's life is not likely to change much—the pushcart man, who will be her fourth "husband," carries the table in which her money is hidden.

Petry convincingly demonstrates how racism and poverty have robbed Min of a positive self-image. She is less convincing in showing that the black male's exploitation of the black female is solely the result of race and poverty. To be sure, the superintendent has lived in the darkness of the basement for years and, deprived of light, has become a deviant. Other black men, equally powerless in the white-dominated society, are rendered incapable of forming healthy relationships with women. Indeed, every black man in the novel is depicted as a victim of "the street," too crippled to enjoy the psychic health necessary to allow them to love and support the black women in their lives. While these facts explain the tragic devastation of Petry's black male characters, they do not explain why black women in her book submit to male control and abuse. For that explanation, we must look at Petry's treatment of cultural assumptions about "woman's place."

That these assumptions are present in the novel is evident in Petry's use of the advice of Mrs. Pizzini, an Italian woman whose husband owns a shop on the street: "not good for the woman to work when she's young. No good for the man" (p. 38). This was the sexual ethos that undergirded American culture in the forties. As the historical overview in chapter 2 made clear, women left their "place" in the home to support the war effort, and at the end of the war, they were advised to return to their "natural" role as wives and mothers in the home. It was during this same period that "the feminine mystique" reached more deeply into the national consciousness. Although Mrs. Pizzini's advice is thoroughly "American," then, it is hardly relevant to black women, and Petry's irony is justified: Mrs. Pizzini can subscribe to the notion of woman's place in the home because racism has not forced her to leave that place for the survival of her family.

From a psychological perspective, however, it does not matter that the advice is irrelevant to black reality, for values that shape the mainstream culture find their way into the consciousness of all members of the society, no matter how far outside the mainstream they may be. While there are polar groups in America—one black, the other white; one male, the other female; and one the haves, the other the have-nots—there is essentially one set of criteria for what is normal and what is deviant. This fact is most apparent in the numerous sociological studies that speak of the "deviance" of the black families that do not conform to America's standards of normality: the woman in the home, the man in the world of work. Such assessments, like Mrs. Pizzini's warning, are examples of what sociologist William Ryan calls the trick of "blaming the victim."[13] Inadvertently, they help perpetuate myths about the black experience, and in so doing, they validate the status quo.

What is Petry's response to the prevailing notion of the forties that a woman's place is in the home? She seems to challenge this cultural assumption indirectly by depicting Mrs. Pizzini as a static character who stays in the same place, doing the same things, and even saying the same things. There is money in her life but no sparkle. Again, in her observations on the filthy-rich white women in whose household Lutie works, Petry calls our attention to their empty existence. Though it is difficult to separate Petry's attitude toward race and class oppression from her attitude toward sexual oppression, we can speculate that the negative portraits of white women who remain in their "place" are comments on the sterility of woman's place. There is no need to speculate on Petry's opinion of the impact the assumption has on black women. She attacks the system for believing in that "place" and denying it to poor black women.

The reality of Min and other black women in the novel bears the imprint of a corollary assumption about woman's place: man should be aggressive, and woman should be passive. Hence Min's "shrinking withdrawal from life."

Thus, racism makes Min subservient to white women, sexism makes her submissive to black men, and economic deprivation makes her, even in her flight from "the street," a black woman who is "going nowhere immediate." It is interesting that this novel of the forties parallels the thinking of black feminists of the seventies in the Combahee River Collective, who write that it is "difficult to separate race from class from sex oppression [in black women's lives] for they are most often experienced simultaneously."[14]

Since victimization of black people in general and black women in particular makes psychic health and economic success difficult, it follows that there can be no winners on "the street." But paradoxically, not all people are losers. Some of the characters in The Street manage to use the system for their own self-aggrandizement. Such a woman is Mrs. Hedges, a "very black woman," who ritualistically sits at the open window of her first-floor apartment, watching the comings and goings of black people. Even on cold days she is there, as if bolted to her place, watching the women passersby with eyes "as still and as malignant as the eyes of a snake":

> They are the lonesome, sad-looking girls just up from the South, or little girls who were tired of going to high school and who had seen too many movies and didn't have all the money to buy all the things they wanted . . . [and] other little girls who were only slightly older who woke up one morning to discover that their husbands had moved out. With no warning. Suddenly. (p. 159)

Mrs. Hedges studies them carefully and, at the propitious moment, calls out, "Dearie . . . I been seeing you go by. And I was wondering if you wouldn't like to earn a little extra money sometime" (p. 157). Mrs. Hedges is a "colored madam" who lures black women into the trap of prostitution. It might be thought that putting a black character who capitalizes on black powerlessness in a novel of protest would dilute the protest, but Petry understands that black participation in the victimization of black people is just a deeper plunge into the same river.

What is most interesting about Petry's presentation of this problem is her emphasis on Mrs. Hedges's sensitivity to her own unattractiveness. Cursed by an "enormous size" (p. 151), she is not considered feminine in a culture that worships slender frames; nor, with her deep-purple blackness, beautiful in a culture that worships whiteness. She desperately wants a man's love, which, she believes, will give her a sense of worth in spite of her ugliness. When she leaves her small Georgia community for Harlem, it is to "find a man who would fall in love with her" (p. 151). Her migration to the North is prompted by sexual desire, not by the dream of escaping racial oppression in "the promised land."

The move is one of several ironies in the novel, for on "the street" even attractive women must suspend their dreams as women as they struggle to survive as blacks—and often the dreams must be suspended forever. Mrs. Hedges learns this soon after she arrives on 116th Street. In her small black community in Georgia, she was a curiosity. In Harlem, she is a monstrosity. On the faces of white people in employment agencies she sees "an uncontrollable revulsion. . . . They glanced at each other, tried in vain to control their faces or didn't bother to try at all" (p. 151). Unable to find work and without the money to return to Georgia, Mrs. Hedges prowls the streets of Harlem, driven by a "gnawing, insatiable hunger." In her abysmal poverty she scavenges in garbage cans for food, and clothes herself in discarded rags. A pathetic contrast to her fantasized image of herself, she wears "thin, ragged clothes that exaggerate her size and discarded men's shoes" that cramp her feet "so that she limped slightly" (p. 151).

On one of her nightly prowls for food, she meets Junto, a white man who is as destitute as she, but whose whiteness is a decided advantage in a racist culture. Because he is both white and male, he has been socialized to be both competitive and powerful. Out of this socialization he converts his foraging into a business. With Mrs. Hedges's help, he collects scraps, sells them, and in time amasses a fortune. The relationship between Junto and Mrs. Hedges is a metaphor for the exploitation of black people. Mrs. Hedges tills, but she does not reap bountiful harvests. Although Junto could not have succeeded without her help, she is definitely less than a real partner. In fact, she is a janitor in one of his many buildings, and the procurer for his lucrative prostitution business.

Mrs. Hedges solicits women so desperate they see no alternative to prostitution—"good girls" whom the environment has corrupted. Petry's one-dimensional image of prostitutes is common to novels of the literary school of naturalism. With a social worker's attention to details of cause and effect, Petry denounces the injustices that force the innocent to prostitute themselves. Three decades later, black women novelists would expand their artistic lens and give us a different image of prostitutes. Morrison, for example, in *The Bluest Eye* (1970) describes a group of black prostitutes—the "merry gargoyles," she calls them—as "whores" who have never been innocent or good and who "hate men, all men, without shame, apology, or discrimination" (pp. 47–48). But Petry's goal as an artist of the forties was to protest the victimization of black people. In her vision, therefore, prostitutes must be victims.

Petry's analysis of prostitution in America is actually more complex than her one-dimensional image of the "ruined" woman suggests. In some ways, she agrees with Maimie Pinzer, a nineteenth-century Jewish prostitute, who wrote that poor women choose "their means of survival from a position of socially structured powerlessness," and their options are always the same: "prostitution, marriage and unskilled menial jobs."[15] But black women in Petry's vision do not have the option of marriage as an avenue to security, since their men are victimized by the same system that victimizes them. Also, they are much more likely to be entrapped in poverty than white women. And finally, their humanity is systematically denied primarily because they are poor black females, and only secondarily because they are prostitutes. So, no matter how similar the sufferings of poor white women and poor black women are, racism makes a crucial difference.

Mrs. Hedges gives little thought to the pernicious life in store for the vulnerable women she is procuring. She is interested only in making money without having to go out into the world and confront the ridicule and revulsion her appearance produces. This need to protect herself at the expense of other women explains why it is she who suggests to Junto that he begin a business of prostitution with her help. Her rationalization reveals how profoundly she has internalized the cultural assumption that men, but not women, should be cared for. Because black men "hadn't got anything out of life and knew clearly that they never would get it," Mrs. Hedges reasons, they need a way "to escape their hopes and fears" (p. 156). Thoroughly conditioned by sexist assumptions about men's needs and women's obligations to meet those needs, she does not realize that black women, too, need an escape. That they are the vehicles for man's escape is an expression of the profoundness of their oppression.

Once Mrs. Hedges has security as a "partner" in Junto's business, she takes her woman's dream out of suspension. Without money, she had no hope of gaining a man's love; with money, she can buy what her physical appearance has denied her. She does not equivocate about her goal: nothing except the presence of a man in her life can validate her and make her whole. More is involved here than the romantic fantasy of a woman in search of a Prince Charming who will make her a queen. In fact, Mrs. Hedges has no such illusions; she knows that she will not be pampered or even loved. She simply wants a man in her life, and with money "she could pick [one] for herself and he would be glad to have her" (p. 152). For her, therefore, economic success is not a means of survival in a racist society. Rather, it is the prerequisite for her dreams as a woman.

The fickle hand of fate—always operative in naturalistic novels—destroys Mrs. Hedges's woman's dream forever. In Theodore Dreiser's *An American Tragedy* fate is a drowning accident; in Richard Wright's *Native Son* it is an accidental suffocation. In Petry's *The Street* it is a raging fire. Mrs. Hedges pushes herself through a narrow aperture in the burning building, feeling her flesh tear and burn. It is significant that even in the midst of this life-and-death situation, her thoughts are on her woman's dream: all she needed "was to get badly burned, and never as long as she lived would any man look at her and want her." Her agony is profound: "No matter how much money she acquired, [men] still wouldn't want her. No sum of money would be big enough to make them pretend to want her" (p. 152).

Miraculously, Mrs. Hedges survives the fire, but she must live the remainder of her life without hair on her head. That Petry chooses baldness as the most damaging scar Mrs. Hedges suffers as a result of the fire underscores the sexual ramifications of the portrait. Hair, of all physical assets, is culturally associated with beauty, softness, and femininity. Many black women, from childhood until death, undergo a painful heat-and-metal-comb process to make their kinky hair more like the soft straight or curly locks of white women. Mrs. Hedges can wear a wig, of course; she can cover her disfigurement with expensive clothes, or even undergo plastic surgery at Junto's expense. But all these efforts would be useless, for she has lost forever the possibility of obtaining a man. So, in her bandanna, she takes up her station at the window of the apartment building on 116th Street in Harlem and holds herself aloof from the horrors of life in that community. Racially and sexually, she is a lost woman.

The sad, lonesome girls in Alice Walker's *The Third Life of Grange Copeland* make their way down dusty rural roads and between vast fields of cotton. Though this masterpiece of southern black literature, as Walker explained in an interview, is "ostensibly about a man and his son," it is "the women and how they are treated that colors every-thing."[16] The colors are the grays of oppression, the blues of loneli-ness, and, for Josie, the most colorful woman in the novel, the reds of passion and anger.

Josie was born on the rich clay soil of Georgia and was reared in a small rural community owned by white men who exact from black sharecroppers a pound of their dreams for every ounce of harvest their labor brings. In this community there are only two roles for women—wife/mother or whore. Josie was socialized to believe that power be-longs to white men, who own the land, and to black men, who own their women. She is as certain of the latter as she is of the former, for she has been reared in a male-dominated home. Her mother is a woman of silence and fear, "a meek woman" who "rarely agreed with [Josie's] father, but never argued with him."[17] Josie is programmed to believe that this is the way things are for women and the way they must remain. Only when she is humiliated and abused as a woman does Josie begin to dream and to plan a new life for herself, but in the new life she leaves the racial boundaries of her life undisturbed.

Pregnant at sixteen, Josie incurs the wrath of her father and is cast out of the house for the shame she has brought to the family. She attempts to regain her father's love at a party she gives in his honor. He takes her gifts, sits proudly amid his circle of male friends like a patriarch whose right to the throne is God-given and beyond chal-lenge, and refuses to acknowledge that the party is Josie's plea for reconciliation. Out of frustration she takes the drinks he refuses to accept from her hands and gulps them down, one by one, until she is intoxicated. She falls "clumsily on her back within the curve of the all-male semi-circle" (p. 40). Judge, jury, and now executioner, Josie's father presses his foot into her shoulder and forbids anyone to touch her: "I hear she can do *tricks* on her back like that" (p. 41). Josie's mother weeps, but she does not challenge her husband's right to hold her daughter under his foot "like a spider deformed and grotesque" (p. 41). Instead, she suppresses her maternal rage and submits to her husband's control.

The cultural assumption that men are women's protectors has no voice in Walker's novel. Perhaps, as Elizabeth Schultz suggests, this assumption figures mainly in fiction written by black men: Frank Yerby's *Health Card*, James Baldwin's *Beale Street*, and John Killens's *Youngblood*, for example. "Black women novelists seem to have less faith [in the black man's role as protector] for they present the black woman as having to protect herself. Her form of resistance is liberating, but it is resistance by reaction, through hatred, anger, and violence."[18] In Petry's portrait of Min in *The Street*, a novel of the forties, and Walker's portrait of Mem in *The Third Life of Grange Copeland*, a novel of the seventies, the black woman struggles alone, and often her adversary is her male "protector." Clearly, this is Josie's tragedy. Receiving no support from her mother as she is crushed under her father's foot, she has to struggle out of bondage alone. Like a phoenix who rises from the ashes with unfurled wings, she soars above male control to become the richest and most powerful black person, male or female, in the community. Her damnation has become her salvation, and she achieved it alone.

Salvation from male oppression, however, is not the same as liberation from sexual assumptions about male control and female surrender. Josie decides that she will never again be controlled or humiliated by a man, but she does not see her particular grievances as emblematic of women's reality. Her response to these grievances is to seek vengeance against those who abused her. If women are bodies to be used by men for their pleasure and then discarded, so be it. Josie intends to make the most of what she is supposed to be. She becomes a prostitute.

In a little shack on the aptly named Poontang Street, Josie does "her job with a gusto that denied shame" and "demands her money with an authority that squelched all pity" (p. 41). In time, having saved her earnings, she moves from the little shack to her own establishment, the Dew Drop Inn, the only house of pleasure in the community. As proprietor and prostitute, she vents her rage at men in the community.

> When they became too old to "cut the mustard" any more, she treated them with jolly cruelty and a sadistic kind of concern. She often did a strip tease in the center of their eagerly constructed semicircle, bumping and grinding, moaning to herself, charging

them the last pennies of their meager old-age savings to watch her, but daring them to touch. (p. 41)

Economic power—so rare for women in the small community—does not liberate Josie. She is respected because she is wealthy, but she is confined to a role named by men for women. She is able to strike out sadistically against men, but she is tragically unable to redeem herself from their image of her as a ruined and worthless woman. She is a prisoner, then, chained by the male community's assessment of her as a sex object. Like Petry's Mrs. Hedges in *The Street*, she is a winner who loses.

Elizabeth Schultz has observed that both the black "respectable woman" and the prostitute are forced to view themselves as sexual objects, removed from the "possibility of growth and freedom."[19] Early in life Josie falls victim to male designs on her physical vulnerability. Walker writes lyrically, "Josie had never been young, had never smelled of milk or flowers, but only of a sweet decay." If someone would "take the trouble to expose inch after inch of her to one bright consuming fire of blind adoration and love," Josie might be "made clean" (p. 42). But the smell of decay lingers, for there is no challenge to sexism in the rural community. Convinced of her irredeemable worthlessness as a woman, Josie plays well the role of a "devouring cat, voracious and sly" (p. 36).

One of the prevailing myths about women is that they are always vulnerable to the tragedy of having loved and lost. By sentimental ballads and fairy tales, girls entering puberty are psychologically prepared for the agony and the ecstasy of romantic love. This myth, like all myths, connects to some extent with truth, and Walker develops the point in her story of Josie. Having lost her first love, Grange Copeland, Josie envelops Grange's son, Brownfield, in unchecked passion. She attempts "to eat him up, swallow him down alive" (p. 36). She pampers him, functioning as both mother and lover. She fights her whorish daughter for his affection. She makes him economically dependent on her, the better to exert control over his life. She uses him for the physical pleasure he gives her. She is, in fact, "masculine" in her relationship with Brownfield: Josie adopts and perfects every posture deemed acceptable for men in their relationships with women. Even the male desire to sleep with virgins (a desire that strokes their egos) is included in Walker's description of Josie: Josie takes pleasure in "screwing" Brownfield because he is "a clean young animal [she and her daughter] had not finished soiling" (p. 41). This is Josie's game, and while it gives her pleasure, it does not fulfill her as a woman. For that, she needs a special love to which "woman gives her all."

But Josie never experiences fulfillment. She "gives her all" to the Copeland men, Grange and his son Brownfield, without realizing that their destruction in the narrow space of race can only deepen her misery in the dark enclosure of sex. As sharecroppers they live in virtual slavery, and they see the world through eyes jaundiced by self-hatred. Grange strikes out at the sharecropping system and at "Captain Shipley" by abusing his wife, Margaret, and using Josie as a salve for his pain. His sorrow is profound, but so, too, is Margaret's. She is weary of endless hours of woman's work in the house and exhausting physical labor in the field. After five years of patience and understanding, she follows Grange's example. She neglects her child; she has affairs. Because she is female, she is vulnerable to additional and even justifiable abuse from Grange. After all, even in the face of her husband's infidelity a woman does not have the right to seek love away from the marriage. Because she is black, she is vulnerable to the lust of Captain Shipley, all the more vulnerable, Walker implies, since her loyalty to Grange would permit her to grant Shipley favors in exchange for reductions in Grange's debt. Predictably, her attempts to steal a little pleasure for her life give her only encompassing misery. When she gives birth to Shipley's child, Grange has an excuse to abandon her. Her guilt and despair lead to her murder of the half-white child and her suicide.

The economic system that once enslaved the father also enslaves the son, for there are few alternatives to sharecropping for black people in the small Georgia town. Like his father before him, Brownfield tills land owned by a white man who enjoys the full harvest of Brownfield's labor. Like his father, Brownfield strikes out at this cruel system by abusing his gentle wife, Mem, and their three children, taking diabolical pleasure in seeing them grovel in fear before him:

> Instinctively, with his own life as an example, he had denied the possibility of a better life for his children. He had enslaved his own family, given them weakness when they needed strength, made them powerless before any enemy that stood beyond him. Now when they thought of "the enemy" their own father would straddle their vision. (p. 86)

Brownfield is beyond salvation because he yields his humanity to external forces and justifies the monster within by placing all blame for his failures on white people. When he moves his family from a decent house in town, which Mem had rented, to a squalid, hay-filled shack owned by Mr. J. L., Brownfield embraces his own damnation.

At this most difficult period in Brownfield's life, Grange returns to do penance for the sins of his first life, the sins which explain, in part, the tragedy of his son. Unlike Brownfield, Grange left the South in search of promises of a new life in New York City, or in search of experiences that could remove his guilt as a negligent father, abusive husband, and defeated human being. He finds neither. In the cold and impersonal world of New York, his blackness is no less despised, his manhood no less questioned. He learns this lesson painfully when he sees a pregnant white woman fall into a pond in Central Park. He attempts to rescue her, but the woman disdainfully refuses to take his outstretched hand. This experience is the beginning of Grange's discovery of self. On the one hand, he feels responsible for the woman's death because he had not insisted that she accept his help. On the other hand, he feels that her death was his liberation. Walker writes:

> The death of the woman was simple murder, he thought, and soul condemning; but in a strange way, a bizarre way, it liberated him. He felt in some way repaid for his own unfortunate life. It was the taking of that white woman's life—and the denying of the life of her child—the taking of her life, not the taking of her money, that forced him to want to try to live again. (p. 153)

It is this desire to "live again" that takes Grange back to the small Georgia town. He reaches out to Brownfield, to save him from crippling self-hatred, explaining that he "used to blame the white folks too. For they *is* the cause of all the dirt we have to swallow." But this attitude is the real danger, he explains:

> "By George, I know the danger of putting all the blame on somebody else for the mess you make out of your life. I fell into the trap myself! And I'm bound to believe that that's the way the white folks can corrupt you even when you done held up before. 'Cause when they got you thinking that they're to blame for everything they have you thinking they's some kind of gods! You can't do nothing wrong without them being behind it. You gits as weak as water, no feeling of doing *nothing* yourself. Then you begins to think up evil and begins to destroy everybody around you, and you blames it on the crackers. *Shit!* Nobody's as powerful as we make them out to be. We got our own *souls*, don't we?" (p. 223)

His sermons come too late for Brownfield, who in Grange's absence had begun "to destroy everybody around" him. His efforts to comfort and feed Brownfield's family only widen the gulf between father and son. His newly discovered humanity only magnifies Brownfield's loss of his soul. Ironically, Brownfield festers in rage. He strikes out at the father whom he fears as much as he loathes by aiming the full barrel of a shotgun at Mem's face and standing without remorse over her lifeless body.

> He wouldn't repent. None of what he had done mattered any more. It was over. What had to happen happened: the beautiful faded, the pretty became ugly, the sweetness soured. He had never believed it could turn out any other way. But what had *she* thought, his quiet wife, when he proved to be more cruel to her than any white man, or twenty? . . . Instead of rage, she had had an inner sovereignty, a core of self, which, alas, her husband had not had. She had possessed an embedded strength that Brownfield could not match. (p. 245)

Following Mem's death, one daughter becomes a prostitute. Another goes insane. Ruth, the youngest, becomes Grange's child, his way to salvation, his "third life." It is this Grange Copeland to whom Josie gives everything. Out of "love," she sells her business and shares the money with Grange. With his money and, mainly, hers, he buys a farm where he "raised *his* own bread, fermented *his* own wine, cured *his* own meat." Finally *he* was *his* own boss—"at least *he* was free" (italics added, p. 156). For Josie, however, there is no freedom. Only with Ruth does Grange share his intimate feelings and only because of her is he redeemed and made whole. Josie plots with Brownfield to have the courts take Ruth from Grange, not realizing that even if Ruth lives elsewhere the new Grange can no longer love the Josie of his past. He can be gentle toward her and even feel the pain of her loneliness, but he cannot love her as she wants to be loved. Nor does she realize that Grange would sacrifice his life for Ruth's chances for a full and meaningful existence. Grange murders Brownfield in the courtroom when he loses custody of Ruth. Having removed the only obstacle to her future, Grange stoically returns to the farm and waits for the posse. Josie is once again alone. In her sixties she is bereft of her fortune and aged out of the "bumping and grinding" that had been her livelihood: "once again she had been used by a man and discarded when his satisfaction was secured" (p. 156). Her father's judgment of her becomes her own: she was "the biggest curse in her life and it was her fate to be an everlasting blunderer into misery" (p. 150).

Walker takes the feminist position that in a sexist culture women are socialized to believe that their lives must be reflectors of the lives of men. But she seems to reject the notion that socialization is the only cause of the differences between women and men. In the images and colors that define women in the novel, there is the implication that the special quality that distinguishes women from men is women's preference for love over power, their delight in giving as opposed to controlling. When black men can be whole in white society and resist "the ostensible psychological necessity to brutalize black women as the only outlet for the hatred, anger, shame and envy resulting from their own brutalization,"[20] black women will thrive because they are so capable of intense love.

In Toni Morrison's *The Bluest Eye* (1970) black women move from light into darkness when they migrate from the rural land of their birth to the industrial Midwest. Set in a small Ohio town in the forties, the novel is the tragic story of eleven-year-old Pecola Breedlove, "who yearns for acceptance into life of pretty dresses and shoes . . . and jewelry, into . . . a Storybook life peopled by a laughing mother and smiling father and friendly playmates." She takes as her ideal, writes critic Joan Bischoff, "the blonde-haired, blue-eyed girl epitomized by Shirley Temple," and reasons that "if she herself were thus given beauty, she would simultaneously fall heir to the rich tangibles and intangibles of the world of her dreams."[21] Imprisoned in both poverty and blackness, she finds her wish fulfilled in insanity. As the earlier discussion of this novel in chapter 3 illustrated, it is her mother, Pauline, who contributes in a major way to Pecola's insanity.

A master at making place function as character development, Morrison begins her chapter on the Breedlove family with a description of the storefront house in which they live. "It is a strange house that does not recede into its background of leaden sky, nor harmonize with the gray frame houses and black telephone poles around it." Rather, it foists itself on the eye of the passerby in a manner that is "both irritating and melancholy" (p. 30). The house is more than a dwelling place; it is the mirror in which the confusion and violence of Pauline Breedlove's life are sharply reflected. In one of the most insightful studies written of *The Bluest Eye*, Joan Bischoff examines not only the symbolic description of the storefront house as a mirror of Pauline's life but also the symbolic heading of the opening chapter. She calls attention to Morrison's clever use of a typical passage from a Dick and Jane primer of the forties, showing a pretty house in which a happy white family lives. In the reader, the passage is a scene of middle-class, suburban white family life. In the novel, the passage is a "distorted run-on. . . . one long collection of consonants and vowels seeming to signify nothing":[22]

Hereisthehouseitisgreenandwhiteithasareddoorit
isveryprettyhereisthefamilytheyareveryhappy

. . . seethecat . . . motherisverynice . . .
fatherissmiling. (p. 8)

This run-on chapter head introduces the empty, misshapen life of the Breedloves and points up the existence of two separate societies in white America. Even when "mother" is present and "father" is smiling, the black family experience is perforated with chaos and violence.

When Morrison describes the Breedloves in the first chapter, we see Pauline, her two children, Sammy and Pecola, and her husband, Cholly, living bleak and lonely lives. Pauline is convinced that they are irredeemably ugly and that the poverty and chaos of their private lives are directly traceable to race and other physical attributes. Morrison writes that Pauline and her family moved into the house "because they were poor and black," but they remain "there because they believed they were ugly" (p. 34). Pauline wraps her blackness, poverty, and ugliness around her "as a mantle . . . as an actor does a prop: for articulation of character, for the support of a role she frequently imagined was hers—martyrdom" (p. 34).

Morrison also writes of Pauline's frustration as an artist denied an outlet for her creativity. As earlier discussions have shown, the thwarted desires of the black woman artist are focal points in several black women's novels. The dilemma is addressed brilliantly by Alice Walker in her essay "In Search of Our Mothers' Gardens" (1974), where she writes of black women of the past, especially in the South, who "stumbled blindly through their lives . . . yielding . . . to the prophecy that they were unworthy even of hope." Many of them were artists, "driven to the numb and bleeding madness by the springs of creativity in them for which there was no release."[23] Without developing the idea as fully as she does in *Sula*, Morrison alludes to Pauline's artistic yearnings. They are not expressed in clay or paints, for Pauline had access to neither during her poor Alabama youth. Neither are they expressed in writing, for Pauline, as the oldest of eleven children, was forced to quit school to tend house for her working mother. Rather, her artistic yearnings are expressed in her delight in arranging things so that the finished product suggests order and beauty:

She loved, most of all, to arrange things. To line things up in rows—jars on shelves at canning, peach pits on the step, sticks, stones, leaves. . . . Whatever portable plurality she found, she organized into neat lines, according to their size, shape or gradations of color. (p. 89)

Pauline's dominant characteristic however, is her overwhelming self-hatred, which precludes struggle of any kind. She is aware of the turning wheels of racial oppression in her life, but she makes no effort to stop the turning. Instead, she oils the axles and polishes the spokes so that the wheels turn more smoothly, more rapidly, and without interruption. She wears her maid's uniform with pride and bows low to the racist demands of the white Fisher family. She does not bemoan her lot in the house of whiteness and plenty. Rather, she smiles as she plays the role of surrogate mother for the Fishers' young daughter, Polly. She struts as she surveys the results of her handiwork—an immaculate house filled with enticing aromas of homemade pies and other dishes the Fishers enjoy. In her storefront house, "irritating and melancholy" in appearance, she is irredeemably ugly. In the Fisher home, she is beautiful and important, made so by the magic of service to white people.

The unmistakable resemblance between Morrison's Pauline Breedlove and the traditional image of the black mammy is surely intentional. As we have seen, the black mammy is a pervasive character in white American fiction. She appears as Dilsey in *The Sound and the Fury*, Berenice in Carson McCullers's *The Member of the Wedding*, Calpurnia in Harper Lee's *To Kill a Mockingbird*, and simply "Mammy" in Margaret Mitchell's *Gone with the Wind*. Whatever her name, and whatever the artistic merit of the book that contains her, she is always a dutiful black female servant who attempts to keep white families from cutting their souls on the shattered pieces of their morally bankrupt lives, while able to place only a thin and soiled bandage on the open wounds of her own family. Morrison uses the image, but she distinguishes between Pauline's reasons for being a mammy and the reasons that inform the myth. Pauline cleans the Fisher home so that its affluence and power are dazzling, and she neglects her own storefront house, letting the dust collect around the frayed furniture in the dreary narrow rooms. Affectionately she gives baths to the Fishers' daughter, Polly, dries her in thick white towels, and brushes the yellow hair as it slips like strands of gold between her fingers. To her own daughter, Pecola, she gives the back of her hand and cutting words of disgust, displeasure, and disapproval.

In one of the most poignant scenes in the novel, Pauline the mammy confronts Pauline the mother. Unexpectedly, Pecola appears at the Fisher home in need of maternal comfort and some whiskey, which she and her friends superstitiously believe will keep them from being "ruined" like the prostitutes in the community. When she accidentally knocks a freshly baked pie off the stove, she incurs the wrath of her mother:

> In one gallop she was on Pecola, and with the back of her hand knocked her to the floor. Pecola slid in the pie juice, one leg folding under her. Mrs. Breedlove yanked her up by the arm, slapped her again, and in a voice thin with anger called her "a crazy fool." (pp. 86–87)

The scene is a powerful statement on racial self-hatred and self-denial: Pauline rejects her own daughter because she has erased from her psyche the line separating reality from illusion, mammyhood from motherhood.

And yet, Pauline Breedlove is not a typical black mammy, for Morrison takes the image and turns it upside down and inside out so that one sees the image of the mammy as it is reflected in the psyche of Pauline Breedlove. Without denying Pauline's dutiful service to the white family, Morrison renders Pauline's understanding of what she does as mammy, and more important, why she does it. She serves the Fishers not out of blind loyalty to white people, but because she believes that *she* deserves some power and peace in life, and it is only in their world of plenty that she can get them. In her mind, then, she is not yielding to powerlessness; she is acquiring power. She is convinced that "power, praise and luxury were hers in this household" (p. 101).

The sexual dimensions of Pauline's life are equally complex and equally tragic. As a woman, she knew bliss in the red-clay, all-black community of the small Alabama town of her birth, where all the colors of spring were in her soul. Her love for Cholly and their relationship of warmth and trust were "like all the bits of color from . . . down home" (p. 91). In Alabama they "loved each other" and Cholly "seemed to relish her company" (p. 92). When they leave the South, the colors of spring disappear from Pauline's life, replaced by a smoke-laden sky and streets paved with concrete.

The negative impact of the North on black families from the South is a common theme in historical accounts and sociological studies. John Hope Franklin writes that "family disorganization and disintegration were a logical consequence of all the social ills associated with the maladjustment in urban life."[24] In *The Negro Family in the United States* (1939), the first serious study of the black family, E. Franklin Frazier develops the same thesis, offering data on broken homes, juvenile delinquency, and "fathers on leave."[25] Since the publication of Frazier's study, sociological analyses have continued to document the detrimental effect of the northern experience on the black family, and they have been reflected in black fiction's "mirror of reality"—dramatically in Paul Laurence Dunbar's *Sport of the Gods* (1906) and John Oliver Killens's *Sissie* (1966). Morrison's portrait of the Breedloves is part of a tradition in black literature.

Where Morrison's novel is different is in its treatment of Pauline's response to the changes the migration has made in her life as a woman. In the South, she had been happy to wait passively on a country road for the magic of love. In the North, Cholly comes and goes as he pleases, gorging himself on the ephemeral pleasures of city life, while Pauline remains confined at home, exhausting herself with the unending tasks of woman's work. She has no economic power, for Cholly decides how the family's money is to be spent and when. Even when Pauline goes out to work as a domestic to add to their income, Cholly retains the power of the purse. The particulars of her life are familiar details in sociological studies of poor black families in which the man—contrary to the myth of the black matriarchy and contrary to the belief that employment brings power—holds unchallenged the reins of power. Racism denies Cholly power in the larger society; sexism gives him power in the privacy of his home.

Another dimension of Morrison's depiction of the Breedloves' alienation in the North is the extent to which Pauline sympathizes with Cholly as he metamorphoses from a gentle man to a drunken wife-beater. When her white employer advises her to leave Cholly, Pauline analyzes her plight not just as a woman abused by a man but, significantly, as a black woman whose man is being psychologically diminished. Pauline's identity as a poor woman produces sympathy for Cholly: "What he gone give me alimony on?" And her allegiance as a black woman causes her to soften her rage: "It didn't seem none too bright for a black woman to leave a black man for a white woman" (p. 95). What is there in life for a black woman, Pauline asks, if not union with a black man? White people simply don't understand what "good a man is." They think he's "good for paying bills" because white men work and white women stay home. For Pauline, who is capable of supporting herself, Cholly is "good for" adding meaning to her life as a woman. He validates her because he is a man, and also because he shares with her a history of racial outrage.

Pauline Breedlove has known only one joy in life, and that joy is associated with her sexuality. In the early days, she recalls, lovemaking with Cholly gave her a sense of power and wholeness she could not otherwise experience:

> When Cholly let go of all he has, and give it to me. To *me*. To *me*. . . .
> I feel a power. I be strong, I be pretty, I be young. . . . And it be a
> rainbow all inside. (pp. 103–4)

When her sexual life with Cholly diminishes, Pauline retreats into religious rationalizing, which convinces her that the sorrow of her life "don't make no difference . . . it is sure to be a glory" (p. 100). But she wistfully longs for the one experience that once gave her "glory" here on earth, an experience associated with her reality as a woman. Sadly she says that the "only thing I miss sometime is that rainbow" of sexual pleasure (p. 104).

From a feminist perspective, Morrison's novel is a study of the various degrees of fulfillment women experience as women. Pauline is at one end of the spectrum. Other women characters are less obviously deprived—at least economically. Some are "comfortable" being completely immersed in motherhood and find peace in resignation to the limitations on their lives. Mrs. McTeer, whose daughters befriend Pecola, is such a woman. She rears her family in rooms "peopled by roaches and mice" (p. 12) and open around windows and doors to the cold wind. She makes ends meet by taking in boarders and by "watching every possibility of excess" (p. 17). Like other women in the community, she dreads the "real terror of life," being put "outdoors," and "having no place to go." Claudia McTeer explains the reality of her mother and other women in the community:

> Being a minority in both caste and class we moved about . . . on the
> hem of life, struggling to consolidate our weaknesses and hang on,
> or to creep singly up into the major folds of the garment. (p. 18)

The second group of women, whom Morrison calls the "sugarbrown Mobile girls" (p. 69), live in better neighborhoods where everyone is employed and where there are nice houses with porch swings and sunflowers and pots of bleeding hearts. These women are poor imitations of what they believe whiteness to be. They have smooth hands and slim ankles. They wash with "orange-colored Lifebuoy soap, dust themselves with Cashmere Bouquet and soften their skin with Jergen's Lotion" (p. 68). Though they marry and have children, they find sex repulsive. At land-grant colleges and normal schools where they are educated, they learn "how to do the white man's work with refinement . . . how to instruct black children in obedience" and how to develop "thrift, patience, high morals, and good manners" (p. 68). They are fake and frigid women who deny their blackness and their sexuality, who try to get "rid of the funkiness":

> The dreadful funkiness of passion, the funkiness of nature, the
> funkiness of the wide range of human emotions.
>   Wherever it erupts, this Funk, they wipe it away; where it crusts,
> they dissolve it; wherever it drips, flowers, or clings, they find it and
> fight it until it dies. They fight this battle all the way to the grave.
> (p. 68)

Women in the third category have no desire for property or rootedness of any kind. These women are prostitutes, embittered and frigid in lovemaking because they choose to be. And they choose to be because they "hate men . . . without shame, apology, or discrimination." Puerto Ricans, Mexicans, Poles, Jews, white men, black men—all men come under "their jaundiced eye" (p. 47).

Regardless of the category in which her women characters exist, Morrison makes an unchanging observation about them: they are removed from the possibility of self-knowledge, self-expression, and freedom. The measure of their lives is the extent to which, in old age, they will be able to look back with satisfaction on their younger years. Walker assesses Josie's life from this same perspective, for she writes of Josie at sixty without economic security and, worse, with no memories of a joyous past. Ann Petry draws Mrs. Hedges and Min as women with burdens so acute that they grow old too fast. All of the women characters discussed in this chapter—those in a novel of the forties, those in two novels of the seventies, those in an urban environment, and those rooted in the dust and clay of the rural South—edge "into life from the back door." It is only in old age that they experience freedom and security. Morrison writes:

> Then they were old. . . . With relief they wrapped their heads in rags, and their breasts in flannel; eased their feet into felt. They were through with lust and lactation, beyond tears and terror. . . . They were old enough to be irritable when and where they chose, tired enough to look forward to death, disinterested enough to accept the idea of pain while ignoring the presence of pain. *They were in fact and at last free* [italics added]. (p. 110)

chapter 5

"JOURNEYING FROM CAN'T TO CAN" AND SOMETIMES BACK TO "CAN'T"

Black Women of Challenge and Contradiction

What about the colored woman? What about her?
—Mariah Upshur in Sarah Wright, *This Child's Gonna Live*, 1969

From the nineteenth century, when Sojourner Truth asked, "Ar'nt I a woman?," to the 1970s, when Shirley Chisholm spoke boldly of the two burdens against which black women must struggle simultaneously, many black women in white America have challenged in various ways the impact that racism and sexism have had on their reality. During slavery their resistance was often subtle—they put glass in the master's food, poisoned animals, broke tools, and feigned illness and ignorance to avoid work; but sometimes it was overt and violent—they ran away from plantations, they killed overseers and masters, and they killed themselves.

In the post–World War II period with which this book is concerned, black women were not unlike their ancestors in bondage: they resisted oppression both covertly and overtly. Many pretended to be ignorant, played clever games of submission, and wore a mask that concealed their true selves when doing so was an advantage. Other women, however, removed the mask and overtly challenged the restrictions placed on their lives. They journeyed from the South to the North in search of the "promised land." In the South and in the North, many of them fought oppression in violent ways. Not all black women incarcerated in the prisons of this nation are there for black-on-black crimes. Some are there because they struck out against whites who overstepped the safe limits of oppression. To this picture should be added the sustained involvement of many black women in the civil rights movement of the sixties and the black power movement of the sixties and seventies, as well as in smaller, but no less important, movements that sought change in their realities.

Throughout this history of challenge and resistance many black women have tended to give up the struggle for change before their goals are realized. They rarely live for themselves alone, so they rarely struggle without thinking of others. Therefore, if their resistance to oppression puts their husbands, children, and communities in jeopardy, they yield. Thus they journey from "can't to can" and then painfully back to "can't."[1]

It is fairly easy to document a tradition of challenge and resistance in the history of black women when we consider racial and class oppression. It is not so easy, however, to document such a tradition when we consider sexual oppression, for in scholarly works, black women are treated mainly as blacks and not as women. Nevertheless, we can make several assumptions, the most obvious of which is that black women who resist control of their lives by one group of "others" will not easily yield to control by another group of "others." A second assumption is that the sensitivity of many black women to sexual oppression early in the history of black America—even during the antebellum period—did not die with the passing of years, for sexism certainly did not fade away in the culture of this nation. Indeed, the challenges to sexism and racism made by black women in the seventies were perhaps explosions of many years of suppressed resentment. One black woman says that "inside all of us is a volcano on the verge of erupting."[2]

We can further assume that the pattern of resisting and then yielding evident in the racial history of black women has been present in their sexual history as well. Indeed, it can be argued that the pattern is even stronger there, for the challenge to sexual oppression raises fundamental questions that affect the women's personal lives, and the persons they challenge are often the men they love and whose children they have borne. Moreover, while they can easily find sup-

port from other black women for challenges to racial and class oppression, they often find themselves alone when they challenge sexual
oppression. In fact, myths about women are so basic to our culture
that women who attempt to reject them totally must reject a part of
who they are. For these reasons, we can assume that many black
women make the journey from "can't to can" and sometimes back to
"can't" not only as blacks but also as women.

The women characters analyzed in this chapter make that journey
in the contexts of race, class, and sex. They are, therefore, unlike the
characters analyzed in the previous chapter, "Going Nowhere Immediate," who lead lives of submission and despair. Nor are they like the
characters who will be analyzed in the following chapter, "Giving Birth
to Self," who sustain challenges to limitations of any kind on their
realities. Rather, their response to their anomalous position in white
America lies somewhere between the two ends of the spectrum of
consciousness. They are lonely women forced by external factors to
"walk backwards nonchalantly on tiptoes into happiness if only for
stingy moments," and as they resist and yield, they seek "to make . . .
sense out of the world/of pain/of lonely."[3] We hear them as they speak
for themselves. Their names are Lutie Johnson in Ann Petry's *The
Street* (1946), Cleo Judson in Dorothy West's *The Living Is Easy* (1946),
Mariah Upshur in Sarah Wright's *This Child's Gonna Live* (1969),
Helga Crane in Nella Larsen's *Quicksand* (1928), Ursula Corregidora
in Gayl Jones's *Corregidora* (1975), and Eva Medina in Jones's *Eva's
Man* (1976).

Lutie Johnson was the first female protagonist in black American
fiction to commit murder as an expression of her rage, and the novel
in which she appears, *The Street*, was the first novel by a black woman
in this country to receive significant literary attention beyond the
decade in which it was published. It has not, however, received literary applause. Robert Bone considers it worthy of comment in *The
Negro Novel in America* (1958), but he calls it a "*roman à thèse . . .
which offers a superficial analysis of life in a northern ghetto.*"[4] Noel
Schraufnagel, in *From Apology to Protest: The Black American Novel*
(1973), praises *The Street's* realistic illustration of "the effects of

environment and oppression on an individual," but considers "the melodramatic conclusion" more appropriate for "popular pulp fiction [than for] a fine novel."[5] Addison Gayle, who rates many black proletariat novels highly for their theme and craft, writes that Petry's work, though "provocative and powerful," is weakened by her failure to develop a "denouement [and] to revarnish her work, add color to her painting." Common to all these critical assessments is a comparison of *The Street* with Richard Wright's *Native Son*. "Change the characters," Addison Gayle writes, and *The Street* becomes "little more than a carbon copy" of *Native Son*: "Both Wright and Petry wrote in the naturalistic idiom; both were interested in the effects of the environment upon psychological make-up of characters; both were aware of the images handed down from the past";[6] and both created anti-heroes driven to murder by the exigencies of black life in white America.

In reciting the similarities between *Native Son* and *The Street*, critics ignore the significance of a major dissimilarity: the sexual identities of the protagonists of the two novels. Wright's protagonist, Bigger Thomas, is male. Petry's protagonist, Lutie Johnson, is female. By definition, then, their realities are different, just as Wright's vision as a male artist is different from Petry's vision. Moreover, Bigger Thomas is a young male in his late teens who has not functioned in the sexual roles of husband and father. Lutie Johnson, on the other hand, is a mature woman in her early thirties who has been married and is the mother of an eight-year-old son. Critics who see Petry's vision as just a "carbon copy" of Wright's ignore the extent to which a character's age, sexual identity, and sexual roles affect his or her reality. Critics do recognize that Petry's aim is to show that a black woman, like a black man, struggles against forces in the environment that would circumscribe her life. However, writing from a male perspective, they ignore the added burdens that being a woman places on her. They do not understand that Petry's decision to place a black woman in an environment like the one in which Bigger Thomas is victimized suggests that Petry intended to document not only the impact of racial oppression on the psychological makeup of her character, but the impact of sexual oppression as well. They fail to understand what Beatrice Royster in her doctoral dissertation observes with skill and sensitivity: "*The Street* is the ambience of tragedy for the black female of the twentieth century"[7] in that it documents the brutal attacks made upon her because she is black and because she is female.

When the novel begins, Lutie Johnson, estranged from her husband, is alone with her eight-year-old son in a world of violence and corruption. Lutie looks for an affordable apartment on 116th Street, in the very heart of Harlem. This is to be only a temporary residence because she intends to fight her way out of poverty into prosperity. The opening scene of the novel, considered by some critics a masterpiece of symbolism and imagery, introduces Petry's "dismal view of human nature" and her belief that "tragic disharmony" characterizes both the universe and human nature. A cold November wind "announces . . . the discord between man and nature"[8] and foreshadows Lutie's struggles in the ghetto. Like a monster with a mind of its own and an indomitable will to destroy, the wind

> did everything it could to discourage the people walking along the street. It found all the dirt and dust and grime on the sidewalk and lifted it up so that the dirt got into their noses, making it difficult to breathe; the dust got into their eyes and blinded them; and the grit stung their skins.[9]

The people on "the street" quickly submit to the wind's onslaught, for they have learned the futility of struggle. Theirs is a conditioned response that has them "stooping" or rushing for cover. As a newcomer to this environment, Lutie has no such conditioned response. She has lived amid opulence, working as a live-in maid for a "filthy rich" white family in suburban Connecticut and, from their matter-of-fact discussions of stocks and bonds, has come to believe in the American capitalist dream. Into her very soul she has absorbed the philosophy that "anybody could be rich if he wanted to and worked hard enough and figured it out carefully enough" (p. 32).

Petry draws heavily on her experiences as a newspaper reporter in the bowels of Harlem. Enraged by what she saw firsthand, she attempts to "show why the Negro has a high crime rate, a high death rate, and little or no chance of keeping his family intact in northern cities." In fact, she succeeds, as Richard Wright does not, in giving us the concrete particulars of this reality. She explains that "there are no statistics in the book . . . not as columns of figures," but they are "present in the background," in the hardships of people "who live in overcrowded tenements."[10] "The street" is a wasteland of human suffering, "bordered by garbage cans" that symbolize how life here is discarded with impunity by a system that "sucked the humanity out of people—slowly, surely, inevitably" (p. 144). On "the street" the women work as domestics, laundresses, or prostitutes; the men work in menial, low-paying jobs, or not at all. The children, left unattended because of chronic family breakdown, begin in their preteens to prepare for a lifetime of taking drugs, pimping, or anything that short-circuits their sordid reality. All the people on "the street" are confined to narrow and suffocating roles prescribed by white America, and too many have "lost the ability to protest against anything" (p. 125).

Lutie Johnson protests against everything that hinders her because of her race. In fact, in attitude and behavior she is a forerunner of the black militant of the sixties, refusing to "scrape and bow" to white people. Her pride will not let her wear the expensive clothes Mrs. Chandler gives her after a few wearings. Her pride will not permit her to laugh and jest with white butchers who, rumor has it, use embalming fluid on the meats sold in Harlem. And her pride will not let her accept change from the hands of a white grocer, "because he was white and forcing him to make the small extra effort of putting the change on the counter gave her a feeling of power" (p. 44). The central point of Petry's racial portrait of Lutie is the character's desire for wider options than those synonymous with the black experience.

Petry foreshadows Lutie's tragedy at the very beginning of the novel with an image of walls that move gradually and persistently to narrow the already small space in which she is trapped: the walls in the apartment "were reaching out for her—bending and swaying toward her in an effort to envelop her" (p. 13). After each new wave of self-confidence—always without cause—Lutie pushes harder against the "bending and swaying" walls. Every time she returns to the apartment after being on "the street," she finds that the "walls seemed to come in toward her, to push against her with more force and persistence" (p. 53). On the night that she emerges from her self-imposed isolation to enjoy a evening of forgetfulness in Junto's Bar and Grill, the walls seem to "walk at" her (p. 56). When she learns that she has no chance of making money singing at Junto's, when she sees her relationship with her son being threatened by their poverty and by her growing impatience, and when her funds are depleted and she can no longer believe in her lofty goals, she realizes that "from the time she was born, she had been hemmed into an ever-narrowing space, until now she was very clearly walled in" (p. 201). The stage is set for Lutie's initiation into a world of violence.

From well-articulated plans for success that would be easy to carry out if she "worked hard enough," she moves to a sense of urgency about the need to fight against the doors that "have been slammed in her face" because she is "poor and black." She would "shove [them] open; she would beat and bang on [them] and push against [them] and use a chisel in order to get [them] open" (p. 118). Lutie is "both a conscious and unconscious fighter and rebel," writes Vernon Lattin, "a rebel, ironically, in the American tradition."[11] The irony to which Lattin refers is present in every scene of the novel and saturates every effort Lutie makes to "fight her way out." She fights for lofty alternatives to the suffocating exigencies of black life, but she does not understand the omnipresent force of "the street" and its various "traps," so she fails to choose the proper weapons for her battle.

The story progresses swiftly to tragedy. Her son, Bub, attempts to earn money decently to contribute to their living expenses, but he falls innocently into a trap the apartment super set for him and ends up in juvenile detention. From this moment on, Lutie's blinding naivete is presented as a tragic flaw in her character. She goes, naively, to an attorney on "the street" for assistance with her son's case, not realizing that neither bond nor legal service is required to get her son out of detention. Naively, she seeks a loan from Boots Smith, a seasoned veteran of "the street," who cannot enter into a contract of dignity, for, as Lutie herself sees, he is a man who has "no softness, nothing to indicate that he would ever bother to lift a finger to help anyone but himself" (p. 98). When he attempts to rape Lutie in exchange for the money, the walls close in on her. Consumed by rage, Lutie strikes Boots Smith again and again, venting her rage against all the forces that have conspired to destroy her. In the end, a murderer, she has no dreams, no plans, and no future. She has learned in the most tragic way, writes Vernon Lattin, that the American Dream that shaped her ambitions was always "itself . . . the spring that operated the trap."[12]

In interviews Ann Petry has emphasized that race stands at the center of her artistic vision. I have already quoted her intention to demonstrate the crippling effects of racism and capitalism on the lives of the people who live in ghettos across America—and this literary goal she achieves brilliantly. The fact that Petry does not speak of sexual oppression in interviews about her novel does not mean that she fails to include it in her artistic vision. It is no accident that she opens her novel with a scene juxtaposing racial oppression and sexual violence, suggesting the forces that will victimize Lutie Johnson. The scene introduces the reader to the filth and poverty of "the street," but its drama is the sexual violence of the superintendent. It is significant that Lutie can tolerate the filth of the apartment, but she is "drunk with fear" (p. 12) of the superintendent's sexual desires. She sees him "eating her up with his eyes" and knows, even when her back is turned, that he was "sniffing on my trail, slathering, slobbering after me like some dark hound of hell seeking out, tonguing along the back of me" (p. 21).

Critics do not overlook the role the superintendent plays in Petry's protest against the environment, but they often see only half of that role. They understand that he symbolizes the ultimate in victimization, for he "has come to represent the underground forces symbolized by the street itself . . . and survives mainly on sexual fantasies," writes Addison Gayle.[13] But critics do not understand that the superintendent's perversity is simply an exaggeration of the sexual exploitation that runs rampant in the ghetto, unchallenged and institutionally supported. Consequently, they fail to see that Lutie, as a *woman*, responds to the first appearance of the superintendent with "*instinctive, immediate fear*" (p. 18, italics added).

This fear is obviously the result of the socialization that teaches black women about their physical vulnerability. We learn that Lutie married at seventeen because her grandmother believed marriage would save her from men like the super. And she has always known that as a black woman she is hated by white women and sought after by white men. In the home of the white family in Connecticut, she is suspect not because she is black and therefore is assumed to be dishonest and lazy (purely racial stereotypes), but because she is presumed to be promiscuous and whorish (racial and sexual stereotypes). White women assume that "all colored girls [are] whores" (p. 31), and white men "ain't never willing to let a black woman alone. Seems like they all got a itch and urge to sleep with 'em" (p. 33).

This image of the black woman as whore is not confined to white people. It festers in the minds of black men and creates a code of sexual behavior that sometimes results in the abuse of black women. Richard Wright alludes to the problems of black women in his moving portrait of Bessie, who drowns her despair in drink and expresses her self-denial in sex that is at best an abusive, pleasurable way for Bigger to assert his manhood. That Wright understands the plight of such women is demonstrated in Bessie's tragic plea for her life:

All my life's been full of hard trouble. If I wasn't hungry, I was sick. And if I wasn't sick, I was in trouble. I ain't never bothered nobody. I just worked hard every day as long as I can remember, till I was tired enough to drop.[14]

But Wright's emphasis is on the forces that thwart Bigger's manhood, not on those that thwart Bessie's womanhood. Ann Petry, on the other hand, reaches into the souls of black women for their peculiar agony. *The Street* is an explosion of the sounds of racial and sexual agony. The sounds from the run-down apartment buildings are the sounds of men beating their wives or abusing their mistresses. They are heard in the super's treatment of Min. They are heard crashing through broken windows as nameless men scream their obscenities at nameless women: "you black bitch, I oughta' killed you long ago" (p. 136). And they are heard in Boots Smith's announcement that he will teach Lutie a lesson. As a man, he does not "take that kind of talk from dames. . . . Not even good-looking ones like you. Maybe after I beat the hell out of you a couple times, you'll begin to like the idea of sleeping with me and with Junto" (p. 265).

The central point of Petry's novel is that poor black women are beaten spiritually and economically by "the street," and because they are women, they are beaten physically by black men. All of the violence on "the street," writes Beatrice Royster, "grows out of, or is precipitated by, sexual encounters between men and women."[15] This does not mean black men are "the enemy." They are not. They are the "other" victims of "the street." Like Brownfield in Alice Walker's *The Third Life of Grange Copeland*, they have been programmed into sexism and destroyed by racism, and the two experiences are inextricable in America. While they elicit Petry's rage, they are within reach of her sympathy.

Petry repeatedly describes women who work and men who do not work, painting a picture of inequality in the thirties and forties that is not far from Sojourner Truth's observation in the nineteenth century that "colored women go out washing, which is about as high as a colored woman gets, and their men go about idle, strutting up and down."[16] But she immediately explains that the men are idle because white people enslave black women in white homes and crush the manhood of black men by keeping them unemployed. This history explains why Lutie's rage is heavily commingled with a sense of guilt. Because she chose to work and function in a role society assigns to men, Lutie believes she was partly responsible for the failure of her marriage.

Lutie's attitude toward "woman's place" is shaped by her middle-class aspirations. Indeed, by calling into question Lutie's strivings for upward mobility, Petry suggests that Lutie is partly responsible for her own failures. Lutie believes that she and her son, Bub, are better than other blacks in Harlem because she has seen inside the workings of white America and therefore knows how to dream the right dreams. The world of stocks and bonds, of luxury and waste, of things and treasures, is the world to which she aspires. She wants Bub to sleep in rooms that are decorated with carpets, curtains, and fine mahogany furniture. She wants him to wear knickerbockers and attend the best prep schools, as the Chandler boy does. And for herself, in her hidden fantasies, she wants to be like the white middle-class women whose lives are glorified in subway ads, magazines, and movies. She believes that women should stay in the home because that is what middle-class white women do. Class, then, causes Lutie to internalize cultural assumptions about both her race and her sex, and it prevents her from seeing the direction from which the light in the tunnel of her darkness might possibly come.

Making it possible for black women to stay in "their place" as women is one of the solutions Petry proposed to the problems of family disorganization and teenage crime she wrote about as a journalist. She believed that if women could stay home and tend the hearth, the family unit would be stronger; and if the family unit were stronger, black youths would be sheltered from the pervasive violence in Harlem. In the novel she implies that if all things were in place for blacks in white America, Lutie would be home and her husband, Jim, would be gainfully employed. Petry's response to "woman's place," then, like Lutie's, is unquestionably tied to the problems of racism and poverty. However, by documenting the double jeopardy of women in white America, Petry was a harbinger of the sexual consciousness that broke through in the late sixties and seventies, prompting black women to question the assumption that race is the only deterrent to their self-actualization. No matter how deeply she felt about the victimization of black men, Petry did not conceal from the reader her observation that black men are yet another force with which black women must contend.

Implicit in every sympathetic portrait Petry draws of victimized men is her conviction that they in turn victimize black women. They use women as buffers against the cold wind of "the street," as givers of pleasure, as money-making objects if they are pimps, and as credentials of their masculinity. Lutie's father, for example, brings "a procession of buxom lady friends" home, exposing Lutie at a young age to the sordid in life and going against "Granny's unconcealed disapproval," because "using women was a way of demonstrating his manhood" (p. 55). The same point is made about Jim, who attempts to regain his lost manhood by bringing in another woman as cook, housekeeper, and lover. All the men in the novel partake of woman's emotional nourishment, woman's body, and sometimes woman's earnings to keep themselves on their feet.

Lutie Johnson's struggle to maintain her dignity as a woman is as difficult as her struggle to achieve the American Dream. In her life they are inseparable struggles, though failure in the one need not preclude success in the other for the black woman. The point critics often miss in their analysis of Lutie Johnson is that she never compromises her woman's pride for her black aspirations. When all the signs indicate that Lutie could, in fact, make her way out of the filth and violence of "the street," she holds fast to her image of herself as a woman of dignity and hopelessly confronts Boots Smith. Surely this fact alone makes the novel more than a "carbon copy" of *Native Son*. As Beatrice Royster claims, *The Street* is one of the most powerful "mandate[s] for black women to dismantle the cloak of blind innocence, to recognize the falsity of the American Dream . . . [and most significantly] to resist exploitation of their bodies by men of all races."[17]

In 1948, two years after Ann Petry wrote *The Street*, Dorothy West published *The Living Is Easy*. Both novels are significant works in black American literary history. Both writers were major participants in the political, social, and literary movements that made the forties such a dynamic period in American history. Petry flirted with Marxism, writing political pieces for *The Amsterdam News* and *The People's Voice*; and West, serving as editor of *Challenge and New Challenge*, worked closely with black and white writers who challenged the mainstream philosophy of American politics. Interestingly, both writers come from middle-class New England backgrounds (Petry from Connecticut and West from Massachusetts), and both women left New England to live and work in Harlem during the twenties and thirties (Petry as a reporter and West as a social investigator). There the similarities end, however, for while Petry used Harlem experiences to draw a convincing portrait of a black woman in revolt, West in her novel made no mention of Harlem.

The setting of *The Living Is Easy* is Boston at the turn of the century, and the protagonist is Cleo Judson, a southern-born black woman who marries the wealthiest black man in Boston. Like Lutie Johnson's, Cleo Judson's struggles are class-oriented, born out of her desire to be accepted into the black "counterfeit Brahmin"[18] society of Boston.

Some critics consider the setting and theme of the novel welcome departures from what they see as the dominance of sociology in black American fiction. In *The Negro Novel in America* Robert Bone praises West's craft in producing a "bitingly ironic novel—of the ruthless success drive of the Negro middle class" that does not subordinate "psychological interest to social criticism."[19] It is a welcome departure also because it does not examine traditional black locales such as Philadelphia, Chicago, or—the cultural capital of black America—Harlem. Instead it describes "the psychological, social and material lives of the small but important Negro populations that have always been scattered throughout New England."[20]

None of the laudatory assessments of the novel mentions its vision of womanhood. Robert Bone alludes to the role of sex in the novel when he calls Cleo Judson a "castrating female" and a woman of "masculine protest,"[21] but he does not explain the source of her protest convincingly. He calls attention to the novel's "touch of primitivism" and to West's "Freudian approaches to personality."[22] In fact, he seems so impressed by West's ability to avoid excessive "social criticism" that he fails to recognize that Cleo Judson, whom he calls the "most fascinating women in recent Negro fiction,"[23] is one of the most sexually hostile women in black American fiction. While it is true that she struggles ruthlessly to become a black Brahmin, a point Bone emphasizes, it is also true that she struggles to control her life and destiny in the same way that she believes men are permitted to control theirs. Unable to do so because she is a woman, she is resentful of what she sees as male power and female passivity. West writes that Cleo Judson "felt the spleen spread to the pit of her stomach. *Men were her enemies because they were male*" (p. 68).

The novel begins after Cleo has left the South of her birth and moved to Boston, where she marries Bart Judson, the wealthiest black man in the city, and gives birth to one child, a daughter named Judy. In the opening scene of the novel Cleo is on one of her many trips to her husband's banana business to cheat and lie for money to meet her extravagant needs. Immediately, Dorothy West introduces the theme of racial denial: Cleo is planning her strategy for the rental of an impressive house as far away from "niggers" as Bart's money and their race will allow, for she disavows any identity with the black people in Boston unless they are Brahmin blacks. She has trained "her tongue to the northern twist, [learned] to laugh with a minimum show of teeth, and [memorized] a new word in the dictionary every day" (p. 25). She has prepared herself to be a member of the black elite of Boston.

In the role of mother, her major goal is to ensure Judy a place "behind the tea tables of Boston," the "impeccable mold" of class and refinement that women of breeding "inherit" (p. 92). Since inheritance is out of the question for Judy, Cleo subjects the child to a rigid program in refinement. She hires a private teacher to give Judy genteel manners and the proper accent; she sends the child to a private school in Brookline, an upper-class suburb of Boston; she teaches the child exercises that will make her Negroid nose more aquiline; and she insists that Judy understand that a "proper Bostonian never showed any emotion but hauteur" (p. 40). Undergirding this program is a lesson in racial denial: Judy must never identify or associate with "knotty-head niggers" who are nothing but "midget comedians" (p. 5).

These maternal goals and Cleo's own obsessive desire to "belong" precipitate her ruthless deception of Bart, for they require more than the allowance she receives for household and family needs. Her goals do not, however, precipitate Cleo's biting and unchecked hostility toward her husband. That facet of her personality—the most dominant in the portrait—derives from her frustration as a female who rejects the assumption that women should stay at home as contented mothers and wives. The dichotomy of man's world and woman's place burns anger into Cleo's soul each time she visits Bart at the market: "Here in the market place was all the maleness of men." Everything in this world represented male strength, male power, and male freedom:

This was their world in which they moved without the command of women. The air hung heavy with their male smell and the pungent odor of their sweat. Their rolled-up sleeves showed the ripples of their hard muscles. (p. 70)

Cleo Judson chafes at the unalterable fact that her "sphere was one untroublesome child who gave insufficient scope for her tremendous vitality" (p. 69).

Realizing that she is bound by tradition and culture to roles that do not name her as she wishes to be named, Cleo attempts to make the best of a necessary evil: she functions in the role of wife, but she uses that role to chart her own destiny and the destiny of her daughter. Though she trains Judy to take the place "behind the tea tables of Boston," at every stage of the training she teaches the girl, in "belittling descriptions of men," that marriage should not be the major goal of her life. It had not been Cleo's goal, but she had none of the alternatives to "woman's place" that she plans for Judy. At the age of fourteen she had been "discovered" by a wealthy white woman from New England who was convalescing in South Carolina. When the woman offered to take Cleo to Springfield, Massachusetts, for proper training and education because she hated "to see this sultry loveliness ripen in the amoral atmosphere of the South" (p. 24), Cleo's life took a turn she had not anticipated or desired. When the benefactress became gravely ill, Cleo moved to Boston, where she lived with another white benefactress. There her duties were similar to those she had had in Springfield. She functioned "like a servant, but she was considered a ward. She was fed and clothed, and given a place at table and a chair in the parlor, except when there was company. At such times she put on an apron, held her proud head above the level of everybody's eyes, and wished they would all drop dead" (p. 29). As an eighteen-year-old arriving in Boston, she had had two goals: first, to run away from her benefactress and then to go on the stage. She imagined herself singing and "kicking her heels on a stage in a swirl of lace petticoats," but she was emphatic about having the stage to *herself.* "She wasn't going to sing an old love-song with any greasy-haired coon. She wasn't going to dance any cakewalk with him either, and let his sweaty hand ruin her fancy costumes" (p. 29).

Cleo's sensuous image of herself on stage is not unlike the way she is seen by the nephew of her benefactress. He had heard about Negroes, especially about voluptuous and passionate Negro women, "and the information was correct." Living in the house with Cleo, he is unable to control his desire. It grew "in his loins and there was nothing he could do to stop it. All he could do was try to keep it from spreading to his heart" (p. 29). Young and naive, Cleo does not understand the young man's pining, but Bart Judson, whom Cleo met by accident in the marketplace, cautions her against remaining as ward in the home: "She was not safe and never would be safe, as long as she stayed within the reach of his clutches. She was too young to be alone in Boston. She had no mother to guide her. She needed a good man's protection. She needed a husband" (p. 34). It is in this context that Cleo becomes a wife. She marries Bart only because "she wanted to get away" (p. 34). It is at first a loveless marriage and a strange one in that Cleo refuses sexual intercourse for two years. When she finally gives in to what she sees as Bart's "superior strength," she "found a weapon that would cut him down quickly and clearly. She was ice. Neither her mouth nor her body moved to meet his and with her eyes opened wide Cleo mocked the busyness below" (p. 35).

Open contempt for men is not an unusual emotion for women who are prostitutes, but Cleo is not a prostitute. From the perspective of some feminists, however, she might be considered a "respectable prostitute" in that she sleeps with Bart not because she is interested in the lovemaking, but because it is a necessary service rendered in exchange for her "woman's" allowance. What makes her unusual is her refusal to pretend. Her sexual disinterest is overt—a display of power—and she makes no excuses or apologies for it. "Men are all stomach," she says with disdain, "and the *other thing*. It would be a happy day for women if both could be cut out" (p. 222).

Robert Bone posits that Cleo's contempt for men grows out of her family experiences in the South.[24] She witnesses her father's devotion to his wife and, most especially, her mother's joy in wrapping her life around her husband. In the kitchen Cleo sees her mother bleach corn in lye water made from fireplace ashes, and as her father spits his tobacco juice in the ashes, the mother, carefully and even tenderly, takes ashes from the center of the pile. Cleo comments that "Mama thought everything about Pa was wonderful, even his spit" (p. 16). West's Freudian approach to personality, to which Bone refers, is demonstrated in the suggestion that Cleo envies Mama's love for her husband. Only at night when her woman's chores are done and the children are asleep is the woman truly happy. Cleo knows "by Mama's silver laughter that she was finding time for Pa," and she is certain that "Mama loved Pa better than anyone. And what was left over from loving him was divided among her daughters" (p. 17).

It is evident that Cleo worships Mama and regrets that of the four daughters only she "looked like Pa." Charity has Mama's softness, Lily the doe eyes and Serena the cherry-red mouth and the dimpled cheeks, and Cleo "looked like Pa." She had not been blessed to be Mama's child, and yet she was the only daughter who knew that Pa was not the head of the house. The house was "run by the beat of Mama's heart" (p. 22). She is rebellious, calling Mama's attention to her, and grinning when the strap is "laid on hard and heavy." She is wild and unharnessed, and yet contemplative. She is burdened by the impermanence of life and the "terror of the future"—the knowledge that nothing lasts, "that sisters turn into wives, that men take their women and ride away, that childhood is no longer than a summer day" (p. 22). She is burdened especially by the terror of Mama's mortality. When Mama is gone, she tells herself, there would be "the look of her and the silver laughter in the daughters whom she had blessed with her resemblance." Cleo promises to keep her sisters with her always. "So long as they were within sight and sound, they were the mirrors in which she would see Mama" (p. 22).

Bone's theory of "the dethroned child" has validity, but it does not and cannot fully explain Cleo's resistance to the traditional woman's role, and for a novel as rich in irony and psychological insight as Bone contends, a one-dimensional picture of the basic personality makeup of the protagonist would be unacceptable. Bone studiously ignores West's allusions to Cleo's sensitivity to the two worlds in society—one designed for men and the other designed for women—

that make the flashbacks to Cleo's southern childhood extremely important. West describes Cleo's interest in climbing trees and hanging from her hands, in fighting boys and in riding a wild stallion. She is a problem child for her parents because they do not know exactly what to do with a girl who is wild, uncontrollable, and bent on mischief. Bone calls Cleo's liveliness "neurotic behavior"[25]—a term steeped in sexism when it is used to describe female behavior that is out of line with cultural expectations. The more usual term for those who exact different standards of behavior from girls than from boys is "tomboy." In a study of tomboyism in American culture, psychologist Janet Hyde writes that "tomboyism . . . is considered a stage to be outgrown because girls must learn to replace active 'masculine' behaviors with passive 'feminine' behaviors." In the absence of wider options for girls whose interests lie in the world outside of dolls, tomboyism is perceived as "a confusion of gender identity."[26]

West writes of Cleo's sensitivity to the existence of two worlds: the "at home" world, where there is "nothing to do," and the world "away from home," where there is action, life, and freedom (p. 12). She depicts Cleo as a girl who has no time "for counting out," figuratively speaking, even when the rules of a child's game call for patient counting. "The wildness was in her, the unrestrained joy, the desire to run to the edge of the world and fling her arms around the sun, and rise with it, through time and space, to the center of everywhere" (p. 13). Whether intentionally or not, West's images of Cleo's behavior in the outside world allude to the character's early resistance to sexual modes that curb her vitality. One such image brings to the reader's mind Candace Compson in *The Sound and the Fury*. Faulkner foreshadows Candace's loss of her virginity—and indeed, her break with southern expectations for women—when he writes of her "soiled panties." West uses a similar image to foreshadow Cleo's later aversion to imprisonment in woman's sphere. After a bold ride on a wild stallion Cleo observes that her injury was "a minor one. She had split the seat of her drawers" (p. 14). The injury is so minor that it does not deter her from climbing a tree and hanging from its limb, with her "drawers" exposed. When a boy laughs at Cleo's behavior ("to him a girl carrying on so crazy cut a funny figure"), a fight ensues and, determined to win, "no matter how," Cleo butts the boy in the groin, "where the weakness of boys was—the contradictory delicacy" (p. 20). These images, unmistakable in their allusions to Cleo's sexual consciousness even as a young girl, foreshadow Cleo's unconventional behavior as an adult and her determination to control Bart Judson, "no matter how." They are the implicit manifestations of Cleo's explicit belittlement of men and pride in women:

> What is there to being a boy? What was there to being a man? Men just worked. That was easier than what women did. It was women who did the lying awake, the planning, the sorrowing, the scheming to stretch a dollar. That was the hard part, the head part. A woman had to think all the time. A woman had to be smart. (p. 21)

These details put Dorothy West in the company of women writers of the seventies who seek to dig down into the psyche of women where a volcano might be waiting to erupt. But West was not a feminist, and consequently she enlarges her portrait of Cleo Judson to include ambiguities that avowed feminists might not acknowledge in the psyche of a woman who is the most anti-male character in any fiction written by a black woman. The ambiguities make for a penetrating psychological study of Cleo Judson. She schemes her husband out of his earnings and robs her daughter of her childhood to become one with a group of people she intensely dislikes. She disavows any interest in the South and any identity with southern blacks, and yet she longs for "the salt flavor of lusty laughter." When she thinks of Bostonians and their inability to respond spontaneously to anything, she feels like challenging their stiffness and formality by "cutting the fool for the hell of it" (p. 44). She subdues Bart Judson with her scorn, yet there are moments when her "ice" comes dangerously close to melting in the heat of the passions she keeps under control. "Her need for love was as urgent as her aliveness," West writes, but Cleo would not face the knowledge that she "was incomplete in herself." As the years of marriage with Bart go on, she begins to listen for his key in the door, and in his absence her life becomes "suspended" (p. 36).

Ironically, the "no matter how" approach Cleo takes to achieve her goals leads to her downfall. Her psychological castration of Bart, her destruction of her sisters' happy marriages, and her theft of Judy's childhood are the sins for which Cleo must suffer. One by one those people who had loved her and whose lives were fractured by her cold, manipulative personality desert her—first her sisters, then her daughter, and finally her husband. But her nemesis is most especially that sin that stands at the center of West's novel: for the sake of her own advancement, Cleo turns her back on the Negro struggle in the South, a struggle that takes the life of the husband of one of her sisters. The punishment she incurs is what she fears most. When Bart's banana business is destroyed by World War I, she loses her status and ends up in a boardinghouse in a poor section of Boston.

Since West's main purpose in the novel is to satirize middle-class blacks whose obsession with class blinds them to the urgency of the racial struggle in the South, she does not use Cleo Judson as her voice in the novel. Cleo's views on class and race are obviously not West's views. Nor are Cleo's attitudes toward men West's attitudes: Cleo's contempt for men is contrasted to Bart Judson's tenderness as a man and to Cleo's sisters' need for their husbands. And yet, for all West's displeasure with Cleo's manipulation of human beings, there is an interesting subtheme that grows—perhaps beyond the writer's intentions—into a fascinating and intriguing picture of a woman who challenges the existence of a "world" for men and only a "sphere" for woman.

Mariah Upshur in Sarah Wright's *This Child's Gonna Live* (1969) also sees two contrasting worlds in black culture—man's world and woman's place—but unlike Cleo Judson, she recognizes that each one is a small and narrow space in the cosmic world of white power. She has no interest in belonging to a social set, for in Tangierneck, Maryland, all black people are in one set, and all struggle to keep their heads above destitution in a "god-forsaken"[27] place. And as the mother of four children and the wife of a "going-nowhere man" (p. 20), Mariah has no obsession except that of freeing her children from Tangierneck's ignorance and poverty. She is acutely sensitive to the racism that holds the black community in fear, but she is equally sensitive to the narrow-mindedness that denies women positions of power. Tired of hearing Jacob and other men in the community talk "about the colored *man's* problems," she boldly asks, "But what about the colored *woman*? What about her?" (pp. 11–12).

In an interview Sarah Wright defined herself as a "housekeeper" and added that "housekeepers and homemakers are workers." Her artistic vision, she explained, "reflect[s] this concern,"[28] this interest in dignifying "woman's work" at the same time that it suggests the need to redefine woman's role in our culture. Like Wright, Mariah Upshur is a "housekeeper and a homemaker," and throughout the novel she is seen doing "woman's work." Sarah Wright devotes two full pages to a list of chores Mariah does in the course of a day. From sunup, Mariah tries

> to fling her whole self into the chores of morning. *Had* to wash up, put on her everyday clothes. *Had* to mix pan of bread, sift a-many maggot out of the flour first. *Had* to find an onion and sprinkle some sugar on it over it, set it out in the yard in good hopes that the sun would come up strong and draw the syrup out of it to ease up Skeeter's chest. *Had* to get those washtubs down from the house.

And the rhythm of unending work continues till sundown:

> [Had to] pump enough water for that bunch of dirty clothes. [Had to go] up and down, up and down, up and down over that scrubbing board. . . . Had to feed those two or three Bantam hens she was saving for a Sunday dinner. . . . Had to look over [the children's] homework. . . . Had to figure out what in the name of God she was gonna feed that bunch for supper. (pp. 24–25)

This is Mariah's life, not Jacob's. He works in the fields and devotes the rest of his life to winning back the Upshur land stolen by Miss Bannie, a white woman who owns Tangierneck. Mariah is enraged by the assumption that she should exhaust herself with never-ending work in the house while Jacob, because he has worked in the fields during the day, sits by idle. He comes home, Mariah tells herself, "to sit with his feet propped up by that stove and see [her] fall right over on her feet with the work in a way of speaking and not do another thing else" (p. 25). This is the pattern of their lives throughout the novel, for Jacob has been socialized to believe that a good man cares for his family and a real man leaves work in the home to his wife. Wright repeatedly shows the tension this division of labor creates. When she is pregnant with her fifth child, Mariah calls out for assistance from Jacob in carrying large tubs of water to the stove. His answer is a telling comment on his sexist posture:

> "Mariah, ain't you got no sense? I done told you a-many a time to set these tubs on the stove and then you tote in the water, in a bucket."

Hurt by Jacob's lack of sensitivity to her physical condition and the chores she has to do daily, Mariah tries to get Jacob to understand she needs his help with the jobs she has to do, not his advice on the way she should do them:

> "How many steps you want me to make, Jacob, 'fore I topple over and die? How many steps? It takes a-many a trip to fill this tub, bucket by bucket, when I set the thing on the stove first. I do it that way when you ain't home, but how come you want me to do it when I ain't able? How come you want me to do it when you're right around here doing nothing?" (p. 35)

Sarah Wright adds to her treatment of sexism a dimension not present in the other novels examined in this book. That dimension is the role of the church in limiting women's lives. In fact, the church is seen as the very seat of sexism and narrow-mindedness in the community. It reinforces the submissiveness of southern blacks by teaching that the Lord will make a way for them somehow and, most especially, by insisting on the need to prove to white people that blacks are moral and decent people who uphold the law and abide by the Scriptures. Women are expected to be the most moral of all because the Bible teaches, and the community believes, that

a woman is a mighty unclean person unless they learn how to
respect their menfolks. Menfolks just have to put up with them. . . .
Women supposed to take to the keeping of the house and not to the
keeping of business outside the house. Suppose to obey their man!
(p. 168)

Wright's indictment of the church is seen less in the men's interpretation of the Scriptures than in the churchwomen's role as judge,
jury, and executioner of any woman who steps outside her God-decreed role. Mariah is such a woman. When she conceives a child out
of wedlock she must go before "the Committee" of churchwomen
who, dressed in white and in self-righteousness, pass judgment on
"hot-behinded" (p. 181) whores. When Mariah explains that her
lovemaking with Jacob in the fields one spring was an expression of
her sexuality, the women remind her that men have a right to their
sexuality, but women must deny what they feel: the Lord forgives the
passion of men, but not that of women.

Sarah Wright's treatment of sexism and religious narrow-
mindedness is inseparable from her treatment of racism, the dominant theme in the novel. The novel catalogues the crimes committed
by whites against blacks. Miss Bannie steals the Upshur land and controls the lives of those who work it. Indeed, in her long black car, she
is the power that controls the whole community. Worse than her control, however, is the violence of hooded white men who come in the
night to burn and to frighten and, in some cases, to kill blacks, both
men and women. Neither this control nor this violence is more devastating than the poverty of the community. Tangierneck is cut off
from other communities—isolated, backward, and poor. Poverty is
manifested in the diet of salt pork, molasses, and bread Mariah's children receive daily. Poverty is manifested in the worms that crawl from
the nose and the behind of one child and in the consumption that
racks the small frames of two other children. It is this narrow, racist,
and dismally poor community from which Mariah will journey from
"can't to can" for herself and for her children.

In several ways Mariah Upshur is a misfit in this community. Racially, she is a misfit because she does not fear Miss Bannie and advises the men to confront the white woman with the sin of her past—

her child by a black man. She wants the community to take an aggressive position on the need for a new school for their children. In general, she would take on the system to make it clear that she is not a "nigger." As Jacob tells his sons, a "nigger is someone who can't do no better" (p. 89). Mariah insists on doing better by journeying from the "god-forsaken" place to the promised land."

She is a misfit also because she sees the community's religion for what it is—self-righteousness, hypocrisy, and narrow-mindedness. The Committee women make pretty things for the church, prepare food for church gatherings, and sit on the mothers' bench attempting to direct the lives of children and other women. After her indictment by the Committee, Mariah refuses to attend church, and in response to comments on her backsliding, she catalogues in her own mind the various sins of men in the community and the deliberate blindness of women to those sins. Wright establishes that Mariah is doing penance for her past sins, and that she is actually far more religious than the women on the Committee. Throughout the novel she prays to God for forgiveness and prepares herself psychologically for the day of judgment before his throne.

Finally, Mariah is a misfit because she will not take a backseat to men. When male leaders in the community, including her father, talk about the problems of men, she risks the back of her father's hand and the anger of the other men by reminding them, again and again, that "colored women" have their own set of problems in Tangierneck and that those problems are as severe as any black men face. During her marriage to Jacob she speaks her piece. He orders her not to seek welfare because it offends his male pride, but she rushes to join the wagonload of women traveling to the city welfare office. He orders her not to work in the fields, but she works anyway because she is saving pennies for her departure from Tangierneck. She is a strong woman whose courage and dream of possibilities for her life make her one of the most magnificent women in the group of characters analyzed in this book. She struggles against nature, against white power, against community women, and against community men— all alone. She never has "time to sew for myself" (p. 94), and she feels that her life "ain't been nothing but wind" (p. 113). But by challenging various segments of the black community and the white system, she attempts to journey from "can't to can."

Her journey is thwarted by her obligations as the mother of five children and the wife of a "going nowhere" (p. 64) man whose history of oppression is her history. She resembles in many ways Helga Crane in Nella Larsen's *Quicksand* (1928), a novel about the racial and cultural identity crisis of an upper-class black woman. Helga Crane escapes the stultifying culture of upper-class blacks by marrying an uneducated preacher who speaks to her intense sexuality. He takes her, and she releases without fear her "long-hidden, half-understood desire."[29] She is a willing prisoner of her passions, for

> night came at the end of every day. Emotional, palpitating, amorous, all that was living in her sprang like rank weeds at the tingling thought of night, with a vitality so strong that it devoured all shoots of reason. (p. 202)

Helga gives birth to four children in quick succession and discovers how tragic has been her devotion to lovemaking with this man who is outside her experiences and her dreams. She is, in fact, "used . . . up" by the children (p. 203). She looks

> in helpless dismay and . . . disgust at the disorder around her, the permanent assembly of partly emptied medicine bottles on the clock shelf, the perpetual array of drying baby clothes on the chair back, the unceasing litter of half-dead flowers on the table . . . and she was thankful, whenever possible, to be relieved from the ordeal of cooking. (p. 205)

Having had "more than enough" of the "quagmire in which she had engulfed herself" (p. 218), Helga decides to take control of her life and journey "from can't to can." Tragically, as she plans the journey, she discovers that she is once again pregnant. The novel ends with Larsen's succinct and compelling statement on the "quagmire":

And hardly had she left her bed and become able to walk without
pain, hardly had the children returned from the homes of the
neighbors, when she began to have her fifth child. (p. 222)

Like Helga Crane, Mariah Upshur must give up her journey toward
brighter horizons because she is burdened by the responsibilities associated with motherhood. She has five children of her own, and the
deaths of two women in the community leave her with three more.
Overwhelmed by the realization that she cannot leave Tangierneck,
Mariah decides that the only journey she is ever going to be able to
make is the journey from life to death. Death is calling her, she tells
herself, beckoning her to come so that she can face judgment for the
sins of her past. Her attempted suicide by drowning is foreshadowed
early in the novel when Wright writes of Mariah's respect for water
as "a bossy thing. Fit anywhere it wants to. Sometimes it goes quiet.
Sometimes it goes noisy. But any way it goes, it takes over" (p. 36). As
Mariah wades into the cold waters of the sound, she repeats the prayer
that has been like a refrain to every scene and conversation in the
novel: "Let my children live." Ironically, it is this passion for her
children's welfare that pulls her back from death into life.

At last this woman of courage, strength, and tenacity makes peace
with her soul. She decides she will no longer contemplate death or
grieve over her past sins. She will find redemption in serving the needs
of her family and dignity in the roles of mother and wife. From a
feminist perspective, however, Mariah has journeyed from contem-
plating "can" to accepting "can't." Wright does not suggest that there
will be changes in Jacob's understanding of Mariah as a woman or
his definition of himself as the man in the family. Mariah will struggle
with Jacob as she has always struggled, and she will challenge the
women of the community as she has always challenged them. With
the death of Vyry, a woman whom the community respects, Mariah
will probably emerge as a leader, but the dimensions of her personal
life will remain the same. This is clearly implied in the closing lines
of the novel. As Jacob, in his way of showing love, reprimands Mariah
for being a "fool woman" going out into the cold waters, knowing
that she can't swim, she answers:

"Jacob, I forgot to put the dough to bake in the oven so you and the children could have some nice hot bread for your dinner." (p. 253)

In *This Child's Gonna Live* we see Mariah, a woman of dignity and compassion, in the home and in the fields, and in both places she sings hymns to the Lord. In Gayl Jones's *Corregidora* (1975) we see Ursa Corregidora in a nightclub or in seedy restaurants, where she sings the blues. Whereas Mariah is religious, rural, and southern, Ursa is worldly, urban, and northern. In addition to these differences, there is the stark difference between the history of oppression that Wright examines and the history of oppression that Jones recounts. In Mariah's world, white people have stolen her family's land and now hold an entire community in the grips of poverty and powerlessness. For Ursa, who lives in a black community that has virtually no contact with whites, the history of oppression is the tragedy of her maternal ancestors, the Corregidora women. The story of the women is told in the late 1940s, but the tragedy began during slavery and lasted through three generations. Corregidora, a Portuguese seaman turned plantation owner, turned rapist, turned breeder of mulatto women, enslaved and exploited the Corregidora women.

The story comes out in monologues that "seep from Ursa's consciousness in moments of psychological stress."[30] Corregidora was a slavemonger who slept with his slaves, sired children by them, and then slept with the children. He was a breeder who sent his women out to sleep with other men so that he would have mulatto children for the market. As the story unfolds throughout the novel in Ursa's subconsciousness, it is a bizarre and horrifying tale of perversity and abuse, a commentary on the sickness of the slave culture. Corregidora slept with his own children, and his wife slept with them as well:

> And you know sometimes the mistresses was doing it too so they could have little pocket money that their husbands didn't know about. And getting their brothers and their brothers' friends and other mens they know, you know, and then they make theyselves right smart money for their purse. Naw, Corregidora's wife didn't do that. She slept with you herself.[31]

From the age of eight, Ursa hears the story of the Corregidora women, from "Great Gram" first and then from her mother, until it becomes an abiding part of her consciousness. Their past becomes her past and, in a terrifying way, controls her present. For her, Corregidora is "the symbolic progenitor of all evil . . . much like the serpent in the mythical Garden of Eden."[32] Most especially, he is a symbol of the evil that is peculiar to the reality of black women: they are bodies to be used and abused. Because of this history of oppression, Ursa is taught that she has a special mission in life: she must "make generations. They can burn the papers but they can't burn conscience. . . . And that['s] what makes the evidence. And that's what makes the verdict" (p. 24).

In a nightclub in Kentucky Ursa's singing is soul-piercing, entrancing, and sensuous. She sings the blues because it is her way of turning pain into pleasure and of freeing herself psychologically from "the tyranny of historical oppression"[33] that Jones sees as peculiar to black women. She fears that the tragedy of her maternal ancestors might find its way out of her subconscious into the center of her life. To the question, "Who are you?" Ursa answers, "I am the daughter of the daughter of the daughter of Ursa of currents, steel wool and electric wire for hair" (p. 75).

Claudia Tate discerns two dramas in the novel: the "internal drama," which deals essentially with the Corregidora legend, and "the external drama," which deals with Ursa's problems with her husband, Mutt Thomas. Mutt is a macho man, insisting on his right to own Ursa. He neither realizes nor cares that her singing of the blues is an expression of her creativity and her way of fingering the scars on her psyche made by the Corregidora tragedy. She is his wife and must therefore obey his orders. When he insists that she stop singing, an argument ensues. He pushes Ursa down the back steps of the nightclub, and the fall results in her having to have a hysterectomy. As "the daughter of the daughter" who must "make generations," Ursa cannot keep her promise to her maternal ancestors. Divorcing Mutt, she "seems to be left with no alternative but to live out her life alone like all the Corregidora women before her."[34]

Claudia Tate posits that Ursa would have been content to remain alone had she not been "frightened by a lesbian encounter while convalescing at the home of a friend." She worries, Tate writes, whether men will still desire her or whether she will "succumb to homosexual embraces."[35] Jones's vision does not easily support Tate's comment on Ursa's fear of homosexuality. It does, however, support the interpretation that Ursa worries about not being desired by men. This point is clear in Ursa's lovemaking with Tadpole, the man who befriends her after the operation. As he takes her, she demonstrates in the sexual act that she still knows how to lie with a man.

Ursa marries Tadpole, but within a short period of time she returns to Mutt, who has never given up sending her pleas for forgiveness and messages of love and need. There is some vagueness in Jones's handling of the relationship between Mutt and Ursa. We feel that Ursa does indeed love Mutt Thomas. The emotional and physical bond between them is obviously strong, for Ursa forgives Mutt for making it impossible for her to keep her mission as a Corregidora woman. We also sense, and Jones develops this point explicitly at times, that Ursa feels the need to hurt Mutt. This point raises a fundamental question about the novel's vision of black male–female relationships. What is the relationship of the Corregidora legend to Ursa's reality as a black woman if not that it is an extreme statement of the exploitation that black women experience beyond slavery with their own men?

Several arguments can be made for this interpretation. One is that Jones weaves the story of white male exploitation of black women throughout the novel, but in her vision of Ursa's life in the 1940s she makes no references to white men and no references to white exploitation. Interestingly, however, sexual exploitation continues into the present. Corregidora forced black women to make generations because he profited from this exploitation. Mutt Thomas accidentally prevents Ursa from making generations because he believes he has the right to control her. His limiting view of women is similar to Corregidora's. Jones writes that Mutt sees Ursa's "pussy . . . as the center of her . . . being," and she adds that Mutt believes it belongs to him and only to him.

Past and present seem to come together as Ursa engages in an oral sex act with Mutt. She gives him, as Great Gram had given Corregidora, "a moment of pleasure and excruciating pain at the same time, a moment of broken skin but not sexlessness ... a moment that stops before it breaks the skin." This is Ursa's power as a woman—and Jones implies, perhaps without intending to, that it is Ursa's only power. In the act that defines the center of her reality according to Mutt, she has the power to kill him: "I could kill you" (p. 212). Clearly, Ursa loves Mutt and wants to be loved by him. Clearly, she desires him physically. But Jones seems to say that because of the lessons she has learned about the historical oppression of black women, Ursa hates Mutt as much as she loves him.

Although these arguments support the interpretation that Jones extends the legend of sexual exploitation during slavery to apply to black women out of slavery, there are perhaps as many arguments to the contrary, for the novel, powerful though it is, often moves in and out of focus. It raises many provocative questions to which it does not give easy answers. In fact, Tate's interpretation of Ursa's fear of embracing homosexuality is precipitated by this shift in focus. Jones treats two lesbian characters with sensitivity, but she steps back from developing them. Our failure to get a handle on the novel that does justice to Jones's vision demonstrates the need for clearly defined and tested approaches to lesbian criticism. With such approaches, we might find that *Corregidora* belongs to the tradition of lesbian or latent lesbian fiction that J. R. Roberts and Barbara Smith celebrate in *Black Lesbians: An Annotated Bibliography* (1981).

Jones's vision of black womanhood is more fully developed in her second work, *Eva's Man*. In fact, in some ways *Eva's Man* is a companion work. The theme of hate and desire is repeated, as are the themes of sexual exploitation and of oral sex as a reflection of a woman's hostility and her power to kill. The vision remains one of horror. Toni Morrison is therefore correct in saying that Jones's writing is "an exception to black women's writing" in that it is "never ... about joy."[36] But it is not just the absence of joy that places Jones's second novel in a category all its own. There is also its preoccupation with raw and crude sexual lust, sexual profanity, and sexual perversion. Jones's artistic mirror is broad enough to reflect everything that happens in the netherworld of sex. Like many female erotic novels published in the sixties and seventies, *Eva's Man* reads at times like the script of an X-rated movie.

The novel is an exception to black women's writing also because it emphasizes sexual victimization almost to the exclusion of any concern with racial oppression. The other black women writers examined in this book allude to sexual victimization, but they do so within the contexts of racism, sexism, and poverty, and they extend genuine sympathy to the black man as a victim turned victimizer. Ann Petry, for example, writing three decades before Gayl Jones, indicts Boots Smith for his attempt to rape Lutie Johnson, but even while doing so, she keeps before the reader's mind Smith's victimization and sense of helplessness. This same posture is present in the fiction of Alice Walker, a contemporary of Gayl Jones. In her first novel, *The Third Life of Grange Copeland*, Walker writes movingly of the tragedy of Brownfield in the corrupt and unjust sharecropping system of a small Georgia town.

Gayl Jones departs radically from this tradition of holding the system at least partly responsible for the black man's victimization of the black woman, and in so doing she adds a fictional dimension to black womanhood that is decidedly new. The black man's brutal victimization of the black woman is the major chord in her work. Some consideration should be given to Jones's opinion that the particulars of the victimization of the black man, which might explain his treatment of the black woman, need not be presented in fiction. "For the black man," Jones says, "his very life is a criticism of the society in which he lives."[37] This same attitude could have been taken by other black women writers who, like Jones, chose to examine the black man's sexual cruelty, but those writers wisely understood that a careful writer never assumes that the reader already knows the particulars that forge a certain kind of personality. The verdict on *Eva's Man* is that its author's neglect of particulars about the black man's victimization results in his appearing to be innately a victimizer rather than a victim turned victimizer unwittingly.

In an interview published in *The Massachusetts Review* Gayl Jones described her novel as "a horror story" that starts with "the telling and sometimes the answers come out of the telling."[38] This is an accurate description of the technique she uses in *Eva's Man*. The story is told in disconnected dialogue, in dreams and fantasies, in fractured time sequences and "hereabout-whereabout" places, in memory and myth, in flashbacks that take the reader into Eva's past, wherein the explanation of the act of violence against her lover lies. Jones further explains that in "using memory and fantasy as well as storytelling," she reclaims Eva Medina's "whole past, and reveals all the things that lead up to . . . her relationship with her lover."[39] The skillfully handled first-person point of view facilitates this reclaiming and, what is most important, humanizes a strange woman.

Eva is forty-three when the novel begins. Her crime took place when she was thirty-seven. For five years she has been in the psychiatric ward of an upstate New York hospital, presenting to all the "Dr. Frauds" who examine her a face frozen in nonchalance, exhibiting neither guilt about the act for which she was committed nor concern for her welfare. As the flashbacks begin, Eva is resurrected from a comatose state into clarity, and the *who* of her identity and the *why* of her act unfold metaphorically and clearly. Dispassionately, she explains, "I opened his trousers and played with his penis. My mouth, my teeth, my tongue went inside his trousers. I raised blood. . . . I squeezed his dick in my teeth. I bit down hard."[40]

The flashbacks, Gayl Jones explains, make a "connection" with Eva's act of sexual violence because all of them are metaphors of the sexual victimization of black women that Eva has witnessed since she was a child. Indeed, the statement that best explains Eva's past and Jones's vision of black male–black female relationships is repeated frequently in disconnected dialogue and fantasy throughout the novel: "all [men] think about is where they going to get their next piece" (p. 154). Jones attempts to dispel the notion that Eva and her lover represent a statement on male–female relationships in the black community: they "stand for themselves, really,"[41] she says. But this disclaimer is hardly convincing in light of the heavy emphasis on sexual abuse that characterizes all the flashbacks and all the dreams. The recurring theme of the novel, Jones's disclaimer notwithstanding, is that black men see black women as sexual objects, "bitches," and "whores" who like to be laid and who will accept abuse.

The first flashback that informs the reader of Eva's exposure to sexual victimization relates to Eva's childhood in a small New York apartment building where she lives with her mother and father. What she remembers most about those years is her mother's preoccupation with the subject of sex, an interest avidly shared by her mother's friend, Miss Billie. In Eva's memory and fantasy the two women talk freely and graphically about sexual perversion, aggression, and violence; about Old Man Logan, who masturbates in the presence of women; and about the day-in and day-out sexual brutality of men that scars the psyches and bodies of women in the community. She is instructed not to let Old Man Logan "mess with you . . . cause he ain't nothing but a shit" (p. 12). Eva begins to see all men as "shit" because in all encounters they seek only "to mess" with women.

The theme of men "messing" with women undergirds all of Eva's experiences as a young girl. When she was only eight, young Freddy Smoot "messed" with her with "a dirty popsicle stick" (p. 13), having learned from his environment that the relationship between men and women is characterized exclusively by sexual encounters in which the man aggressively demands service and the woman, upon pain of a beating, delivers. He takes a dirty popsicle stick and moves it around under Eva's pants as she, following his orders, "squeezed him like a milkweed" (p. 13). Here "dirty" symbolizes the baseness of sexual encounters in the community; and the "popsicle stick," something one finds in a filthy gutter, stands throughout the novel for man's erection, and in this instance for the pervasiveness of sexual abuse that is part of the consciousness even of the very young.

The popsicle experience, one of several incidents of sexual victimization, is followed by others in which Eva is pursued, cornered, fondled by young boys or by older men who are acting out the culturally defined behavior of their sex. From all these encounters (and there are many) Eva develops a fear of men. As she recalls her experiences with her "man" in a cheap hotel room, she realizes at age forty-three that "fearing is a better word" for her emotional response to men. All of them are "old shits" who want only "to mess" with women.

In her discussion of black female adolescence Joyce Ladner writes that by the age of eight, a black girl in the ghetto has "a good chance of being exposed to rape and violence,"[42] and this experience plays a decisive role in the girl's definition of womanhood. Jones's fictive world mirrors the real world Ladner and other sociologists have studied. In the sanctity of her home Eva sees sexual encounters as very natural occurrences in the life of her mother. She recalls in the psychiatric ward that her mother took a lover who was ten years her junior, a musician who possessed the sexual prowess associated with that profession. Only in her memory and fantasy does Eva understand what she could not understand as a young girl: her mother's interest in Tyrone was entirely sexual. The relationship had nothing to do with her mother's need for companionship, for tenderness, or for a broader definition of self. It was rooted purely in sexual desire. Tyrone came into their private lives to "mess" with her mother at her mother's invitation. The trauma of the relationship is that it makes Eva available to Tyrone: he begins in small ways to teach Eva about her sexuality, and eventually attempts to rape her.

Since "all men think about is where they going to get their next piece" (p. 151), Eva is taught to avoid them. And yet, she hears her mother and Miss Billie express concern about Miss Billie's daughter, who, at twenty-seven, has not slept with a man. Whereas early promiscuity is frowned upon, validation of self in sexual encounters with a man is expected. In the cultural ethos of the community, a woman without a man is either insane or lesbian. These fears for Eva are created by her propensity for staying at home. At seventeen, she should have had "the meat and the gravy too," and Mrs. Medina encourages her daughter to go out into the world of womanhood.

The sexual mother is certainly unusual in black fiction. And in black American poetry mothers are so devoted to their responsibilities—making those great sacrifices for their families—that they often repress or conceal their sexuality. But many sociological studies of black women as mothers give a different picture. Joyce Ladner, Camille Jeffers, Carol Stack, and others write of the exposure of young girls to the sounds of lovemaking, an exposure that is often created by the exigencies of poverty that deprive women and men of privacy. In the novels examined in this study—and in all other novels written by black women from 1853 to the present—the only mothers whose sexuality is central to their lives are Jones's Mrs. Medina and Toni Morrison's Hannah Peace (to be discussed in the following chapter).

Two images of women dominate *Eva's Man*. One—hardly new to black literature—is the image of the "whore." The word is used loosely throughout the novel to refer to all women, but, significantly, it is used by men only. Men don't cajole women; they coerce them. Men don't "jive talk" women; they humiliate them. Men don't "make love" to women; they "fuck" them. This damaging picture of male–female relationships precludes any saving graces that might move those relationships to a level in which the women's personhoods are respected and their sexual services appreciated and revered. Whether they are wives or mothers, "good" women or "bad," all women in the eyes of men in the novel are "whores" and "bitches."

Again, it is significant that Eva hears the words "whore" and "bitch" in the sanctity of her own home. She often heard her parents making love, but there is one experience she remembers vividly and with horror. "He had her arm and he was undoing her blouse," she recalls. "Then it was like I could hear her clothes ripping . . . now he was tearing that blouse off and those underthings. I didn't hear nothing from her the whole time. I didn't hear a thing from her." What she hears is her father saying, again and again, "Act like a whore, I'm gonna fuck you like a whore. You act like a whore, I'm gonna fuck you like a whore" (p. 37). Her mother's silence is sufficient evidence either of guilt or of submission to masculine strength.

When she becomes a woman, Eva searches for something that challenges "whoredom" as an unavoidable reality for women and "fucking" as the unalterable posture men have toward lovemaking. But she cannot escape the image, for it is in the ethos and culture. Wherever she goes, she is labeled a "whore and a bitch" simply because she is a black woman. She explains to the psychiatrist that her lover, Davis, simply assumed that she was "that kind of a woman." All men, she continues, saw her that way. "Always . . . Always. No matter what I . . . They all would" (p. 171). She is uncertain of what she can do to relieve herself of this burden, to exorcise this curse from her life. Simply by walking, talking, breathing—simply because she *is*— she is a "whore" or a "bitch" in the eyes of black men.

The second image that dominates *Eva's Man* is that of "the queen bee." The queen bee is the alternative to the oppressive forces that push women into whoredom. In the eyes of the community the queen bee represents a posture toward men no normal woman would want to adopt. Eva is told by her mother that the "queen bee" is a woman "sucked hollow by a man" (p. 73). She stings men out of anger or out of her desire for something more than the abuse they offer. She is a "queen bee because every man she had ended up dying." Miss Billie explains, "I don't mean natural dying, I mean something happen to them. Other men know it too, but they still come" (p. 30). They have to "be stung by the bee before they can see" that women are more than whores. They believe that all women need "the fork" between their legs, but the queen bee teaches them that the breasts they suck contain blood. She is a Medusa, really, whose strange eyes invite them to a world of pleasure and then turn them to stone.

Myths and fantasies, dreams and memories come together in Eva's mind to paint a horror picture of male–female relationships that reflects the institutionalized devaluation of black women that began in slavery. Then "every black woman was, by definition, a slut according to the racist mythology; therefore, to assault her and exploit her sexually was not reprehensible and carried with it none of the normal communal sanctions against such behavior."[43] According to bell hooks, most people, even a highly respected scholar such as Susan Brownmiller, "tend to see devaluation of black womanhood as occurring only in the context of slavery. In actuality, sexual exploitation of black women continued long after slavery ended and was institutionalized by other oppressive practices"[44] so integral a part of American culture that they cause black women to doubt their own morality. Gayl Jones weaves this history of devaluation into her story of Eva Medina, who learns to doubt her morality in a black community where sexual exploitation of black women is commonplace. In an interview with Claudia Tate, Jones explained that the images in the novel show "how myths or the ways in which men perceive women actually define their characters."[45]

Eva's response to these myths is her encounter with Davis in a cheap hotel room where every word, movement, color, and odor suggest horror, perversity, destruction, and death. It has all the makings of a gothic scene, but instead of ghosts and unsolved mysteries and forebodings, there are sexual victimization and sexual violence. All her life Eva had heard about and seen the dangers of men and sex. Finally, she finds herself confronting both. Driven by forces she cannot control, Eva walks into the pits of whoredom. Davis makes love to her when she is bleeding. He "fucks" her and calls her "bitch" repeatedly. He refuses to let her comb her hair, refuses to let her leave. She is like an animal he rides again and again, beating her with a whip of verbal abuse, demanding that she not whinny or slow down. He keeps her in the cheap hotel room as an animal is kept in a cage, and brings her dinners in a greasy bag from the restaurant. The dinners symbolize the coarseness of the encounter, for they are always cabbage, sausage, and horseradish that look "like Baby's doodoo" and that fill Eva with gas. Impressed with his own sexual prowess and convinced that all women want to be "had" by men, Davis believes he is doing Eva a favor. After all, he tells her, "she ain't been getting it" (p. 7). And when he takes her, he goes in "like he was tearing something besides her flesh" (p. 51).

At Eva's trial, those who will decide her fate are men who do not understand her strange past. Those who will decide whether she is sane or insane are also men who do not understand the woman's rage within her soul. Their very simple explanation of her actions is that she killed Davis because he was "cheating" on her or because he was sexually cold toward her: "hers was a crime of passion, and his was a crime of coldness" (p. 82). As her past is reclaimed, Eva understands that she castrated Davis and poisoned him because "he came to represent all the men she had known" (p. 81). Her act of violence is an extreme expression of the rage of which Anaïs Nin writes. When women are engulfed by "angers that have come from damage that has been festering, from anger that hasn't been expressed, or anger that is not understood," the result is "an explosion."[46]

Elvira, the lesbian who shares the prison cell with Eva, understands Eva's rage and her silence following Davis's murder better than the experts trained to explain human behavior. Their common identity as black women is more of a bond than their sexual preferences are barriers. Elvira calls Eva "honey" and gives her the first taste of unqualified love. She taunts Eva with her open legs, and Eva remembers her mother's teaching that "once a woman opens her legs, she can't close them" (p. 142). Elvira turns the statement a different way: "once a woman closes them, do they stay closed?" (p. 142). She offers Eva an alternative to sexual victimization, and in embracing Elvira, Eva moves from "can't to can" in sexual fulfillment. Only when Eva embraces lesbianism does she hear and speak sweet words. Jones ends the novel:

> "Tell me when it feels sweet, Eva. Tell me when it feels sweet, honey."
> I leaned back, squeezing her face between my legs, and told her,
> "Now!" (p. 177)

chapter 6

GIVING BIRTH TO SELF

The Quests for Wholeness of Sula Mae Peace and Meridian Hill

"I don't want to make somebody else. I want to make myself."
— Sula Mae Peace in Toni Morrison, *Sula*, 1973

"You are free to be whichever way you like, to be with whoever, of whatever color or sex you like—and what you risk in being truly yourself, the way you want to be, is not the loss of me. You are not free, however, to think I am a fool."
— Meridian Hill in Alice Walker, *Meridian*, 1973

The emerging sexual consciousness of black women in the nation is reflected in the work of Alice Walker and Toni Morrison. Walker, a gifted and prolific writer, became "within a relatively short space of time . . . a touchstone in black literature, especially that created by female writers."[1] In 1968, still in her twenties, she published her first book of poetry, *Once*. In 1970, not yet thirty, she published her first novel, *The Third Life of Grange Copeland*. Since then, she has written a collection of short stories, *In Love and Trouble* (1973); two volumes of poetry, *Revolutionary Petunias* (1973) and *Goodnight, Willie Lee* (1980); a second novel, *Meridian* (1976); and the third novel, *The Color Purple* (1982), which won a Pulitzer Prize. Mary Helen Washington writes that "from whatever vantage point one investigates the work of Alice Walker—poet, novelist, short story writer, critic, essayist, and apologist for black women—it is clear that the special identifying mark of her writing is her concern for the lives of black women."[2] Like Langston Hughes in the twenties and thirties, Alice Walker in the sixties and seventies displayed her talents in various genres and, also like Hughes, became admired by colleagues and respected by critics:

> Hardly any conference or seminar on Black American literature can be called viable without proper attention being paid to Walker's visionary plots, her laconic style impacted with a premature wisdom, her fervent regard for history . . . or her perceptive and fertile analysis of continuing social dramas.[3]

Toni Morrison is the empress of black women's fiction, a master of her craft, and the creator of some of the most complex and intriguing women in American literature. In the space of twelve years she wrote four major novels. *The Bluest Eye* was published in the same year as Walker's first novel, *The Third Life of Grange Copeland*. That was 1970, the beginning of the decade in which black women would follow the advice Shirley Chisholm gave in the sixties on the need to speak truthfully and courageously about their plight as women.

If Walker explores "the oppressions, the insanities, the loyalties, and the triumphs of black women,"[4] Morrison illuminates in the lives of imaginary women the presence of "beauty, love" or, more often, "the absence of [love]."[5] Before her debut as a novelist, Morrison was a senior editor at Random House, where she was instrumental in publishing a number of significant works by black writers such as Henry Dumas, John McClusky, and two literary powerhouses, Toni Cade Bambara and Gayl Jones. She was a major black thinker and doer in this position, but it is as a novelist that she has made distinctive contributions to a deeper understanding of the black experience, most especially that which shapes the lives of black women. In 1973, her second novel, *Sula*, was published; in 1978, her third, *Song of Solomon*; and in 1981, her fourth, *Tar Baby*. Morrison was the first black novelist in America since Richard Wright to have her work chosen as the main selection of the Book-of-the-Month Club.

Morrison is hailed as the creator of three complex women—Eva Peace, Sula Mae Peace, and Hannah Peace—affectionately called "the Peace women." Walker is hailed as the creator of Mem Copeland, Josie, and Meridian, women of the soil whose uniqueness is unsurpassed in American literary history. Morrison is a northern writer; Walker southern. Their literary visions are shaped by these different perspectives, and yet Walker and Morrison speak a similar truth and create women who are spiritual sisters.

Walker's Meridian is a young, pure, saintly woman of the South who has functioned in the roles of wife and mother. Morrison's Sula is an "evil" and defiant woman of the Midwest who has been neither wife nor mother. What they have in common is an intense desire to give birth to themselves as persons. Their individual quests for selfhood are precipitated by different personal needs and reflect different attitudes toward the human condition. The stages of their journeys toward selfhood and the people they love and leave along the way are, therefore, decidedly different. But the goals of their quests are the same—a clearer understanding of self and expanded room in which to hum their own melodies and sing their own lyrics.

Set in a small, semirural community in Medallion, Ohio, and covering a time span of five decades (1920 to 1965), *Sula* is the intriguing story of Sula Mae Peace, an acutely sensitive, enigmatic, and defiant woman whose nonconformity is a "living criticism . . . of the dreadful lives of resignation other women live."[6] Joan Bischoff compares Morrison's protagonist to Henry James's Maisie of *What Maisie Knew*. She is "the modern preternaturally sensitive but rudely thwarted black girl in today's society."[7] As a young girl she so startles the community with her extreme emotional impulses that her growth into a "strange, strong and independent woman" is all but predictable. She rejects "behavioral standards of all kinds" and attempts to "rely solely on herself."[8] It is to herself and only herself that Sula wishes to be good, for early in life she adopted the philosophy that "being good to somebody is just like being mean to somebody. Risky. You don't get nothing for it."[9]

Sula challenges the limitations on her individuality and, to the consternation of the community, openly and hostilely disregards time-honored conventions and traditions. She becomes an outsider with "a quality of abandon."[10] At twenty-seven, she takes pride in being a single woman and says, with strong conviction, no man "ain't worth more than me" (p. 124). Instead of actively seeking lovers and stroking them into matrimony, or letting them stroke her into matrimony, she sleeps with men as if she were "trying them out and discarding them without any excuse the men could swallow" (p. 99). She uncategorically rejects the standards others use to measure her life, insisting on the right to create a "version of herself she could reach out to and touch with an ungloved hand" (p. 104). This version of herself is decidedly not the traditional view of woman as wife and mother. Both roles, in her opinion, are coffins in which a woman's self is buried and never exhumed.

Before she introduces Sula to the reader, Morrison gives a life-throbbing picture of the community in which the drama of defiance takes place. It stands "in the hills above the valley town of Medallion and spread[s] all the way to the river" (p. 63). It is connected to the valley by one road only, which is shaded by beeches, oaks, and chestnuts. Strangely, this community "in the hills" is called "the Bottom." "It all started," Morrison writes, as "a joke," a "nigger joke" about a white farmer who convinced his ignorant and unsuspecting slave, to whom property had been promised with freedom, that the land in the hills was not only "the fertile valley," but also, from God's vantage point, "the bottom of heaven." With its rows of shacks and "its hilly land, where planting is backbreaking, where the soil slides down and washes away the seed all through the winter" (p. 5), the Bottom is closer to hell than to heaven. But the name remains unchanged, and from generation to generation the people repeat the joke with "wet-eyed laughter," concealing "the cruelty of their fate" (p. 4).

A community that is the opposite of what its name suggests, that yields to "the cruelty of its fate," that accepts what is, though its "wet-eyed laughter" reveals its awareness that a challenge is needed—such a community casts Sula's challenge to convention and tradition in sharp relief. For in this culture of sameness and boredom, defiance is neither understood nor tolerated. The profoundness of Sula's defiance is a reflection of the sharp contrast between who she is and what the Bottom decrees for its women. Place in *Sula*, therefore, is significant to the credibility of the character and the realism of the plot. The same point should be made about the function of time in the novel. Although a woman like Sula would be startling in any era, she is fascinatingly unique in a semirural town during the thirties, forties, and fifties when the nation's conscience did not bear the imprint of women's struggles for wider options in their lives.

As Morrison analyzes Sula's growth from childhood to womanhood, she analyzes as well the three individuals who shape Sula's personality, values, and defiant posture toward life. Significantly, all three characters are women, and each offers Sula different responses to womanhood. The most influential and intriguing of the three women is Sula's grandmother, Eva Peace, who was discussed in chapter 3. When Sula is introduced in the novel, she is a child of three who has moved with her widowed mother into the home of her grandmother. The move is a decisive point in Sula's life in that it introduces her to various kinds of strangeness. The grandmother's house itself is a strange structure, with "many rooms that had been built over a period of five years to the specifications of its owner, who kept on adding things: more stairways ... more rooms, doors and stoops" (p. 26). No one asks questions about the strange house, just as no one asks questions above Eva Mae Peace, "the creator and sovereign of this enormous house," who sits in a wagon on the second floor, "directing the lives of her children, friends, strays, and a constant stream of boarders" (p. 26). Fewer than nine people in the town can remember when Eva had two legs, but no one ever asks how she lost her leg. There is something about Eva's ability to control, to dominate, to command attention that makes her disability glamorous. In a "rocking chair top fitted into a large child's wagon," she is enthroned as the sovereign of the house and the community (p. 26).

It is in this strange house of strange boarders lorded over by a strange and domineering woman that Sula Mae Peace grows into a woman. She grows without the sustaining love that is essential for healthy socialization, for Eva Mae Peace, despite all her gestures of magnanimity toward "strays," is unable to embrace her granddaughter with warmth and affection. Sula's life, like the lives of Eva's boarders, is an arrangement that requires control, not love, and Sula is lost in the noise and numbers of the strange house. Hannah, Sula's mother, is guilty of indifference: her "relationship to [her daughter]," Morrison explained in an interview, "is almost one of uninterest. She would do things for [Sula], but she's not particularly interested in her."[11] She tells a friend, "I love Sula, but I just don't like her" (p. 49). Sula over-hears her mother's pronouncement and runs "flying up the stairs. In bewilderment, she stands at the window fingering the curtain edge, aware of a sting in her eye" (p. 49). Months later, when Hannah burns to death, Sula watches, not because fright has paralyzed her, but be-cause she is "interested" (p. 67).

Never knowing the security of love or the warmth of a home envi-ronment that identifies her as central to that environment, Sula un-derstandably becomes estranged and impulsive. She cuts off the tip of her finger to deter an attack by a group of tough boys, she watches as a boy from the community drowns in a lake after he slips from her hands, and she witnesses the burning death of her mother with curi-osity and detachment. She grows into a "strong, strange and inde-pendent woman" because, as a young girl, she had already begun a journey of defiance.

In the "house of many rooms" Sula learns about women's roles and women's sexuality. By Eva, who engages in a good deal of coquettish play with men in spite of her age (she is well into her eighties), Sula is taught that a woman's role is to attend to the needs of men.

> [Eva] fussed interminably with the brides of the newly wed couples
> for not getting their men's supper ready on time; about how to
> launder shirts, press them, etc. "Yo' man be here direc'lin. Ain't it
> 'bout time you got busy?" (p. 36)

Though Eva's disappointment in romantic love years earlier made her the shaper of her own reality, it has not diminished her belief in the institution of marriage and the service of women. She hates only one man, her former husband, Boy-Boy. Her relationship with other men, Morrison explains, is characterized by "a concentration of manlove" (p. 36).

From Hannah, Sula learns about the sexuality of women. Young, voluptuous, and, in her sexual appetite, insatiable, Hannah "would fuck practically anything" (p. 37). Her interest in men is purely physical, however, for Hannah is "a daylight lover," making love "behind the coal bin, in the pantry, up against the shelves . . . or on the flour sack just under the rows of tiny green peppers." As soon as the lovemaking is over, Hannah wants her lover to depart. What Sula remembers most about Hannah's relationships with men is that Hannah emerged from the lovemaking as if nothing had happened. For her, "sex was pleasant and frequent, but otherwise unremarkable" (p. 38).

Two versions of womanhood, then, inform Sula's adolescence. One, the posture of her grandmother, pays deference to men as persons of importance in the home who should be pampered the way a woman pampers a child. The other shows a woman attending to her sexuality, wrapping herself around the bodies of men, demanding and giving nothing except pleasure. Both images, Morrison writes, illustrate that "the Peace Women simply loved maleness, for its own sake" (p. 35). As an adolescent, Sula rejects both images—the caterer to men and the whore—and begins a journey toward self-exploration that will widen her options as a woman.

At the age of twelve, Sula begins an intense friendship with Nel, the third woman in her life. Each girl receives from the other the security, love, and identity painfully denied them in their homes. "They found relief in each other's personality," Morrison writes, as "solitary little girls of profound loneliness. Daughters of distant mothers and incomprehensible fathers (Sula's because he was dead; Nel's because he wasn't), they found in each other's eyes the intimacy they were looking for" (p. 45). In a provocative essay entitled "Toward a Black Feminist Criticism," Barbara Smith writes that the friendship between Nel and Sula is an example of "the necessary bonding that has always taken place between Black women for the barest survival. Together the two girls can find the courage to create themselves."[12] For Sula, in particular, the friendship fills the vacant spaces in her life and gives her a kindred soul with whom she can share the fantasies she enjoys "in the attic behind a roll of linoleum" (p. 44).

Together Sula and Nel enter puberty. Together they discover boys. Together they become aware of their own sexuality. Their young bodies throb with excitement as they walk invitingly past groups of men who "draped themselves" in front of the Elmira Theatre, Irene's Palace of Cosmetics, the pool hall, the grill, and other sagging business enterprises whose descriptions make Morrison's sense of place so strong and effective in the novel. Together the girls listen eagerly for the profane phrase "pig meat," which, when uttered by one man in particular, Ajax, suggests "a nastiness impossible to imitate" (p. 43). In this environment Sula learns that to be female is to be wanted in this way, and that to be complimented is also to be insulted. Her budding sexuality makes her study "the cream colored trousers . . . where the mystery curled," for she is certain that in "those smooth vanilla crotches . . . lay the thing that clotted [her] dreams" (p. 43).

In seven years this "new theme of men" for Nel matures into a proposal from Jude, a hardworking hotel waiter who presses Nel into settling down. It is not difficult for Nel to fill the traditional role for women in the community, for, unlike Sula, she has "no aggression" (p. 72). In spite of her closeness to Sula, she has never liberated herself from the cultural assumptions about woman's place and is therefore unable to see the strongly limited role Jude intends to assign her in his life. Morrison makes her most explicit and sarcastic statement on the sexism of some black men when she writes that Jude "needs some of his appetites filled, some posture of adulthood recognized, but mostly someone to care about his hurt, to care very deeply." He wants Nel to enlarge his life, even if it means diminishing her own. "The more attractive [marriage] becomes, the more seriously he pursues Nel"; and the more he pursues her, the tighter the net of submission in which she will be caught. Morrison writes:

> Whatever his fortune, whatever the cut of his garment, there would always be the hem—the tuck and fold that hid his raveling edges; a someone sweet, industrious and loyal to show him up. . . . The two of them would make *one Jude*. (p. 71; italics added)

Sula slips away mysteriously from their wedding reception and is not seen in Medallion for ten years. Her departure completes the first layer of Morrison's multidimensional portrait of Sula Mae Peace.

This phase of Sula's life encompasses her experiences from age three to age nineteen, and it focuses on her relationships with the three women in her life—Eva, Hannah, and Nel. There are clear signs in this phase that Sula will grow beyond the confines and definitions of conventional womanhood, and one is her birthmark, which "spread from the middle of [Sula's eyelid] toward the eyebrow." Resembling "a stemmed rose, the mark gave Sula's otherwise plain face a broken excitement" (p. 45). On the one hand, it is a traditional symbol for womanhood—a rose, suggesting softness, fragrance, fragility. On the other hand, its keloid appearance suggests toughness, resistance, and struggle, all "masculine" qualities. Morrison writes, foreshadowing Sula's strangeness, that the mark "will grow darker" as the years pass (p. 45).

Ten years after her abrupt departure from Medallion, Sula returns, and with her comes a plague of robins. Every inch of the Bottom is covered by puddles of their "pearly shit" (p. 78), a striking image that Morrison uses to underscore the chaos and confusion that the defiant Sula brings with her. The nature of her strange personality cannot be ignored by the people in the Bottom or explained as a youthful phase that will pass, for Sula is now a mature woman. The fact of her abiding strangeness is emphasized by the change in Sula's birthmark: it has deepened in color.

Sula immediately begins to shock the community with her profound disdain for all their institutions and traditions, and she takes sadistic delight in the agony and discomfort she produces in them. Women go to church in their finest clothes, carrying platters of steaming food. Sula goes "without underwear" and picks at the food they have prepared. They believe she is "laughing at their god" when in fact she is laughing at the emptiness of their lives. She seduces their husbands and then discards them like well-used toys that are not worth being handled again. The men come to hate her because it is rumored that she sleeps with white men, an egregious sin in the black community. And the women hate her because her very presence is a critical commentary on their reality. At twenty-nine, "she has lost no teeth, suffered no bruises, developed no ring of fat at the waist or pocket at the back of her neck" (p. 99). She seems untouched by the "vulnerability" that has allowed them to be scarred.

All that Sula and Nel shared as friends bent on creating "something else to be" has disappeared in the waste of Nel's submission to her vulnerability as a woman. "Talking to Sula had always been a conversation with herself," Nel remembers of those old days, but in maturity Nel is shackled by woman's work while Sula is still in possession of the dream of "something else to be." As Nel talks to Sula in the kitchen of her home, she listens "to the crunch of sugar underfoot that the children had spilled" or busies her hands with ironing clothes, folding diapers, or cooking. Just as Jude planned, she has become, "the tuck and hem of his garment." When Sula seduces Jude, and Nel discovers them naked on all fours in the bedroom, Nel is devastated, not only because Sula has betrayed her, but also, and more acutely, because she recognizes she has had "no place to be" (p. 92).

Sula has little sensitivity to the problems black men face in a racist society. Indeed, she rejects the assumption that they have a difficult time because they are black. When Jude capitalizes on this assumption, making it an excuse for his demands on Nel's sympathy ("white man running it—nothing good"), Sula ridicules Jude's pansylike posture and says that black men are far better off than black women. In fact, the only speech Sula delivers in the novel reveals her disgust with black men's exploitation of black women. The speech is so powerful that it is worth quoting in full:

> "I don't know what the fuss is about. I mean, everything in the world loves you. White men love you. They spend so much time worrying about your penis they forget their own. . . . Now ain't that love? . . . Colored women worry themselves into bad health just trying to hang on to your cuffs. Even little children—white and black, boys and girls—spend all their childhood eating their hearts out 'cause they think you don't love them. And if that ain't enough, you love yourselves. Nothing in this world loves a black man more than another black man. . . . So, it looks to me like you the envy of the world." (p. 89)

Because they surrender themselves to men who know only their own names and not the names of their women, black women incur Sula's disgust and disdain. They are pitiful creatures who refuse to see "the slant of life that made it possible to stretch it to its limits." They are "spiders . . . whose only thought was the next rung of the web, who dangled in dark dry places suspended by their own spittle." They are "merely victims," she says, who know "how to behave in that role" (pp. 103–4). In no sexual role are they women of dignity and wholeness. Women "with husbands had folded themselves into starched coffins, their sides bursting with other people's skinned dreams and bony regrets." Women without husbands are equally pathetic, for having internalized the assumption that a woman without a man is incomplete, they are "like sour-tipped needles featuring one constant empty eye." And those with children are "like distant but exposed wounds whose aches were no less intimate." Motherhood's only contribution to women, Sula believes, is that it keeps them from committing suicide: "they had looked at their children . . . and one clear young eye was all that kept the knife from the throat's curve" (p. 105).

If her racial assessment of black men indicts their immaturity and dependency, her sexual assessment indicts their inability to translate "the nastiness" of "pig meat," which had fascinated Sula in her puberty, into excitement and satisfaction for her. Men foolishly believe they are giving Sula something she wants, and, most unforgivable of all, they believe they must be in control. They want to be above her, determining the rhythm of her pleasure and the moment of the orgasm, which never comes. She resents that they see her as a sexual object, not as a person who has ideas and dreams. In Sula's eyes, they merge

> into one large personality: the same language of love, the same cooing of love. Whenever she introduced her private thoughts into their rubbings or goings, they hooded their eyes. They taught her nothing but love tricks, shared nothing but worry, gave nothing but money. (p. 104)

Barbara Smith interprets Sula's attitude toward men and her rejection of traditional sexual roles as expressions of latent lesbianism. If one takes several poignant quotes about Sula's hostility toward men out of the novel, Smith's thesis seems to be supportable. The most conspicuous of such quotes is Sula's realization that "a lover was not a comrade and could never be—for a woman" (p. 104). Referring to this quote, and to Morrison's "consistently critical stance" toward men in the novel, Smith writes, "Sula's presence in her community functions much like the presence of lesbians everywhere to expose the contradictions of supposedly normal life."[13] She continues, "The novel is exceedingly lesbian in the emotions expressed, in the definitions of female character and in the way the politics of heterosexuality are portrayed."[14] Smith's argument is interesting and, on occasion, comes close to striking a convincing note, but it is contradicted by Morrison's own explanation of the forces that drive Sula into strangeness and rebellion. Rather than latent lesbianism, Sula's problem is her frustration as an artist who has no channels for her creativity:

> Had [Sula] paints, or clay, or knew the discipline of the dance, or strings; had she anything to engage her tremendous curiosity and her gift for metaphor, she might have exchanged the restlessness and preoccupation with whim for an activity that provided her with all she yearned for. And like any artist with no art form, she became dangerous. (p. 105)

On one level, the word "artist" means a person who is gifted with creativity and requires a medium in which to express that creativity. If Sula had had meaningful outlets for her creativity, Morrison suggests, she could have been a painter, a dancer, a musician—that is, an artist in the usual sense of the word. Sula's latent creativity is a thematic thread in the novel, since the absence of an "art form" is the cause of her "restlessness and preoccupation with whim." On another level, "artist" loosely suggests a vision of life that is uncluttered by things, time-honored assumptions, other people, place, time, and circumstance. As this kind of artist, Sula does not depend on others but moves in a sphere of feeling and thinking that is continuously expanding toward the birth of self. Sula, then, is frustrated because she is a creative woman in the usual sense and also because she is a free-spirited soul.

As an artist without an art form, Sula is indeed "dangerous." She watches with interest as her mother burns to death, she commits her grandmother to a nursing home (a cardinal sin in the black community), and she breaks all the rules that reflect the community's traditional values. But Morrison is less convincing in her depiction of the impact that racism and sexism together have on Sula's defiance. She writes of Sula's discovery that being "neither white nor male" means denial of "freedom and triumph" (p. 106), but she gives the heavier influence to sexual restrictions, not racial restrictions. To be sure, racism is woven into the fabric of the novel, for it is racism that creates the "nigger joke" that in turn creates "the Bottom." However, it is sexism that Sula challenges in her determination to create herself.

When Sula speaks despairingly of black women's self-denial, she means their willing submission to black men. When she chafes at the notion of "full surrender" and speaks of the irony and outrage of "lying *under* someone" (italics added, p. 106), she means sexual surrender. When she demonstrates the "self" she has created, she does so in a black environment in relationships with black men and black women. And when she reneges on her promise to create "something else to be," she does so in surrender to a black man. This surrender—the third phase of Morrison's richly layered portrait of Sula—is the most conclusive argument against Barbara Smith's thesis of latent lesbianism.

When Sula tires of the boredom of the Bottom and longs for some way out of her own dissatisfaction, she becomes fascinated with Ajax, the symbol of male sexuality in her adolescence. She remembers him as a man who pronounced "pig meat" with nastiness unsurpassed. She was fascinated with him when she was twelve and he was twenty-one because "his vanilla crotch" seemed to conceal the most perfect manifestation of the mystery. When he visits her, unexpectedly and out of curiosity about the strange woman in the Bottom, she takes him immediately into the pantry, as she had seen Hannah do with so many men, stands "wide-legged against the wall and [pulls] from his track-lean hips all the pleasure her thighs [can] hold" (p. 108).

Sula has seduced men before, but the experience of lying with Ajax is different. With him she is free to be a woman with thoughts, plans, and desires that are not wedded to sex. He loves her passionately and expertly, and he courts her with presents that are not the traditional "woman's gifts" of money and perfume. He senses the artist in her and showers her with gifts that show his sensitivity to her free-spirited soul. He gives her a "jar of butterflies . . . and let[s] them loose in the bedroom" (p. 109). He does not talk "the same language of love" that has so consistently made men "one large personality" of dullness for Sula. He respects Sula's mind, and "thinking she was possibly brilliant . . . he seemed to expect brilliance from her, and she delivered" (p. 110). The sexist approach to women confers upon men the obligation to protect women because they are frail, or to pamper them because they are like children in their inability to plan their own lives. This is the opposite of Ajax's attitude toward Sula. He assumes "that she was both tough and wise" (p. 119). With joy, he meets her insistence on protecting herself and expressing her wholeness. He likes her "to mount him so he could see her towering above him" (p. 111). And thus is Sula, for the first time in her life, released from the ritual of masturbation. In every coitus with Ajax she experiences "the high silence of orgasm" (p. 112).

Ironically, Sula's surrender to Ajax places her inside the circle of women she had rejected and humiliated. She begins to discover what those women discovered years ago—possessiveness. Morrison writes that "Sula was astounded by so new and alien a feeling." Like the women she once dismissed as "spiders," Sula begins to prance for Ajax and to decorate herself in a way that emphasizes her body and not her mind. Her typicality is tragic. She stands before her mirror— the symbol literature has long used for women's mindless devotion to their own attractiveness—and traces with her finger how "the laugh lingers around her mouth" (p. 113). She becomes so obsessed with being "feminine" that she joins community women who sit for two hours in beauty shops preparing themselves for sacrifice, having forgotten that she had once been a threat to these same women. The extent to which Sula gives her mind over to puerile "women's concerns" is symbolized by the green ribbon she ties neatly in her hair and by the pleasure she receives from doing "woman's work." On one visit, Ajax finds the bathroom gleaming, the bed made, and the table set for two.

In an interview Morrison explains that "the very thing that would attract a man to a woman in the first place might be the one thing she would give over" once she falls in love.[15] In Sula's case, she gives up her independence, her toughness, and her wholeness to become Ajax's woman. The metamorphosis is a large, threatening cloud on the horizon for Ajax. In low tones of desire, Sula murmurs, "Lean on me," having forgotten that a whole man in search of a whole woman does not desire "a hem and a tuck and fold" in his life. And finally, Sula makes the fatal error of asking Ajax where he has been. She has finally internalized the assumptions about woman's role and behavior in relationships with men, and she has ended her journey toward selfhood. She must now surrender to Ajax physically as she has surrendered in other ways: Ajax "dragged Sula under him and made love to her with the steadiness and intensity of a man about to leave" (p. 115). Having forgotten that she has the right to "create something else to be," Sula is left alone. She has "loved and lost" (p. 122).

After Ajax's departure, Sula is a woman of the blues, but she is not typical even in this regard. When a woman sings the blues, she moans and groans in loneliness, singing the low notes of regret and the high notes of another time with another man. This is Sula's song only temporarily. She sings all the songs there are, and in the final days of her life, she sings the song of both death and freedom that only a broken woman still bent on wholeness can sing. She dies slowly of cancer, as proud in death as she was in life. When Nel visits her, she hears the old Sula of their childhood speaking of triumph: "my lonely is mine" (p. 124).

Devotion and sacrifice rather than alienation and hostility are the themes of Walker's story of Meridian Hill. Meridian is a woman who embraces her community and on its behalf begins a strange "pilgrimage" of sacrifice. She is not a Sula. There are no strange marks on her face. There are no puddles of "pearly shit" made by robins that accompany her on her "pilgrimage." There are no church fairs she disrupts and there are no women who can say that Meridian lay with their husbands and discarded them. Meridian is a child of the soil—pure, innocent, and loving. Both characters journey toward independence and wholeness, but Meridian begins her journey under circumstances that are antithetical to Sula's.

Sula grows up in a family of relative hardships. Meridian grows up in an intact family of the lower middle class. Sula's mother is an uneducated woman of insatiable sexuality. Meridian's mother is an "educated woman," but a "willing know-nothing,"[16] a woman of ignorance and frigidity. Sula never knew her father, his death having taken place when she was three. Meridian knows and adores her father. He, too, is educated—a history teacher in the local school—and he is a "dreamy ambitious person . . . who walked over the earth unhurriedly as if conscious of every step and the print his footsteps would leave in the dirt" (p. 40).

Walker reverses the traditional images of the father as the harsh and distant parent and the mother as the all-embracing friend. Mr. Hill is concerned about people and devoted to causes. Mrs. Hill is concerned about herself and the theft of her life by marriage and especially by motherhood. He sings, she moans. He embraces, she rejects. He loves, she hurts. He stretches himself toward the sun. She imprisons her soul in a dark cave of sour memories. As a child, she ran from her father's beatings. As a teenager, she ran from the sexual desires of white men. She was determined to become a schoolteacher, but her father was determined that she would learn to do only what women are meant to do: "cook collard greens, shortbread and fried okra" so that "some man might have her" (p. 122). As an adult, she feels compelled to marry and become a mother, only to discover that the agonies of her present equal the agony of her past. When Meridian hears her mother's memories, she "weeps and wishes that she had not been born to this already overburdened woman" (p. 122).

As a young girl, Sula is exposed to her mother's trips into the coal bin and the pantry, where she pulls from the bodies of men all the pleasure they can give. Meridian has no such experiences. The prudish Mrs. Hill never uses the word *sex* in Meridian's presence. Instead, she impresses on her daughter the necessity of being "sweet," not realizing that Meridian has no understanding of the caution against sex that the expression intends. Meridian's early exposure to sex, however, is more complete than Sula's. As a young girl Sula only *imagines* what happens between men and women, whereas Meridian *sees*.

The lascivious Dexter, the local funeral parlor director, pursues Meridian when she is only twelve. Meridian goes to the funeral home and lets Dexter suck her breast and touch "the bottom of her panties. She could sit, holding his head against her breasts—while he busily and noisily sucked—and feel the hot throbbing of his passion almost enter her." She is excited, for her sexuality has already been awakened, but "in the end his obesity . . . is distasteful to her" (p. 59). He is insistent on conquering Meridian, for his pride in being a skillful "lover" has been damaged by her rejection. To convince Meridian of the desirability of sex, he arranges for her to witness his assistant's seduction of another schoolgirl. The scene, vividly and graphically described, is at once humorous and resoundingly critical of man's attitude toward woman. The assistant uses his voice and his body to ride the young girl with supercilious vanity, and then coldly pushes her aside when his performance ends. Meridian is unimpressed, even repelled by the scene. What she remembers most is "the greedy, obscene and ugly" face of the man and the young girl's ignored need for tenderness afterward (p. 60).

Being a spectator is one thing; being a participant is quite another. As both, Meridian is naive, unaware of her physical vulnerability and essentially uninterested. No one in her family has taught her "what to expect from men, from sex." As a result, when she acquires a young boyfriend, Meridian has sex as often as "her lover" wants it, "sometimes every single night."

> And, since she had been told by someone one's hips become broader after sex, she looked carefully in her mirror each morning before she caught the bus to school. Her pregnancy came as a total shock. (p. 53)

Meridian drops out of school, marries her lover, and awaits the birth of her son. Her whole life has been changed—and by an experience she did not enjoy.

In the chapters that deal with Meridian before she calls herself whole, Walker questions the relative importance of sex in a woman's life, suggesting that the notion that a woman lives for sexual pleasure is a sexist myth, celebrating the power of man's potency. She alludes to this myth in the scene in which the funeral director's assistant seduces the schoolgirl. Having taken the girl and given what he considers an expert performance, the assistant is convinced that he owns the girl forever. For Meridian, the delivery of her body and soul requires more "gifts" than those the assistant can offer women. In fact, Meridian sees sex as a "sanctuary." Only when she is sexually active with one boy, becoming his girl in the eyes of the community, can she get over her fear of men. Only in this "sanctuary," Walker explains, can Meridian "look out at the male world with something approaching equanimity, even charity; even friendship" (p. 53).

At sixteen, Meridian is married, pregnant, and singularly bored by her life. Pregnancy is as negative an experience for her as it was for her mother. It changes her physical appearance, making her once velvety skin "bloated, tight" (p. 56). Marriage is also a negative experience—a long, unbroken stretch of emptiness and sameness. Her husband, because he is a male, remains in school in spite of his new roles as husband and father. Meridian, because of the swollen stomach that she carries as innocently as she had engaged in the experience that caused it, remains at home, and there she receives a different kind of education. She learns that a wife is forever turning in the small confines of home, doing for others. She does not take to housekeeping, and, in time, her ineptitude at tasks a woman is expected to perform well displeases her young husband. He is bothered by Meridian's

> ironing of his clothes, and even her own, which she did not do nearly as well as his mother; the cooking, which she was too queasy to do at all; and the sex, which she did not seem interested in. (p. 57)

When she becomes a mother, Meridian is a younger version of Mrs. Hill. She is exhausted by caring for the baby, who gasps, screams, twists, and turns, robbing Meridian of her rest. "It seemed to her that the peace of the dead was truly blessed, and each day she planned a new way of approaching it"; it is only out of her "reliance on suicide" that she maintains her sanity (pp. 63–64).

Meridian's mother and other women in the community attempt to dissuade Meridian from leaving her husband and child. They explain that Eddie is a "good" man. He does not beat her or cheat on her—implying that, as a man, he has the right to do both, and that she, as a woman, has the obligation to adjust her needs to providing for his. They do not understand, and Meridian cannot explain, that her need for something else in life is not contingent on what Eddie does or does not do. He cannot measure the width of her dreams or chart the course of her journey toward their realization. A woman is not always necessarily frustrated because her man is "bad" or fulfilled because he is "good." Rather, she can be frustrated because the culture gives women few alternatives to traditional wifehood and motherhood. Meridian cannot be a wife because she sees the role as demanding submergence of her self in perfunctory expressions of love and togetherness. Moreover, she has found no man in her backward town whose intelligence and vision of possibilities for growth complement her own need to "ask impossible questions" and courage "to pursue seemingly absurd paths."[17]

Burdened by a guilt she feels for stealing her mother's life, she has no interest in being a mother. "In giving life to children who were both unwanted and unappreciated by society," black women in Walker's vision have also had to give up much of their own lives to sustain those children. "The children know they survive only because their parents committed acts of extraordinary suffering."[18] Meridian's guilt for causing her own mother's suffering and the emptiness she believes will always be hers in marriage precipitate her departure from the small Mississippi town. She commits the cardinal sin of giving up her child for her own dreams. When she leaves to attend college in Atlanta, Meridian Hill begins the first stage of her journey toward wholeness.

As its name suggests, Saxon College is a metaphor for white Anglo-Saxon values that have seeped into the thinking of middle-class blacks. The school emphasizes self-aggrandizement in a capitalist economy and ladyhood in a sexist society. Walker is sternly critical of Saxon, which represents, of course, the historically black southern colleges in the sixties. In her vignettes of campus life, Walker portrays the school's stress on the acquisition of things and status, and its insistence that its female students play circumscribed roles: "The emphasis at Saxon was on form, and the preferred 'form' was that of the finishing school girl whose goal . . . was to be *accepted* as an equal because she knew and practiced all the proper social rules" (p. 91). The real life that Meridian witnesses in the streets of Atlanta is ignored by the curriculum at Saxon, and new definitions of the role of women are anathema to Saxon's program for "ladies." The school condones anything as long as it is done "with white gloves" (p. 91). Meridian and other like-minded students decide that they have two enemies: "Saxon, which wanted them to become something—ladies—that was already obsolete, and the larger, more deadly enemy, white racist society" (p. 91).

It is at Saxon that Meridian becomes friends with Anne-Marion, a character who is central to Meridian's development. The friendship between the two girls is very different from the friendship between Nel and Sula. As Eva Peace observes, Sula and Nel merge into one personality. Anne-Marion is not the other side of Meridian, or vice versa. They are two distinctly different individuals, as evidenced most clearly in their response to the civil rights movement, in which both are involved during their years at Saxon. Anne-Marion says she is able to "kill" for the revolution and chides Meridian for her inability to "kill." By juxtaposing the two women, Walker is able to distinguish between the noise of faddish militancy and the silence of genuine devotion to the struggle. Actually, Anne-Marion is lying about her ability to "kill": Meridian "knew [Anne-Marion's] tenderness, a vegetarian because she loved the eyes of cows" (p. 14). She lies, Walker explains, because she takes her posture toward the revolution from the rhetoric of group thinking rather than from a deep well of concern for her people. Unlike Anne-Marion, Meridian struggles for the hard answers to perplexing questions about the past, the present, and the future. Whereas

> Meridian is always groping for answers even to the point of illness, Anne-Marion is confident, practical, unquestioning. Meridian is compelled to seek the answer to the dilemma of human beings' injustice to each other, but Anne-Marion is content with being the victor rather than the victim.[19]

A true revolutionary, Meridian is held by something that rejects violence as the approach to change. That something is the music of her people, the music of a culture that has been rooted in love. Walker's poetic evocation of black culture is worth quoting in full:

> Meridian alone was holding on to something the others had let go. If not completely, then partially—by their words today, their deeds tomorrow. But what none of them seemed to understand was that she felt herself to be, not holding on to something from the past, but held by something in the past: by the memory of old black men in the South who, caught by surprise in the eye of a camera, never shifted their position but looked directly back; by the sight of young girls singing in a country choir, their hair shining with brushings and grease, their voices the voices of angels. When she was transformed in church it was always by the purity of the singers' souls, which she could actually *hear*, the purity that lifted their songs like a flight of doves above her music-drunken head. If they committed murder—and to her even revolutionary murder was murder—*what would the music be like?* (pp. 27–28)

When Meridian makes a commitment to revolution by joining the civil rights movement while she is a student at Saxon College, she is introduced to both the ecstasy and the agony of love. In the movement, she meets Truman Held, a Che Guevara type of revolutionary who speaks French and sings the praises of "sisters" who are African queens. He hails Meridian as a black queen who will ascend to her deserved throne when, together, they build the black nation, but the beauty of his rhetoric is belied by his desertion of her. After Meridian becomes pregnant with his child, Truman leaves her for a white exchange student named Lynn Rabinowitz. The relationship between Meridian and Truman is the focal point of Walker's analysis of sexism and racism as both work to create the black woman–black man–white woman triangle. The relationship illustrates the "prone" position of all woman in the Student Nonviolent Coordinating Committee (SNCC) during the civil rights movement, but it is a tragic statement on the vulnerability of black women to deep racial and sexual pain.

In the novel the conflict between black women and white women is not in any way similar to the problem black women have with their "madams." In *Meridian*—at least on the surface—class is not a factor, for black women in the civil rights movement are essentially the white women's equals. The conflict is a reflection of the "sickness" to which Eldridge Cleaver refers and the dilemma Shulamith Firestone discusses. Simply stated, black men—some, many, or a few, it does not matter—want white women because they are the closest thing to power black men can get in white America. Black women understand what white women represent in the lives of black men, but they also have their own view of what white women are and are not in white America. They see white women as "spoiled" females who have never had to be responsible for their own lives and who do not want to be. From her grandmother and mother Meridian has learned that white women are "frivolous, helpless creatures, lazy and without ingenuity" (p. 104). This same assessment is made in June Jordan's poem "What Would I Do White?":

> I would do nothing
> That would be enough.[20]

Meridian has her own assessments, based on what she observed in her hometown:

Who would want to kiss [white girls]? What were they good for? What did they do? They only seemed to hang about laughing, after

school, until when they were sixteen or seventeen they got married.
Their pictures appeared in the society column, you saw them
pregnant a couple of times. Then . . . they sank into a permanent
oblivion. (p. 105)

This view of white women is presented satirically in an incident
involving Meridian and black children in a small southern town where
Meridian lives as a saint, as a remnant of the civil rights movement,
which had once sent hundreds of volunteers into oppressed black
communities. The children are anxious to see "Marilene O'Shay, One
of the Twelve Human Wonders of the World: Dead for Twenty-five
Years Preserved in Life-like Condition." She is "A Goddess," "Obedi-
ent," "Pure," "Beautiful." She is dead because her husband killed her
when she betrayed him with another man. It is he who takes her
body from small town to small town to exhibit at moneymaking
shows. Only on Thursday can she be seen by blacks. Marilene O'Shay
is a symbol of "the white woman protected, indeed mummified, by
the sanctimonious rhetoric of her society, but losing even these questionable privileges when she exercises her sexual freedom."[21]

In her portrait of Lynn Rabinowitz, Walker reaches beyond this
sort of stereotype into the complexity of white guilt, showing a woman
who in the final analysis is perhaps the most tragic woman in the
novel. Lynn gives herself to Truman, has his child, and walks beside
him in the civil rights movement, only to be discarded when the
movement changes its song from "We Shall Overcome" to "Power to
the People," and becomes the black power movement. She sacrifices
herself on an altar of guilt, giving in to Truman's abuse and even to
rape by one of his friends, who had lost an arm in the racial struggle.
After the rape, Lynn kisses the stump of her victimizer. Walker is sympathetic toward Lynn, who represents white women driven by racial
guilt to be what black women are supposed to be: "prone" in relationships with men.

Black women are not guilty; they provoke guilt because they have
fought against racial oppression throughout this nation's history.
Their posture as soldiers, however, does not save them from sexual
exploitation: black men play racial games to exploit black women

sexually. Mr. Raymond is a case in point. A black nationalist of the 1920s, he is hardly distinguishable from the Truman Helds of the sixties. A teacher at the college, he calls Meridian into his office and preaches about the "Race as if it were a lump of homogenized matter that could be placed this way or that way, at will, to effect change" (p. 108). He talks emotionally about protecting the virtue of black women from white men, and recites for Meridian the number of "black women who had reported rape at the hands of white men in the years between 1896 and 1963" (p. 108). He is a scholar on the subject, and yet he sees Meridian, who earns money by performing small tasks for him, as little more than a body he has the right to fondle and exploit: "each day when she rose to go . . . he clasped her in his arms, dragging her away from the door, the long bones of his thighs forcing her legs apart, attempting to force her to the floor" (pp. 109–10).

Truman's sexism is more sophisticated than Mr. Raymond's crass attempts, in his old age, to make his "limp" penis once again express his manhood, for Truman speaks French, is well read, and is a revolutionary of the sixties. He does not attempt to rape Meridian by using his superior strength. He rapes her devotion to the struggle so that he can rape her body. His sexism is expressed also in his concept of the ideal woman—a virgin—though he himself has deflowered many women and moved on. (So "Where was the virgin to come from? Heaven?" [p. 140].) Truman wants a virgin because he will accept nothing less than what the culture says he deserves. He wants this virgin to be "a woman to rest in, as a ship must have a port. As a train must have a shed" (p. 139). His definition of the role of woman is Jude's definition in Sula. Only the metaphors are different.

Like many black feminists of the seventies, Walker refuses the obligation to hold her woman's rage in check until the black man's rights to manhood—total manhood—are ensured. She conveys this attitude in the story of Mem Copeland when she gives Mem the courage to refuse to walk forever in the crevices of Brownfield's self-destruction. The abuse of black women at the hands of black men is, of course, one of the central themes of The Third Life of Grange Copeland. It is not the central theme in Meridian, but it is there, directing the course of Meridian's life and the profundity of her pain.

The abuse is not physically violent, for class is a major determinant of the way in which sexism is expressed. Truman is not destroyed, as is Brownfield, by a vicious sharecropping system. Instead, he is confused and spiritually broken by everything in white America that makes all black people suffer from the problem of "double consciousness" of which W. E. B. DuBois wrote in 1898.²² Truman is black, but his psyche is white-directed. Meridian suggests as much when she observes that "from a distance both Truman and Lynn looked white" (p. 112). Ironically, she makes this observation as she keeps her appointment with an abortionist, who promises to tie her tubes free of charge if he can get "in" on the "extracurricular activity." The abortion is a metaphor for the injury black women suffer because they are physically vulnerable and not respected in a sexist culture. As Truman tosses his head in the wind, riding free-spirited in Lynn's car, Meridian's pain flows in buckets of blood. "It enrages her that she could be made to endure such pain, and that Truman was oblivious to it" (p. 112).

After this ignominious experience, Meridian makes the second of three moves in her life. She leaves Atlanta and settles in a small Mississippi town distinct only for its backwardness and blatant racism. Here she does penance for stealing her mother's life. Here she struggles with the bitterness she feels as a woman used and discarded by a man. Here she searches for answers to the "dilemma of human beings' injustice to one another."²³

When Meridian takes up her life in Mississippi, the civil rights movement is over, but the dreams from which it was born, and ideals and the dream it inspired, remain a part of her consciousness. She is a revolutionary—a remnant of the movement—whose courage is all the more remarkable because she believes she is slowly dying. She has strange dizzy spells, painful headaches, and violent seizures. Frequently she is carried motionless on the shoulders of community people to be placed in the narrowness of her cluttered shack. In her analysis of Meridian's illness Walker connects Meridian's past to her present. She first mentions the severe headaches when Meridian is confronted with the question, "Can you kill for the Revolution?" She writes of Meridian's thinning hair when Meridian speaks of her deep love for Truman in a conversation with Mrs. Hill. And early in Meridian's relationship with Truman, Walker alludes to Meridian's psychological distraction, for no matter what was being said, Meridian always "seemed to be thinking of something else." There was about her

> something dark . . . a shadow that seemed to swing, like the
> pendulum of a clock, or like a blade, behind her open, candid eyes.
> (p. 139)

All signs of Meridian's illness reflect the guilt created by the collective history of black women. Through what Barbara Christian calls "a mind-voice which directs the flow of thought and action,"[24] we move back in time and forward and back again, so that the past and the present come together to explain Meridian's vision of the future.

In the final section, we see the beginning of Meridian's journey from illness to health. Her health returns in stages. At a memorial service for a civil rights leader, Meridian finds herself answering affirmatively the question that has been a refrain in the novel: "Can you kill for the Revolution?" She is moved by the beauty of the black church, the only place left where black people can

> congregate, where the problems of life were not discussed fraudu-
> lently and the approach to the future was considered communally,
> and moral questions were taken seriously. (p. 203)

She is also moved by the presence of the father of the slain leader, whom she calls, symbolically, the "son's father," suggesting a parallel between the slain Christ and the death of the leader. And she is moved by the father's words, which come "from a throat that seemed stoppered with anxiety, memory, grief and hope" (p. 202). His words are these three: "my son died" (p. 202). As she listens to the songs of the people, the sermons, and the sincerity of "brothers and sisters," she is converted to a new approach to the revolution:

The people in the church were saying to the red-eyed man that his son had not died for nothing, and that if his son should come again they would protect his life with their own. "Look," they were saying, "we are slow to awaken to the notion that we are only as other women and men, and even slower to move into anger, but we are gathering ourselves to fight for and protect what your son fought for on behalf of us. If you will let us weave your story and your son's life and death in what we already know—into the songs, sermons . . . we will soon be angry, so angry we cannot help but move." (p. 240)

The conversion lifts a weight from Meridian's soul. She feels a "breaking in her chest," Walker writes, "as if a tight string binding her lungs had given way, allowing her to breathe freely." She finally understands that she must respect her life and "not . . . give up any particle of it without a fight to the death, preferably not her own" (p. 204). In making a promise to kill for the revolution, she takes her first step toward health.

The promise to kill brings Meridian to a fuller understanding of her role in the revolution, and a deeper understanding of the cause of her illness. She has not wanted to face that she does not belong to the future, but is "left, listening to the old music beside the highway." What she will give to the revolution will be the strength of "memory songs." It is significant that Walker does not use "sorrow songs"—she is emphasizing hope. Meridian "will come forward and sing from memory songs the people will need once more to hear." It is the music that holds

the people together, and if any part of it is lost the people suffer and are without soul. If I can only do that, my role will not have been a useless one after all. (pp. 205–6)

When Meridian resolves the conflict regarding her role in the revolution, she finds a way to repay the debt she owes her maternal ancestors for their collective history of sacrifice. But there remains the cure for her suffering as a black woman abused and used by Truman. He seeks her out in the small Mississippi town as a man ravaged by guilt. He deserts Lynn and their child, Camara. Even when Camara is brutally murdered, Truman is unable to speak the truth to himself: he loves Lynn, and only the antiwhite rhetoric of the black power movement keeps him from expressing his love. He turns to Meridian because she comes from a long line of Harriet Tubmans—strong, understanding, and self-sacrificing women. She is "a woman to rest in, as a ship must have a port. As a train must have a shed" (p. 139). Unlike the Truman of yesterday, who spoke French and in his Che Guevara clothes talked in macho language of the "African woman" he could sexually satisfy, the Truman who searches out Meridian is devastated by confusion and guilt. He leans on Meridian so that she can "help [him] through this shit" (p. 123).

Meridian's response to Truman's plea shows how definite Walker is about the black woman's need to distinguish between what she must do for the race and what she cannot do, as a person, for black men. The two needs, though created by the same culture, do not have equal weight in Walker's vision. Meridian feels sorry for Truman, but like Mem Copeland in *The Third Life of Grange Copeland*, she does not explain away Truman's weaknesses as a man. "Of all the savage nibblings of racism," Walker suggests, "the most poisonous bite is the abnegation of responsibility for one's own soul."[25] By refusing to be a "port" or a "shed" in his life, Meridian forces Truman to realize

> that the most effective way to control anyone is by confusing his or her sex definitions according to the norms of society. The masculine thrust in this society manifests itself in forms of power and acquisition, [while] the feminine thrust manifests itself in passivity, chastity and demure beauty.[26]

Truman must understand the extent to which he has permitted his name for himself to come from a society that is both racist and sexist. He has believed that a woman's love flows into a man's life "like a special sun, like grace" (p. 223). He asks for that kind of love from Meridian. She forgives Truman and pities him, but knows the "sun" and the "grace" in his life must come from his own search for wholeness. She sets him free, and in so doing, she frees herself of the bitterness and pain she has felt as a woman used and discarded:

"You are free to be whichever way you like, to be with whoever, of whatever color or sex you like—and what you risk in being truly yourself, the way you want to be, is not the loss of me."

In the final chapter of the novel Walker shows Meridian emerging from her shack, free of headaches, seizures, guilt, bitterness, and confusion. Her hair is no longer thin; it is a soft wool that frames her "thin, resolute face." She is "strong enough to go" from the small town of Chickowema out into the world of health. In the eyes of Truman, we see the magnificence of Meridian's wholeness: "Meridian would return to the world cleansed of sickness." Truman will take her place in the small town, and tomorrow "the people would come and bring Truman food" (p. 226). Meridian does not have all the answers for Truman, as she does not have all the answers for herself, because the search for wholeness and for answers to the problem of human injustice is an individual search—in Barbara Christian's words, "a continuing process rather than an adventure that ends in a neat resolution." Truman's sickness clearly is a part of that "continuing process." Christian writes:

Walker's ending suggests that even Meridian's dearly won salvation is not sure unless we others sort out the tangled roots of our past and pursue our own health. In other words, until the pattern of this society is transformed, no part of it is free and it cannot be free unless each of us pursues our own wholeness. By making the end of the novel the beginning of another such quest, Walker invites us to use the novel as a contemplative and analytical tool in our own individual search. For the questions that she gives flesh to in the novel, questions that are rooted in this country's past, persist in the present.[27]

The differences between Sula's quest for a version of herself she could touch with an ungloved hand and Meridian's quest for health are major ones. Meridian is a child of the race whose mind and vision of life are shaped by the collective consciousness of her people. Sula is the child of Eva and Hannah, whose lives, though clearly shaped by race, are more decidedly shaped by sex. *Sula* is, then, more about sexual consciousness than about racial struggle. The time of the novel—the thirties, forties, and fifties—and the setting—a small midwestern town—make it different from *Meridian*, which is set in the South during the height of the civil rights movement. In spite of these differences, however, *Sula* and *Meridian* are very similar because both are stories of black women who will not be restricted to narrow definitions of themselves as women. This similarity cuts across time, place, and even circumstance. Sula challenges the assumption that a woman should be the "tuck and hem" of a man's garment. Meridian challenges the assumption that a woman should be a "special sun" in a man's life. In their individual challenges, each woman creates "something else to be."

We can conjecture that had Sula lived in a different place, and certainly at a different time—one that offered the civil rights movement, for example, as an outlet for her defiance and creativity—she might have been able to sustain her own version of self. Implicitly, Morrison's portrait is a criticism of an environment that offers no alternatives to wifehood and motherhood, to suffocation and sacrifice. A corollary to this observation is that, without the movement and without an education, Meridian could have become like Mrs. Hill, a woman who knows suffocation is "all deliberate" but who lives nonetheless a life of blind sacrifice.

On another level, both *Sula* and *Meridian* are about the human need for wholeness, for in both novels we see how race and sex also fragment the lives of men. Ajax wants to be free to be himself no less than Sula does. Truman Held, in the final chapters of the novel, does penance for his failure to say no to external factors that name him. Unquestionably, their realities are no less eclipsed by race and sex than are the realities of the women. We can say, then, that while the controlling statements in the two novels are about black womanhood, the subsidiary statements are about all people, regardless of sex or race: the "special sun" in our individual lives must come from within our souls and must challenge the darkness in which the essence of our humanity is hidden.

chapter 7

THE SPACE AND
THE ENCLOSURE

The Collective Vision of Black Women

what i can be even i can not know.

—Carolyn Rodgers, "I Have Been Hungry," 1968

To understand the dark enclosure, and therefore, the double jeopardy of black women, we must examine their pain in the narrow space of race, for it is here that they learn the meaning of force, of conflict, and of unending struggle, all three of which affect the lives of those they love—their children, their husbands, and other family members. And it is here that they develop approaches to life that affect the way they see themselves and the way they function in the dark enclosure.

Without pitting sex against race, or vice versa, the women novelists never equivocate on the harsh exigencies of life in the narrow space and never minimize how profoundly those conditions cause suffering in the dark enclosure. Numerous instances have been discussed in the preceding chapters of this study. Pauline Breedlove, for example, suffers intensely because, in the narrow space of black powerlessness, her life is ravaged by stark poverty and by the effects of imposed inferiority. This fact alone explains her attitudes toward herself, toward her husband, and toward her children. Mariah Upshur says that her life "ain't been nothing but wind" because, in the narrow space, she is powerless against the malnutrition to which her children are subjected and against a superstructure of exploitation that questions her husband's manhood even as he demonstrates in his backbreaking work that he is twice over a man. Mem Copeland moves from one manure-filled barn to another because a vicious sharecropping system keeps black people, and especially black men, in servile dependence akin to slavery. And finally, Eva Peace has "no time" for loving her children because racism and poverty make bare survival a phenomenal task.

When we read these novels and others that illuminate the narrow space, we understand how profound is the suffering of black people. We see black women, along with their men, standing in the center of the space, laboring in darkness to open their lives to light. And we understand that since all their suffering begins in the narrow space, wider options for black women must be brought about as much in the space as in the enclosure—and most definitely *first* in the narrow space. Black feminist thinkers of the seventies say as much when they write that black women will not gain their emancipation at the expense of their men or, more cogently, that wider options for black women, of necessity, mean wider options for black men. As separate as they are, the narrow space and the dark enclosure are inextricably bound together, for race, sex, and class are interdependent in white America.

We must go beyond the narrow space deep into the dark center of the enclosure to understand the extent to which sexism exacerbates the effects of racism, or how the two work together as major determinants of the lives of black women. That journey begins, as Mary Helen Washington writes, when we attempt "to finger the grooves of . . . the scars" on the lives of *women* characters in selected black women's fiction. As we fingered those "scars" "until we [knew] the designs by heart,"[1] we made several interesting discoveries, some already mentioned. First of all, we discovered that sexual reality for black women is greatly exacerbated by their racial reality and never completely separate from it. Second, we discovered that black women often confuse what they experience in this special world with what all black people experience in the narrow space of uncertainty and powerlessness. And finally, we discovered that it is often in the enclosure that women experience their deepest and most permanent scars, for it is here that they are in conflict, not with a white-controlled system, but with black men who shatter their dreams of love and acceptance.

In *The Street*, a classic protest novel of the forties, Ann Petry illumines both the narrow space and the enclosure in her attack on the capitalist system's exploitation of black people in ghettos of the North. She establishes a cause-and-effect relationship between what the system does to black men and what they in turn do to black women. The men are victims whom harsh reality causes to become victimizers of their women. Petry does not perceive them as the major oppressors of black women. Racism and poverty are. Therefore, when Lutie Johnson strikes Boots Smith in rage, she indicts him as a representative of many black men on "the street" who exploit black women, but she lands her heaviest blows on the system that makes black men and black women antagonists in the suffocatingly narrow space, creating thereby the special dark enclosure of pain for black women.

Emphasis on the capitalist system as the cause of conflict between black men and black women also shapes visions from the fifties, but the emphasis is less intense, given the waning of protest in that decade. In *Maud Martha*, for example, protest against race and class is subdued as Gwendolyn Brooks analyzes, from a positive perspective, the "kitchenette" culture of Southside Chicago, an economic half-step above the culture of "the street." Racism created the culture, but a strong sense of community and the workings of survival motions save Maud Martha from the despair and violence that engulf the characters in Petry's novel. Nothing, however, can save Maud Martha from the "grooves . . . of scars" made by the system's definition of beauty in white terms. The ache in her soul is a woman's ache because she cannot close the distance between her appearance and the ideal of white beauty. When her husband is cold, insensitive, and even rejecting, she forgives him because he is a psychological captive of a white-oriented value system.

In *Brown Girl, Brownstones*, also from the fifties, Paule Marshall's sympathy for black men, her understanding of the forces that produce the defeated black man, is expressed in the contrasting portraits of Deighton Boyce and his wife, Silla. Deighton is warm, gentle, and affectionate. Silla, on the other hand, is hard, distant, and fiercely ambitious. Her fury comes from the lingering pain of the death of her son but in a more immediate way from her frustrations with her husband's lack of ambition, his dance-and-play games with long shots for success, and his indiscreet infidelity. He dresses in silk shirts, spends days with his "concubine," and whittles away his future and his family's future on empty fantasies that can never be realized in white America. She works long shifts in the factory in the hope of saving enough money to buy a brownstone. Marshall writes of Silla with understanding, but of Deighton she writes with deep compassion, for he has been turned from pride and a sense of accomplishment by the omnipresence of white power, first in Barbados and then in Brooklyn.

As early as the late sixties, and most definitely by the seventies, the victimization of black men no longer obscured the harsh and heavy lines of the enclosure in which black women are placed. Black women writers, like black women activists, began to answer the question Mariah Upshur raises in *This Child's Gonna Live*: "but what about the colored woman?" In the first major black woman's novel of the decade, *The Third Life of Grange Copeland*, Alice Walker answers the question, but not without an understanding of what has happened to "the colored man." Her moving portraits of Grange Copeland and his son Brownfield, both victims of a vicious sharecropping system, are obviously attacks on the narrow space in which black people, regardless of sex, dance with only shadows of dreams and trudge wearily through a journey of hopelessness. Walker sympathizes with black men, but she does not excuse them for destroying their gentle and devoted wives. Grange is held accountable, and his conscience is ravaged, for the suicide of his wife, Margaret; and Brownfield, whose brutality lies at the center of the novel, is not forgiven for his murder of Mem. Toni Morrison in *The Bluest Eye* writes sympathetically of Cholly's pain when mocking white men turned their flashlight on his lovemaking, but his pain does not make the reader forget the loneliness and alienation Pauline feels in the cold steel town of Lorain. In these novels and others, black women are damaged persons not only because they are black and often poor but also because they mix the colors of their dreams in black men's cups of victimization and sexism. The line between sexual oppression and racial oppression is so thin as to be, at times, indistinguishable.

In novels written later in the seventies, victimization of black men is no longer the axis on which the abuse of black women turns and, accordingly, the assumption that sex is the "lesser question" is no longer without challenge. Sula's denigration of Jude, who seeks stroking and indulgence because "the man" is at his throat, is similar in tone to the writings of Barbara Sizemore, Frances Beal, Pauli Murray, and other feminist thinkers of the decade. However, whereas these thinkers admit that there are racially imposed shackles on the lives of black men, Sula seems to make mockery of the notion of injured black men. In her opinion, they have more than their share of love and attention and a chance for flight and freedom. When she sees victimization in the Bottom, she sees black women, "spiders" on a rung, who are slowly and silently "dying" without having lived. Eva Medina, in Gayl Jones's *Eva's Man*, has a similar vision of black reality. In the black world in which she seeks "alternatives to brutality"[2] for black women, she sees women who are forced to become bitches or whores or, rejecting those images, queen bees and Medusas whose lives are synonyms for isolation and loneliness.

But there are no monolithic statements on sexism in the black experience. Not all black men victimize their women. Not all are cold, selfish, rejecting, or, for that matter, broken. Walker writes of the sexism of Truman Held, who believes that women are to be "had," and if they are virgins prized, but "had" nevertheless, but she also writes with tenderness of the sensitivity of Mr. Hill, who cried when he broke into his wife's body. Marshall paints tenderness and affection into her portrait of Deighton Boyce, and Louise Meriwether writes of "Daddy's" laughter and the sweet tinkling of the piano. Jude speaks to Sula's mind and delights in having her on top of him. Bart Judson is an unselfish and humble man who is victimized by a cold and manipulative wife. Black men in black women's fiction are not always *the* enemy.

Black men in the novels, as a rule, do not see black women beyond the services they render to others, most especially to men. They see a house cleaned, meals prepared and served, and children tended to, rather than the women who have performed the chores. They understand money problems and racial problems rather than the problems of their women that go beyond money and race. They see bodies to be had rather than minds to be respected and aspirations to be encouraged. They believe that husbands and wives should share the responsibilities associated with families, but they do not themselves share by performing traditional women's roles in the home. They understand that pain is real and deep, but they do not disengage themselves from their own pain long enough to recognize the pain their women suffer. In a word, they fail to see the small, dark enclosure within the narrow space. They do not know that they are sexist. And significantly, they are not sexist because they are black or even because they are victimized. They are sexist because, as men, they are socialized to be sexist. Sexism has no respect for race or class, just as racism has no respect for sex.

It goes without saying that sexism is far more complex than love battles between men and women. Along with racism and class, sexism is a part of an infrastructure that affects every aspect of a black woman's life. For this reason, it is important, as Zillah Eisenstein writes, to avoid "seeing sex or class, or race or class, or sex or race" and study instead "the process and relations of power."[3] It is equally important to avoid seeing male-female conflicts as the only manifestations of the sexual arm of "the process." But there is a logical explanation for what seems to be undue emphasis on male–female conflicts in the novels. The women writers, as artists, are interested in the particulars of a woman's life that define her in relation to others and, in doing so, define her within her own psyche. Given the cultural weight of a woman's "place," those particulars are dramatically vivid in the "inside" world. It is the inevitability of what Cleo Judson calls woman's "sphere" that keeps women apart from the world in which male power reigns often unchallenged.

The black women in the novels discussed in this study do of course leave the "sphere" to participate in the labor force, working mainly as domestics or clerks. There are no characters who are professional black women actively participating in the "outside" world. The focus of the writers is on nonprofessionals, a focus that lends support to Claudia Tate's opinion that black women writers are "concerned with a kind of folk heroine and have not, as yet, dealt with the college-educated black woman who is, by fact of her education, encountering all kinds of additional problems."[4]

In spite of pain in the dark enclosure, a recurring theme in the novels is black women's love for black men. Pauline Breedlove's fantasy about being Jean Harlow is the only instance of a black woman looking longingly at a white man, but even here the white man is not sexually desired. In fact, as Morrison handles the fantasy, we see that Pauline is interested in being Jean Harlow because Harlow embodies beauty, power, and security. The love she receives from Clark Gable is only one expression of the contrast between her life and Pauline's life. Lutie Johnson is taught as a young girl that she should not let white men bother her, and as an adult woman she would rather lie with a snake than sleep with a white man. Significantly, when she attempts to borrow money for her son's bail, she goes to Boots Smith although she knows that it is Junto, the white man on "the street," who owns everything. A third example is found in *Sula*. When people in the Bottom want to prove that Sula is evil incarnate, they spread the rumor that she has committed the worst sin of all: she has slept with white men.

Studying race and sex in the same context shows that triumph in one dimension of "double jeopardy" is juxtaposed and, in some instances, challenged by defeat in another. Women can challenge racial limitations and achieve in spite of them at the same time that they are submitting to sexual limitations, or vice versa. This dynamic of failure and success—challenge and submission—is particularly dramatic in portraits of women who are mothers, since the legendary black woman of strength and achievement against insurmountable odds is more often than not a mother. If one looks through the veil of motherhood at the behavior of Mem Copeland in *The Third Life of Grange Copeland*, Meridian in *Meridian*, or Eva Peace in *Sula* one sees the "sturdy black bridges" of which Carolyn Rodgers writes. They are the women who are "resilient and hardy," and like "midnight birds" they are "yearning and impatient."[5]

But because they are bridges over the treacherous waters of race, class, and sex, the major chord of maternal triumph becomes only one of several chords in a sorrow song. Mem Copeland is an exemplary mother, but outside the role she is destroyed by male abuse. Meridian's grandmother has reason to recite her success in "turning corners and reachin' landin's" as a mother, but outside the role she tastes the acidity of her husband's hostility to wider options for women. And Eva Peace makes the phenomenal sacrifice of a leg for the welfare of her family, but she is half a person because she encloses her feelings behind an impenetrable wall of hatred for the man who abandoned her. Often, then, when the women soar as mothers into seeming triumph above race and class, their wings are clipped in flight and, sexually, they are plunged into sorrow.

Not all women are exemplary mothers. In *Meridian*, for example, Mrs. Hill anchors Meridian's spirit in guilt and her own maternal posture in distance. Brilliantly, Alice Walker depicts Mrs. Hill as a woman whose serenity and independence have been robbed by the sexual role of mother. Thus she irons into her children's clothes the "starch" of her sexual anger and continues to cry inside, "It's all deliberate." Pauline Breedlove, as a mother, is psychologically cruel, adding her own brand of rejection to racial pressures that make Pecola long, tragically, for blue eyes. Morrison explains that Pauline is damaged by her inferior status as a poor black woman in a white world of wealth and also by her husband's failure (or inability) to compensate in their love relationship for what she experiences in the outside world. In these examples, and in others, the women are not negligent mothers. Indeed, they are "good" mothers in that they attend to the physical needs of their children, and, although they do not demonstrate affection, they love them. But they can not travel the emotional miles from indifference to involvement, from maternal frustrations to maternal fulfillment, because as blacks and as women, they are "damaged persons."

The maternal missions of the women characters reflect the double-edged nature of their reality and also the significance of their sexual vulnerability. Boys receive the message of preparation for survival and success in a white world, with the emphasis on dealing with "*the* man" and the system. Girls get a very different message, given the emphasis on winning in "a man's" world rather than "*the* man's" world.

Mrs. Medina and Eva's other mother give Eva one lesson for the future: "don't let men mess with you," suggesting that her identity as a woman rather than her identity as a black person is the problem. Silla Boyce and Henrietta Coffin stress the importance of an education, and in the same breath they warn their daughters that their sexual vulnerability is the greatest threat to this goal. If socialization is a comment on reality, and it is, then one could argue that black women perceive sexual vulnerability, not racial oppression, as the greater danger in their lives. Racism is, of course, involved here, and in a major and decisive way. It determines where the women live, what kinds of jobs and salaries they receive, what monsters will stalk their children's future, how they and their men are treated and, as a result, how they are treated by their men—in a word, the parameters of their lives. But racism alone does not explain the women's sensitivity to their sexual vulnerability. This sensitivity supersedes race at the same moment that it intersects with race. It supersedes race because it is a biological fact that is not contingent on race. It intersects with race because one of the results of racism and sexism in the black experience is that black women are more physically vulnerable because they are perceived by the larger society and, more tragically, by their own men as devalued sex objects.

Their double identities, along with the problems of their men in white America, add another dimension to their socialization: they must be independent. Unlike most white women, they are taught that no one will adore them, revere them, care for them, and protect them. There are no pedestals in their reality and no crystal stairs. Because they are black, they can expect nothing from white America except what they manage to acquire through miracles, hard work, and sometimes game playing. And because they are female, they can expect very little from their men, even if they play a woman's game of coquettish indulgence.

Independence, however, is not the same as selfishness, and self-sufficiency is not a mirror image of egotism, for the women have the ability to be self-sacrificing at the same time that they are self-sufficient. This fact is an unchanging feature in the novels: the women are rarely seen doing for themselves. They are rarely happy in the "inside" world, but they are always there, serving their husbands and children. They do not shop for themselves, collect things for themselves, or spend time on themselves. Mariah Upshur's sigh, "no time to sew for myself," is a good description of the extent to which most of the women are depicted as other-directed. Somehow, all of them, regardless of class, manage in the crises of their personal lives to keep in focus their role as keepers of the "inside."

"The subject of the black woman's physical beauty," writes Mary Helen Washington, "occurs with such frequency in the writings of black women that it indicates that they have been deeply affected by the discrimination against their skin and texture of their hair." The "color theme," she continues, "almost always plays at least a peripheral role in the lives of imaginative women created by black women writers."[6] Washington's thesis is supported by the color and hair problem in *The Bluest Eye*, *Maud Martha*, *Corregidora*, *The Living Is Easy*, and, for Mrs. Hedges, in *The Street*. But it does not surface in *Eva's Man*; *Sula*; *Brown Girl, Brownstones*; or *The Third Life of Grange Copeland*. Walker dismisses "color" as a problem when she writes of Mem's interpretation of color as something done to flowers.

One would be foolish, of course, to ignore the impact that the specter of white beauty has on the thinking of black women. It is an intrinsic part of their socialization, and even when they cope with their blackness, it is an ever-present ache in their souls. They know that they are devalued because they are black women. But without denying its weight in the lives of black women, the women writers move us beyond this problem to the larger and more complex problem of sexism, which cannot be traced to color or other physical features. Sexism is not fed or created by men's interest in beauty, though their vanity makes them believe they should have only those women who are beautiful. Rather, sexism is fed by men's assumption that, as men, they should have dominant roles in society. To be sure, there is a mixed and intricate picture here, in which a multitude of factors are at play—color, hair texture, race, class—and none can be extricated from the total picture without distorting the truth. But we must be sensitive to proportion, as the women novelists are, and in our sensitivity, recognize that black women in the novels, though often not pleased with the way they look, experience "loss, isolation, vulnerability and victimization," even when they are beautiful, because they are hostages in a racist and sexist culture. Black men might use the color and hair problems as excuses for their abuse of black women, as does Brownfield when he reminds Mem that she is not white, but the single most decisive factor in their attitudes is their socialization in a sexist culture.

Perhaps William Grier and Price Cobbs are correct in their claim that narcissism is absent in black women,[7] for the women in the novels have little interest in expressing their "femininity" in traditional frills and frivolities, in wardrobes of sheer garments and dressers cluttered with makeup that colors cheeks and enlarges eyes. Obviously, for poor black women, time and money are deciding factors. And yet, we can challenge the novels' failure to include in the portraits of black women, even those who are poor, the women's interest in their appearance. It is not true, as many of the authors imply, that this interest is subdued in black women. The flourishing market of special cosmetics for black women and cheap ones for poor black women proves otherwise. The cheap clothing stores that pepper black communities prove otherwise, as does the presence of beauty shops within shouting distance of one another. No woman who is socialized in this culture of eye cosmetics, silky fabrics, and alluring perfumes can fail to be affected in some way by the institutionalized and profit-oriented promotion of American femininity. We could argue, in fact, that black women, more than white women, might seek aids to femininity because they have been denied beauty in white America.

Black women's interest in being "pretty" and "attractive" in a "feminine" way is not completely excluded from the visions. In *Brown Girl, Brownstones* and in *Corregidora*, women are seen flocking to beauty shops where they sit for hours enduring the heat of metal or chemicals that will improve the appearance of their hair. In *The Street*, Lutie Johnson expresses her desire to be more than a struggling mother by flirting with a reflection of a "feminine" self in a mirror as she prepares to make her debut as a nightclub singer. The most convincing statement on the effect of the femininity market on black women is given by Toni Morrison, for she uses Sula's desire to be feminine, as it is defined in American culture, as a sign of Sula's destruction. When Sula seeks to hold Ajax in a relationship of possessiveness, she joins other women in the beauty parlor, decorates her hair with ribbons, and scents the bedroom with fragrances. Seeing Sula behave like a typical woman, Ajax mounts her, rides through her pleasure, and abandons her.

While the novelists pay only minor attention to these concerns, they pay preeminent attention to other criteria of femininity, criteria that determine how a woman should function rather than how she should look and, in a sense, that determine the darkness of the enclosure. The women in the novels want to be dainty, soft, winning, coquettish, demure, sweet—all criteria of femininity. They want to be supportive rather than domineering. If it is true that black men are socialized to be sexist, it is also true that black women are socialized to be feminine, or to internalize sexist assumptions about the appearance and behavior of a successful and desired woman. The novelists' visions support this fact, as evidenced, among other examples, by Mrs. Hedges's concern about her enormous size, Eva's belief that women should coquettishly pamper their men rather than openly compete with them, and Nel's decision to be "the tuck and hem" of Jude's garment rather than "something else" more fulfilling.

Being a woman and being feminine are two different experiences in the novels, and it is the former that most engages the attention of the writers. To be a woman is to be legitimized in a relationship with a man. To be a woman is to be a mother, a wife, and/or a lover. To operate outside these roles often brings censure from the community. To challenge these roles is to enclose oneself in loneliness and isolation. This was the dilemma of Eva Medina. In a sense it was the dilemma of Mrs. Hill, who functioned in the roles of wife and mother without acknowledging their significance. It was the dilemma that made Sula, who would create a different version of herself, a pariah in the Bottom. And it was the cultural lesson, accepted by most black women, that made Eva explain that what Sula needed to do most was to make babies.

Like their white counterparts, black women are victims of the concept of romantic love. They, too, have sung the songs, recited the poems, seen the movies, and read the romance magazine stories about "the man I love." They, too, have been fed from the "staples"[8] of American mythology about the magic of romantic love. Because of their location in the narrow space of powerlessness, perhaps black women need the magic in a special way, but ironically, it is often because of this location that they discover there is no magic at all. Toni Morrison best explains the tragedy of this concept in the lives of black women. Like the concept of physical beauty, she writes, the concept of romantic love is a destructive force in civilization. It is presented as such in most of the novels. It colors Pauline Breedlove's fantasies and poses her idle at a country fence waiting for a man to make her whole. It causes Josie to forget her victory over a community of exploitative men and rush head-on into victimization at the hands of that special man. It makes Nel relinquish her claim on the right to create "something else to be," and it turns Sula 180 degrees from independence, freedom, and unlimited expression of self. For the women, to be loved by a man is to know one is alive.

Belief in the concept of romantic love does not, however, make the women empty-headed, dizzy, pining souls who are stagnant in life, singing the blues for a man who has gone. Men come into their lives, often they conquer, often they exploit, often they leave having conquered, but in their leaving they cannot look back at women so devastated by disappointment in love that they cease to function. With the exception of Margaret in *The Third Life of Grange Copeland*, who commits suicide, the women rise from the ashes of unrequited love and male abuse to put the pieces of their lives back in place. The scars are real, deep, and lasting. Often the women never love again, or they box their lives in loneliness and isolation, in cynicism and hostility. But they continue to be pragmatic women who get on with the business of living and coping. Their resilience in the enclosure is forged by their reality in the narrow space, for what they experience as blacks prepares them to confront problems peculiar to women.

In the novels written in the seventies, the sexuality of women, or more specifically, their experience with sexual lovemaking is treated with honesty, frankness, and bitterness. Again, race, class, and sex are involved in the quality of the experience, for "coitus is never in a vacuum."[9] The myth of the sexually talented and sexually eager black woman is examined critically, resulting in the conclusion that black women are sexually active on the one hand and spiritually frustrated on the other. Josie bumps and grinds with great skill, but she wants more than the pleasure of the act itself. She wants to be cleansed, and that takes love, acceptance, and tenderness. Sula sleeps with men but gets no pleasure from the experience because their monotonous love tricks deny the existence of her mind. Mrs. Hill can not separate the act from the consequences of the act—pregnancy and motherhood—which imprison her in unfulfilling, noncreative duties. Meridian finds the nights with Eddie only exercises in duty and mechanics because he is too limited to understand that there is a larger world of possibility than the one they know in the small Mississippi town. And finally, at the extreme end of the spectrum is Cleo Judson, whose still face mocks the "busyness" below because men are her enemies "because they are male." Sex in many of the relationships is an unremarkable experience that comes with the role of wife.

These black novels make no allusions to new definitions of female sexuality like those made in many white feminist writings in the seventies. Criteria for orgasms are not treated from a biological or physical perspective. Sexual gymnastics are neither the problem nor the solution, for black women are not searching for new ways of making love. The old ways work when one essential is in place. Predictably, that essential is recognition of the women's need to be appreciated and loved and respected, to be valued not for what they do, but for what they are as persons. Mem enjoys lovemaking with Brownfield when he basks in her intelligence, in her humanity, and in her character, which makes her outstanding in the community. Meridian is bored by nights with Eddie, but in her first coitus with Truman, she ascends into bliss because she believes he loves her, respects her mind, and more important, is committed to the noble cause of the civil rights struggle. The strongest statement of the significance of this woman's essential in lovemaking is given in Morrison's portrait of Sula. When Ajax listens to Sula and respects what she says, Sula forgets the eclipsed joy of masturbation and ecstatically plunges into thrilling rides above Ajax. For men, coitus is merely physical. For black women, when it brings pleasure, it is a harmonious blend of what they can physically enjoy and what they emotionally need and desire. Therefore, black men in the novels are sexually potent only when they stroke the souls of women as expertly as they stroke the thighs. The collective and individual visions of the women, regardless of time, class, or region, are pictures of victimization, isolation, loneliness, and loss. The women understand that theirs is a difficult and complex reality. However, like Pauline Breedlove in *The Bluest Eye* and Min and Mrs. Hedges in *The Street,* the women sometimes fail to understand that what they experience as women is a cultural phenomenon. They perceive the sexual dimensions of their suffering, but they do not always realize that other women are in the enclosure with them. Rather, they see the enclosure as the result of their own peculiar reality.

Other women, however, understand that they are not alone in the enclosure, just as they are not alone in the space. They understand that other black women turn the same corners and tiptoe through the same morass of limitations and powerlessness. But understanding the problem is one thing and talking about the problem is another altogether. In most instances, their anger is turned inward, and black men, as a result, rarely have an opportunity to hear women out on matters that are peculiar to the reality of double jeopardy. Women turn their anger inward because they are socialized to believe that their agony is second to the agony of the race and second to the agony of their men. Consequently, they often persevere and suffer in silence. And for those unique women such as Mariah Upshur, Sula Peace, Eva Medina, and Eva Peace, turning anger outward results in further isolation and deeper agony.

What is more surprising about the portraits is that even when the women understand that they share a sisterhood of oppression, they often do not act on the belief that "sisterhood is powerful." They do not come together to talk about their common history and their common reality. When they do attempt to communicate as women, they fail to sustain the sisterhood. Mariah Upshur and Vyry in *This Child's Gonna Live* are kindred souls, seeking wider options for their lives, but the intensity of sexism and religious backwardness in Tangierneck keeps them in separate camps. Meridian and Anne-Marion in *Meridian* touch each other's version of self, but the versions are in conflict on an issue that is fundamental to the black liberation struggle in which both are involved. And finally, Sula and Nel in *Sula* are so close they are like "two throats and one eye," but what they are as sisters is ultimately destroyed by Nel's acquiescence to woman's "place" in a web of spiders and Sula's intense desire to cut the web where it holds women dangling from the frailest of threads.

In her second work, *Midnight Birds* (1980), Mary Helen Washington writes that "one of the most important themes in women's literature [is] women's reconciliation with one another."[10] She gives as an example of this theme the final act of Ntozake Shange's choreopoem, *For Colored Girls.* In the scene of reconciliation, seven women characters who have experienced different kinds of abuse come together and sing, "i found god in myself and i loved her fiercely." Washington writes that "reconciliation [in the play] is finally and completely a feminine and a feminist act."[11] *Sula,* also, Washington writes, is a work in which this theme is developed. She quotes Morrison on this point:

> But black women have always had that, they have always been
> emotional life supports for each other. That's what I was trying to
> say in *Sula,* when Nel discovered that it was not her husband that
> she had missed all those years, but her friend Sula.[12]

While it is true that there has been a "communal network"[13] in the lives of black women, it is also true that there has been hostility among them, a paradox ignored by some black feminists as they write of the power of sisterhood. In some ways, failure to acknowledge that the corrupt society in which we live has created tension among black women is not unlike the failure of black women prior to the seventies to acknowledge publicly that some black men oppress black women. Both are the results of a "sacred cow"[14] attitude toward black women and black men, respectively. In the larger truth, we must include some discussion of a breakdown in the "communal network" once black women stop being "young girls" and become competitors in the adult world for men, for jobs, for status in organizations, and for status in the community. Audre Lorde writes of the failure of black women to acknowledge the anger, hostility, and suspicion we have against each other. "It is easier," she explains, "to examine anger in situations less emotionally loaded, for instance in relationships with white women, which do not threaten genuine self-exposure," but few black women in this country give to their sisters "acceptance, gentleness, enough space to consider change, room to be wrong." Her honesty is a cry for healing:

> I don't like to talk about hate. But the anger between Black women is the tip of an iceberg, the understructure of which is hatred. From the moment she is born, a Black woman in America becomes vulnerable to hatreds that amount to a societal death wish—for her color, for her sex, for her effrontery in daring to presume she has any right to live in racist sexist America. . . . Echoes of this hatred return as anger in our dealings with each other, for each of us bears the face that hatred seeks.[15]

Unless we deal with this hatred, as Mary Helen Washington writes in her first book, *Black-Eyed Susans*, we will "settle for some idealized nonsense about black women and remain deprived of real characters from whom we could learn more about ourselves."[16]

Several of the novels analyzed in this book allude to tension among women characters. In fact, the deeper we travel into the authors' visions, the more we realize that the hardships of black life often push women apart and arrange them in the narrow space and in the dark enclosure as antagonists. Josie ignores the agony of Mem by stretching herself into Brownfield's life. The women in the church flagellate Mariah Upshur verbally and physically and keep her forever in doubt about her morality. The concubines of Deighton Boyce and James Coffin are not ignorant of their participation in the destruction of families that involve not only wives, but children as well. Regardless of the reason that drives Sula to make a point about the empty lives of women in the Bottom, she is the cause of Nel's agony. And finally, Mrs. Hedges, who realizes that women are vulnerable because they are women, lures her sisters in oppression into the worst trap of all—prostitution.

Hostility between black women and white women is a common theme in the novels for reasons discussed in the historical overview. Indeed, white women, more than white men, are the perpetrators of exploitation. Nancy Hoffman is therefore correct in advising white women who teach black American literature to be prepared to be "the enemy."[17] And yet, even on the issue of white women, there is no monolithic statement in the novels. In the forties, white women are madams. In the fifties, they are women of beauty, floating like abstractions in the "other" world. But in the seventies, they are sometimes only passing subjects of conversations or they are not mentioned at all. In *Meridian*, which suggests a new treatment of white women, they are sisters in oppression. Lynn Rabinowitz, whom Alice Walker depicts with compassion and understanding, is victimized because she is white in a world of black rage and female in a movement dominated by sexist men. Walker's sensitivity to Lynn's tragedy supports Washington's thesis that "wrongs acknowledged and challenged, silence broken, signal a distinct change for the relationship between black women and white women."[18]

The women's coping mechanisms vary from novel to novel, but all of the women bleed, and real tears wash salt into gaping wounds. Margaret Copeland is driven to suicide, and Lutie Johnson and Eva Medina to murder. Cleo Judson schemes and plays games to maximize her chances for more power and influence. Pauline Breedlove becomes a self-righteous woman whose religion saves her from insanity. Josie bumps and grinds her way into economic security, playing the game and losing even as she wins. Eva Peace retreats from the world of spontaneous and honest feelings, and her granddaughter, Sula, strikes out against every vestige of sexism or any barrier that will keep her from "catching the slant of life." Regardless of their mechanisms for coping, all of the women, except Lutie Johnson in *The Street*, are at their weakest in their need for love. The tragedy of their lives as black women is that they are socialized to believe that they will ultimately be abandoned, neglected, mistreated, or abused by men, and ultimately most of them are.

What they desire as black women is not unfamiliar in studies of the black experience. They want to be relieved of the strains of poverty.

They want their children's horizons unfettered by anything other than their own potential and dreams. They want their men to realize the fullest expression of manhood. In a word, they want to be free to live outside the narrow space. What they desire as black women is expressed very well by Washington. They want "solitariness, a space and time for themselves, they want to be free of male domination, the need to be the Angel in the House at the cost of [their] creativity."[19] However, they are essentially traditional in their approach to their reality. They do not seek new definitions of sex roles. Most of them, in fact, are willing to observe the old rules, if, in doing so, they are free of victimization. Their desires for wider options, when examined closely—both in the narrow space and in the dark enclosure—are essentially what Gayl Jones calls "alternatives to brutality." They want love, acceptance, respect, and, for several of the women characters, the freedom to express their creativity. Even when they realize that the old rules are by definition obstacles to these desires, most of the women would rather take their chances with the old rules and struggle in small ways for a new reality. They live what most women live—lives of contradiction. For black women, the contradiction is the result of their loyalty or conditioning (or both) in the space and in the enclosure.

In her prefaces to *Black-Eyed Susans* (1974) and *Midnight Birds* (1980), Washington writes of distorted images of black women that "abound like weeds in this society."[20] Only in fiction written by black women, she posits, is the complexity of black womanhood truthfully and sensitively presented, for as "dynamic interpreters of their own lives," black women writers choose "some brand-new" images of black women: "black-eyed susans" of "hardiness and resilience" and "midnight birds" of "yearning and impatience."[21] This statement should not be construed to mean that black women writers ignore and discard traditional images that have constituted a national mythology about black womanhood. As artists, they understand that while "self and image are not the same . . . they can not live apart from each other."[22] Images, even when they are false, are the public mirrors in which we first see ourselves as others see us and, are, therefore, the starting places for our definitions of ourselves. If we deny the existence of public images before they are replaced by more truthful ones, "the self becomes a jibbering ghost, immured in its watchtower, unable to reach the world."[23] Moreover, public images are so fundamental a part of our reality that to repudiate them totally is tantamount to repudiating a part of ourselves.

Choosing new images of black women must be seen as a first and very necessary step toward bringing together in the same place public images of black women and the women's authentic selves in the anticipation, though never the certainty, that the authentic selves will gain a firmer hold in the national consciousness than the images. However, it is a first step and, as such, it must rely on old images. For this reason, it is not true that "one does not see in the black woman as portrayed by the black woman writer any such perversions as the super sex object, or the domineering matriarch, or the evil black bitch."[24] In fiction, as in real life, some black women are those so-called perversions, for myth and truth, image and self, are often one and the same reality. Pauline Breedlove in *The Bluest Eye* is at times a self-effacing mammy. Josie in *The Third Life of Grange Copeland* and Hannah Peace in Sula are at times super sex objects. And Cleo Judson in *The Living Is Easy* often behaves like a castrating matriarch and, sometimes, like "an evil black bitch."

The presence of these women in black women's fiction does not altogether contradict Washington's thesis that black women writers choose new images of black women. Rather, it heightens our appreciation for the special way the writers use old images as they draw bold lines of black women's humanity. In their inside rendering of familiar, traditional, or even stereotypical images, we find complex and sensitive women who, as individuals, are larger than the images and more sensitive to their humanity than national interpretations of black women suggest. The unique contributions of black women's fiction to our understanding of black women's reality is, therefore, not new images, but a new and deeper understanding of old images and familiar myths. The writers move us through images and myths so that they can enlarge hidden dimensions where matriarchs, mammies, super sex objects, and even evil black bitches, in the sphere of the authentic self, are often "black-eyed susans" and "midnight birds."

Perhaps discussions of these "perversions" and feminist analysis of literature are mutually exclusive, especially if we as black feminist writers take the position that our task is to counter negative statements about black women with positive statements, or create new myths about black women that would render old myths powerless. Such self-consciousness and deliberate creation of myths, however, would be tantamount to an overkill and, as well, misrepresentation of truth. We succeed in raising the consciousness of black people in general by admitting that there are, in fact, problems within the race that must be addressed, regardless of their cause. And we succeed in raising the consciousness of black women in particular by admitting that we have internalized myths about our reality. As a result, we sometimes see ourselves as others see us and we sometimes suffer from low self-esteem. We cannot cure an illness by denying that we suffer from its symptoms.

And yet, illness is not all there is to our reality as black people in white America. There is a strong sense of ourselves as a community of people with a rich heritage, a positive present, and a promising future. We want to see our health and our wholeness as the foreground and background of artistic pictures of the black experience. We know there are black women in real life who are not chosen as models for imaginary characters in much of the fiction written by black women today. We have lived with them in our communities. We have worshiped with them in our churches and studied with them in our schools. We have ridden the back of the bus with them, spent hours of laughter with them in beauty shops, and gossiped with them in neighborhood laundromats. We have grown up with their daughters and married their sons. We have seen them age, slowly and with dignity, and we have heard them remind us, affectionately, that they knew us when we were all legs and pigtails. No one ever abandoned them or beat their heads, and they never abandoned or abused their loved ones. They were never unsure of their goals or visibly depressed by any aspects of their lives. They were, as my mother says of herself, women with "a single eye on success."

Some of them were prim and proper women who decorated church pews with colorful hats and white gloves. They never missed school meetings, they took their time fingering fruit in white-owned stores, they blushed when they talked about their husbands, and they preened when they talked about their daughters and sons. Some of them were exceedingly vain women who never knew that black women are not supposed to be beautiful. And still others were proud women who, like my grandmother, wore their blackness and independence at cocksure angles of defiance. They lived in insular black communities where there was warm laughter, where there was gentle nurturing, where there was protection from the world outside. They never opened their doors to social workers or traveled downtown to welfare offices for food stamps or more forms on top of forms. In more than a few cases, at least in the Deep South, many of them never knew "madams." Rather, they knew poor white women across the tracks and around the corner with whom, in spite of segregation, they sometimes shared stories about children (a game of boasting that black women often won), swapped mason jars, hoed in adjacent gardens, cut patterns from discarded newspapers, and "talked Bible."

And there were professional black women who lived in the "pretty" houses we passed as we walked the long way to segregated schools past the "better" schools closed to us. They were the schoolteachers, social workers, secretaries, funeral parlor receptionists, piano teachers, and wives of doctors or lawyers. By definition, their lives were complex and, from the perspective of nonprofessional blacks, most intriguing. And there were the men who, together with these women, built strong families capable of overcoming adversity with dignity. They were role models of hard work, decency, and caring for young boys and examples of good husbands for young girls who fantasized about marriage. They never raped their daughters, abused their wives, or failed to be vigilant in their guard over the lives of all the children in the community. Where are these flesh-and-blood people from our childhood and our adulthood?

As the collective vision of black women's novels shows, these people are in the literature, but they share the canvas with negative images that disturb us and, more painfully, that "prove" myths about the black experience to be truths articulated by our own writers. And so we desire to select proper material for black artistic visions. But there has never been a time in the history of literature when readers select material for writers. There will never be a time. There can never be a time. There should never be a time. Nor has there ever been a time when all readers have been satisfied with all the literature of a culture. If black women writers dealt mainly with laughter, black readers would ask about our pain. If they dealt mainly with professional blacks, we would speak of the dignity of the poor. If they wrote of tenderness in love relationships, we would remember the many instances of sexual exploitation we witnessed or heard talked about in our communities. If they wrote mainly of achievements without struggle and pain, we would charge them with forgetting from whence they came. As black readers, we can wish for that "other" story (and there is always that "other" story), but we should evaluate literature only on the basis of its connection to truth and its ability to help us see humanity and the human experience with deeper insight and sensitivity. We cannot deny that the visions of the women writers discussed in this book are familiar, poignant, powerful, and real.

Perhaps our desire for the "other" story is a subconscious wish for material that would make us feel better about what *other* people are told about our reality, not about what *we* know to be real and whole. Perhaps, too, it is a desire for material that would better serve "personal and political presuppositions." Deborah McDowell discusses the danger of this control and cautions black feminist critics against leaning on "one individual persuasion." She speaks mainly to lesbian critics, but her points apply to all feminist critics. We must guard, she writes, against reading literature

as though it were polemic.... Using literature to make what is essentially a political point, we find ourselves virtually rewriting a text, ignoring certain aspects of plot or characterization, or oversimplifying the action to fit our "political" thesis. Then we are neither practicing honest criticism nor saying anything useful about the nature of art, or about art, or political persuasion, for that matter.[25]

I agree with McDowell, but I believe there are few, if any, discussions on any subject that cannot be construed as political in nature and intent. This is particularly true of discussions about subjects rarely handled in scholarly disciplines. Whatever is new or different is perceived in the mainstream of scholarship as political. *No Crystal Stair* is "political" in that it is a revisionist approach to criticism about black women's literature. It challenges the assumption that black women writers write only about the black experience, not about the black woman's experience. My "individual persuasion," then, has been obvious: to convince, or persuade, the reader that "double jeopardy" is a dominant theme in the writings of selected black women writers from 1946 to 1976.

This "persuasion" did not require a rewriting of any of the texts, for in all the novels discussed *race* and *sex* draw distinct lines marking the women's realities. The writers illuminate the dark enclosure of sex at the same moment that they move us through the narrow space of race. What we learn in their visions is the irrefutable fact about the lives of most black women in white America. Life for them "ain't been no crystal stair." We feel the razor-sharp points of "tacks and splinters," trace the difficult journeys from "landin's" to "corners," struggle in the "dark" with complex women in search of freedom and dignity. The women have reason to explode and build for themselves a place in the sun, for the enclosure is the farthest distance from the large circle of power and influence. And yet, perhaps because of their condition in the enclosure, they are almost always struggling to improve the quality of life in the narrow space. They rear children, stroke or struggle with their men, battle with other black women, stay sane, and continue to dream. They are "tall" and "impervious," and when we *see* them beyond myths, we are "renewed."[26]

AFTERWORD

By the mid-1960s, when the intellectual currents of Black Revolution were becoming apparent, the demand for a "new Black History" was already being heard. The leading proponents of "Black Consciousness" seemed to say that the pride, respect, and self-esteem that were vital to their movement necessitated a revision of the way blacks had been treated in traditional American history as well as in traditional Negro history.

However, once black history and black studies were established as proper enterprises throughout most of American academia, new questions arose as to their meanings and orientations. Was black history, for example, simply a darker imitation of traditional white history, i.e., was it simply the story of great black men? In other words, like mainstream American history, was it both elitist and sexist?

Many in the "new Black History Movement" obviously wanted to believe that black history was different. And, there could be persuasive arguments that black history was classless, since almost all blacks, since slavery, had shared common degrading experiences. Similarly, it could be argued that there was no place for sexism in black history, because of the toils and oppression of men, women, and children alike.

With respect to sex, it was indeed true that in the colonial and antebellum eras, the names of Phillis Wheatley, Sojourner Truth, and Harriet Tubman were seen frequently alongside those of Jupiter

Hammon, Richard Allen, and Frederick Douglass. In the postbellum periods, Ida Wells Barnett, Anna Cooper, and Mary Church Terrell emerged, as did Booker T. Washington, John Hope, and W. E. B. DuBois. And in the present times, Fannie Lou Hamer and Coretta Scott King have found a place in our history with Malcolm X and Martin Luther King Jr.

Therefore, it has been argued that the equality of the sexes, at least in leadership, can be seen much more clearly among blacks than among whites. On the other hand, there have been pictures of the dominating black matriarch, both in slavery and in freedom, and of the ruthless, brutal, and shiftless black male, especially in freedom.

In *No Crystal Stair*, Gloria Wade-Gayles is very conscious of American history and black history in general and of black women's history and studies in particular. She skillfully employs a knowledge of economics, sociology, and psychology in her quest to understand and help others understand the place of black women in American life and history from the end of the Second World War to the crest of the civil rights movement and, more especially, their unique reality in American culture.

The period she has chosen is an ideal one to demonstrate the emergence of new vicissitudes in the black experience, which continue to dominate black lives even today. This period, of course, is the time of the last great migration from the South, the opening of new political and economic opportunities in the North, the birth of the modern civil rights era, and the explosion of Black Revolution and Black Consciousness. As in earlier times, we see in these periods strong, black, female leadership, both in individuals from Mary McLeod Bethune to Fannie Lou Hamer, and in organizations from the Neighborhood Union to the National Council of Negro Women. On the other hand, none of these reached the public significance of Martin Luther King Jr. or the male-dominated NAACP. And many important black women, such as Etta Moten of the Southern Christian Leadership Conference, remain almost invisible.

So it was that black women scholars in the last five or ten years have been able to point out correctly that, even at leadership levels, the roles of black women have often been subordinated, at least in historical and other literature, to those of black men. But more important, these scholars have tended to suggest that black women, generally, suffer disabilities and discriminations on account of both race and sex, suffering some of the latter at the hands of black men. These occurrences and their effects on the social, physical, mental, and fiscal well-being of black women have been, as Wade-Gayles recounts, the subjects of numerous scholarly works by black and white women in recent days.

No Crystal Stair is a welcome addition to this growing body of literature, particularly because of the different approaches and perspectives it brings and the judicious balance it achieves. Many of the previous studies on black women have been flawed because they have been too one-dimensional. Some have been strictly fictional; others have been mainly historical; some have had an anti-male tone. A few have tried to link black women and white women in a common tale of oppression. Wade-Gayles harmoniously interfaces fiction with the latest and most reputable of historical, economic, psychological, and sociological studies to create the real environment out of which black women come.

While recognizing the special disabilities and responses of black women in American society and the role that black men have played in some of that oppression, the work commendably points to the real culprit—a system of exploitative capitalism, controlled by white males. And in this exploitation, the grievances of black women and white women are not identical, for white women do not suffer the legacies and the realities of white racism.

In this book, then, we have the best of two worlds—an updated synthesis and analysis of race and sex as expressed in a wide selection of black women's novels as well as a scholarly treatment of those two variables in the life and history of contemporary black women. Although, indeed, this study confirms that black women have not climbed a crystal stair, it does illuminate the paths they have been treading in their quest for self-fulfillment and racial and sexual equality.

Alton Hornsby Jr.
Editor, *Journal of Negro History*

NOTES

Introduction to the Revised Edition

1. Gloria Wade-Gayles, *No Crystal Stair* (New York: Pilgrim Press, 1984), 20. Emphasis added.

2. Beverly Guy-Sheftall, Introduction, *No Crystal Stair*, xiv.

3. Smith, "Towards a Black Feminist Criticism," quoted in *No Crystal Stair*, xiv.

4. Guy-Sheftall, Introduction, *No Crystal Stair*, xiii.

5. Barbara Smith, "Doing Research on Black Women," *Women's Studies Newsletter* 4 (spring 1976): 7.

6. Toni Cade Bambara, ed., *The Black Woman* (New York: New American Library, 1970), 7.

7. Wade-Gayles, *No Crystal Stair*, 12.

8. Beverly Guy-Sheftall, *Words of Fire: An Anthology of African-American Feminist Thought* (New York: The New Press, 1996), 18.

9. *Studies in Black American Literature*, vol. 1 (Greenwood, Fla.: Penkevill Publishers, 1984), 5.

10. Houston Baker and Patricia Redmond, *Afro-American Literary Study in the 1990s* (Chicago: University of Chicago Press, 1989), 1.

11. Paula Giddings, "The Last Taboo," in *Words of Fire*, 219.

12. Alice Walker, *In Search of Our Mothers' Gardens* (San Diego: Harcourt Brace Jovanovich, 1983), ii.

13. Guy-Sheftall, *Words of Fire*, 19.

14. Patricia Hill-Collins, *Black Feminist Thought* (New York: Routledge Press, 1990), 164.

15. This metaphor, created by bell hooks and used as a subtitle in her brilliant analysis of black womanhood in patriarchy, was very popular during the eighties and into the nineties. However, with the deeper understanding of systems of oppression in our nation comes, I submit, a need for a new metaphor. This one is problematic in

that moving from margin to center does not call attention to the fact that the center must dissolve if marginalization is to be eliminated.

16. Wade-Gayles, *No Crystal Stair*, 3–4.

Introduction to the First Edition

1. *Signs* 6 (winter 1980): 282.

2. This quote comes from Annis Pratt's "The New Feminist Criticisms: Exploring the History of the New Space," in *Beyond Intellectual Sexism: A New Woman, a New Reality*, ed. Joan T. Roberts (New York: David McKay, 1976), 10.

3. Smith, "Towards a Black Feminist Criticism," *Conditions: Two* (1977): 27–28.

4. Ibid., 32.

5. Deborah McDowell, "New Directions for Black Feminist Criticism," *Black American Literature Forum* 14 (October 1980): 153.

6. Ibid., 158.

7. Cheri Register, "Literary Criticism," *Signs* 6 (winter 1980): 270.

8. McDowell, "New Directions for Black Feminist Criticism," 156.

9. Ibid., 155.

10. Mary Helen Washington, Introduction, *Black-Eyed Susans: Classic Stories by and about Black Women*, ed. Mary Helen Washington (Garden City, N.Y.: Anchor Books, 1975), 4.

1. The Narrow Space of Race, the Dark Enclosure of Sex

1. Langston Hughes, "Mother to Son," in *Black Writers of America: A Comprehensive Anthology*, ed. Richard Barksdale (New York: Macmillan, 1972), 518.

2. Gerda Lerner, *Black Women in White America: A Documentary History* (New York: Random House, 1972), ix.

3. Michele Wallace, "Black Macho and the Myth of the Super Woman," *Ms.* 4 (January 1979): 45.

4. See Angela Davis, *Women, Race, and Class* (New York: Random House, 1981).

5. Zillah R. Eisenstein, "Some Notes on the Relations of Capitalist Patriarchy," in *Capitalist Patriarchy and the Case for Socialist Feminism*, ed. Eisenstein (New York: Monthly Review Press, 1979), 47.

6. See Beverly Guy-Sheftall, "Interdisciplinary Approaches to Incorporating Southern Black Women's History into the Study of American History" (paper presented at the Annual Conference of the Association for the Study of Negro Life and History, Philadelphia, October 1981).

7. Elizabeth Cady Stanton, quoted in Chafe, *Women and Equality: Changing Patterns in American Culture* (New York: Oxford University Press, 1977), 47.

8. Maya Angelou, *I Know Why the Caged Bird Sings* (New York: Random House, 1970), 92.

9. Elizabeth Cady Stanton, quoted in Chafe, *Women and Equality*, 46.

10. For an interesting discussion of the problems created by this analogy, see bell hooks, *Ain't I a Woman: Black Women and Feminism* (Boston: South End Press, 1981).

11. Chafe, *Women and Equality*, 46.

12. Calvin Hernton, *Sex and Racism in America* (New York: Grove Press, 1965), 125.

13. Diane Lewis, "A Response to Inequality: Black Women, Racism, and Sexism," *Signs* 3 (winter 1977): 347.

14. See Marabel Morgan, *The Total Woman* (Old Tappan, N.J.: F. H. Revell, 1973).

15. "Combahee River Collective," in *But Some of Us Are Brave: Black Women's Studies*, ed. Gloria Hull et al. (Old Westbury, N.Y.: Feminist Press, 1982), 16.

16. This phrase is Georgia Douglas Johnson's description of the task of the black woman writer. See Jay Saunders Redding, *To Make a Poet Black* (College Park, Md.: McGrath, 1939), 25.

17. Zora Neale Hurston, *Their Eyes Were Watching God* (Boston: Lippincott, 1937; reprint, Greenwich, Conn.: Fawcett, 1965), 16.

18. Sarah Wright, *This Child's Gonna Live* (New York: Dell, 1969), 11.

19. Daryl Dance, "Black Eve or Madonna? A Study of the Antithetical Views of the Mother in Black American Literature," in *Sturdy Black Bridges*, ed. Roseann Bell et al. (New York: Doubleday, 1979), 123.

20. Chafe, *Women and Equality*, 59.

21. Barbara Smith, "Doing Research on Black American Women," *Women's Studies Newsletter* 4 (spring 1976): 4.

22. Tillie Olsen, *Silences* (New York: Delta/Seymour Lawrence, 1965), 6.

23. Alice Walker, quoted in "Combahee River Collective," in *But Some of Us Are Brave*, 163.

24. Langston Hughes, *The Big Sea* (New York: Hill & Wang, 1940), 228.

25. Ibid.

26. Claudia Tate, ed., *Black Women Writers at Work* (New York: Continuum, 1983), xix.

27. Ibid., xx.

2. A Historical Overview: Black Women in White America, 1946–1976

1. See Brisbane, *The Black Vanguard* (Valley Forge, Pa.: Judson Press, 1970).

2. William H. Chafe, *The American Woman: Her Changing Social, Ecomomic, and Political Roles, 1920–1970* (New York: Oxford University Press, 1972), 136.

3. Ibid., 139.

4. Ibid., 142.

5. Ibid., 143.

6. Delores Aldridge, "Black Women in the Economic Marketplace: A Battle Unfinished," *Journal of Social and Behavioral Sciences* 21 (winter 1975): 52.

7. Chafe, *The American Woman*, 142.

8. See Chafe, *The American Woman*, and John Hope Franklin, *From Slave to Freedom* (New York: Random House, 1969).

9. Chafe, *The American Woman*, 191.

10. Lerner, *Black Women in White America*, 239.

11. Brisbane, *The Black Vanguard*, 87.

12. Information on court cases, demonstrations, and numbers of black male and black female leaders in a synthesis of data found in *The Black Almanac*, ed. Alton Hornsby (New York: Barron's Educational Series, 1972), 80–104.

13. A good study of the burdens of black women in northern ghettos is Horace Cayton and St. Clair Drake, *Black Metropolis*, vols. 1 and 2 (New York: Harcourt, Brace & World, 1945).

14. Chafe, *Women and Equality*, 94.

15. Chafe, *The American Woman*, 210.

16. Helene Deutsch, from *The Psychology of Women: A Psychoanalytic Interpretation*, vol. 1 (New York: Grune & Stratton, 1944), quoted in Chafe, *The American Woman*, 209.

17. June Sochen, *Movers and Shakers: American Women Thinkers and Activists, 1900–1970* (New York: Quadrangle, 1974), 202.

18. Chafe, *The American Woman*, 231.

19. Sharon Harley and Rosalyn Terborg-Penn, eds., *The Afro-American Women: Struggles and Images* (New York: Kennikat Press, 1978), 24.

20. Gary Null, *Hollywood: The Negro in Motion Pictures* (New York: Citadel Press, 1975), 121.

21. After her role in *Mildred Pierce* (1945), Butterfly McQueen vowed that she would never play the degrading role of Aunt Jemima again. She kept that promise.

22. Herbert Gutman, quoted in bell hooks, *Ain't I a Woman? Black Women and Feminism* (Boston: South End Press, 1981), 84.

23. June Sochen, *Her Story: A Woman's View of American History*, vol. 2 (New York: Alfred Publishing, 1974), 368.

24. Barbara Christian, *Black Women Novelists: The Development of a Tradition, 1892–1976* (Westport, Conn.: Greenwood Press, 1981), 90.

25. hooks, *Ain't I a Woman?*, 86.

26. Frances E. W. Harper, quoted in Chafe, *Woman and Equality*, 54.

27. This information is a synthesis of facts found in Hornsby, *The Black Almanac*, 80–104.

28. W. E. B. DuBois, *The Souls of Black Folk* (Boston, 1898; reprint, New York: Fawcett, 1963), iv.

29. Barbara Sizemore, "Sexism and the Black Male," *The Black Scholar* 4 (March/April 1973): 4.

30. U.S. Department of Labor, *Handbook of Labor Statistics*, 75–79.

31. Walter Allen, "Family Roles, Occupational Statuses and Achievement Orientation among Black Women in the United States," *Signs* 4 (summer 1979): 679.

32. Pauli Murray, "Jim Crow and Jane Crow," in *Black Women in White America*,

ed. Gerda Lerner, 584–88 (New York: Random House, 1972), 597.

33. Margaret Wright, "I Want the Right to Be Black and Me," in *Black Women in White America*, 607.

34. Murray, "Jim Crow and Jane Crow," 596.

35. Carolyn Rodgers, "I Have Been Hungry," in *How I Got Ovah* (New York: Doubleday, 1976), 49–50.

36. Michele Wallace, "A Black Feminist's Search," in *But Some of Us Are Brave*, 6.

37. Hernton, *Sex and Racism in America*, 7.

38. Ibid., 17.

39. Chafe, *Women and Equality*, 110–11.

40. hooks, *Ain't I a Woman?*, 110.

41. Ibid., 109–10.

42. Amiri Baraka, in hooks, *Ain't I a Woman?*, 95.

43. Wallace, "A Black Feminist's Search," 10.

44. Don Lee, "BLACKWOMAN," in Lee, *Don't Cry, Scream* (Detroit: Broadside Press, 1969), 55.

45. Loren Miller, "Farewell to Liberals," in *Black Protest: History, Documents, and Analyses*, ed. Joanne Grant (New York: Fawcett, 1968), 437.

46. Charles Silberman, "Crisis in Black and White," in *Black Protest: History, Documents, and Analyses* (New York: Fawcett, 1968), 438–39.

47. Lewis, "A Response to Inequality," 349.

48. Sizemore, "Sexism and the Black Male," 4.

49. See Aldridge, "Black Women in the Economic Marketplace," 48–62.

50. Murray, "Jim Crow and Jane Crow," 587.

51. Bambara, ed., *The Black Woman*, 7.

52. Angela Davis, quoted in Acklyn Lynch, "Notes on Black Women Writers of the Past Two Decades," in *Frances, Zora, and Lorraine: Essays and Interviews on Black Women and Writing*, ed. Juliette Bowles (Washington, D.C.: Howard University Press, 1979), 52.

53. Shirley Chisholm, "Sexism and Racism: One Battle to Fight," *Personnel and Guidance Journal* 51 (October 1972): 125.

54. Shirley Chisholm, *Unbought and Unbossed* (Boston: Houghton Mifflin, 1970), xxi.

55. Fannie Lou Hamer, "It's in Your Hands," in *Black Women in White America* (New York: Random House, 1972), 609.

56. Betty Friedan, *The Feminine Mystique* (New York: W. W. Norton, 1963), 55.

57. hooks, *Ain't I a Woman?*, 124

58. Angela Davis, *Women, Race, and Class* (New York: Random House, 1981), 70.

59. Adrienne Rich, "Disloyal to Civilization: Feminism, Racism, and Gynephobia," *Chrysalis* 7 (1979): 23.

60. hooks, *Ain't I a Woman?*, 124.

61. "Combahee River Collective," in *But Some of Us Are Brave*, 19.

62. Robert Staples, "The Myth of the Black Matriarchy," *The Black Scholar* 1 (January–February 1970): 9.

63. Stokely Carmichael, quoted in Robin Morgan, "Know Your Enemy: A Sampling of Sexist Quotes," in *Sisterhood Is Powerful*, ed. Morgan (New York: Random House, 1970), 35.

64. Sizemore, "Sexism and the Black Male," 3.

65. Alice Walker, "He Said Come," in *Revolutionary Petunias* (New York: Harcourt Brace Jovanovich, 1971), 50.

66. Nikki Giovanni, "Beautiful Black Men," in *The Black Poets*, ed. Dudley Randall (New York: Bantam, 1971), 320.

67. Wallace, "Black Macho and the Myth of the Superwoman," 75.

68. Ibid., 79.

69. Ibid., 83.

70. Wallace, "A Black Feminist's Search for Sisterhood," 21.

71. "Combahee River Collective," in *But Some of Us Are Brave*, 19.

72. Truth, "I Suppose I Am About the Only Colored Woman," 566.

73. See the results of the Virginia Slims poll on black women's support of women's liberation in Chafe, *Women and Equality*, 125.

74. Chafe, *Women and Equality*, 147.

3. The Halo and the Hardships: Black Women as Mothers and Sometimes as Wives

1. Adrienne Rich, *Of Woman Born: Motherhood as Experience and Institution* (New York: W. W. Norton, 1970), 15.

2. Ibid., 23.

3. Monta Crane and Betty Scott, compilers, *Along the Way* (Coshocton, Ohio: Shaw-Barton, 1977), 16.

4. Simone de Beauvoir, quoted in Sochen, *Movers and Shakers*, 201.

5. Rich, *Of Woman Born*, 5.

6. Ibid., 39.

7. Zillah R. Eisenstein, "Some Notes on the Relations of Capitalist Patriarchy," in *Capitalist Patriarchy and the Case for Socialist Feminism*, ed. Eisenstein (New York: Monthly Review Press, 1979), 47.

8. Rich, *Of Woman Born*, 20.

9. Ibid., 24.

10. Ibid.

11. Joyce Ladner, *Tomorrow's Tomorrow* (New York: Doubleday, 1972), 63.

12. Robert Staples, "The Myth of Black Matriarchy," in *The Black Family*, ed. Robert Staples (Belmont, Calif.: Wadsworth Publishing, 1971), 158–59.

13. Daniel Thompson, *Sociology of the Black Experience* (Westport, Conn.: Greenwood Press, 1974), 81.

14. Maya Angelou, quoted in *Jet*, 13 December 1973, 48.

15. Andrea Benton Rushing, "Comparative Study of the Idea of Mother in Con-

temporary African and African-American Poetry," in *Frances, Zora, and Lorraine*, ed. Juliette Bowles (Washington, D.C.: Howard University Press, 1979), 3.

16. Carolyn Rodgers, "It Is Deep," in *Sturdy Black Bridges*, 377.

17. Dance, "Black Eve or Madonna?," 127.

18. Ibid., 131.

19. Thompson, *Sociology of the Black Experience*, 81.

20. Christian, *Black Women Novelists*, 205.

21. Ibid., 240.

22. Alice Walker, *Meridian* (New York: Harcourt Brace Jovanovich, 1976), 39. Subsequent references to this work are given by page number in text.

23. See Camille Jeffers, *Living Poor* (Ann Arbor: University of Michigan Press, 1967).

24. Christian, *Black Women Novelists*, 220.

25. Ibid., 138.

26. Ibid., 139.

27. Morrison, *The Bluest Eye* (New York: Pocket Books, 1976), 5. Subsequent references to this work are given by page number in text.

28. Robert Steptoe, "Intimate Things in Place: A Conversation with Toni Morrison," *Massachusetts Review* 9 (autumn 1977): 478.

29. Rich, *Of Woman Born*, 168.

30. Jeffers, *Living Poor*, iv.

31. Rich, *Of Woman Born*, 151.

32. Jesse Bernard, *Marriage and Family among Negroes* (Englewood Cliffs, N.J.: Prentice-Hall, 1966), 108.

33. Christian, *Black Women Novelists*, 140.

34. Ibid., 68.

35. Ibid., 70.

36. Gwendolyn Brooks, *Maud Martha* (New York: Harper and Row, 1953), 5. Subsequent references to this work are given by page number in text.

37. Louise Meriwether, *Daddy Was a Number Runner* (New York: Pyramid, 1970), 39. Subsequent references to this work are given by page number in text.

38. Paule Marshall, *Brown Girl, Brownstones* (New York: Random House, 1959), 4. Subsequent references to this work are given by page number in text.

39. Christian, *Black Women Novelists*, 220.

40. Ibid., 226.

41. Toni Morrison, *Sula* (New York: Bantam Books, 1973). Subsequent references to this work are given by page number in text.

42. Steptoe, "Intimate Things in Place," 478.

43. Ibid.

44. Michele Wallace, *Black Macho and the Myth of the Superwoman* (New York: Dial Press, 1978), 66.

45. Ashley Montagu, *The Natural Superiority of Women* (New York: Macmillan, 1968), 12.

46. Grace Lounsberry and Grace Honet, "Principles of Perception in Toni Morrison's *Sula*," *Black American Literature Forum* 13 (winter 1979): 128.

47. Ibid.

48. Christian, *Black Women Novelists*, 180.

49. Ibid., 182.

50. "Interview with Alice Walker," in *Interviews with Black Writers*, ed. John O'Brien (New York: Liveright, 1973), 192.

51. Alice Walker, *The Third Life of Grange Copeland* (New York: Harcourt Brace Jovanovich, 1970), 44. Subsequent references to this work are given by page number in text.

52. Zora Neale Hurston, *Their Eyes Were Watching God* (Greenwich, Conn.: Lippincott, 1937; Fawcett, 1965), 16.

53. Daryl Dance, "Father May Bring Home the Bacon, but He Don't Cut No Ice: The Economic Plight of the Father Figure in American Literature," in *Journal of Afro-American Issues* 3 (summer/fall 1975): 298.

54. Ron Karenga, "In Love and Struggle: Toward a Greater Togetherness," *The Black Scholar* 6 (March 1975): 18.

55. Eldridge Cleaver, *Soul on Ice* (New York: McGraw-Hill, 1968), 72.

56. Shulamith Firestone, *The Dialectic of Sex: The Case for Feminist Revolution* (New York: William Morrow, 1970), 108.

57. Hernton, *Sex and Racism in America*, 61.

58. Washington, ed., *Black-Eyed Susans*, xxii.

59. Toni Morrison, quoted in Renita Weems, "Artists without Art Form," *Conditions: Five* (1979): 53.

60. Walker, "In Search of Our Mothers' Gardens," 66.

61. Interview with Alice Walker, *Encore* 2 (April 1973): 41.

62. Carrie McCray, "The Black Woman and Family Roles," in *The Black Woman*, ed. LaFrances Rodgers-Rose (Beverly Hills, Calif.: Sage Publications, 1980), 72.

63. Barbara Smith in *Frances, Zora, and Lorraine: Essays and Interviews on Black Women and Writing*, ed. Juliette Bowles (Washington, D.C.: Howard University Press, 1979), 33.

64. Jessie Bernard, "The Impact of Sexism and Racism in Employment Status and Earnings," in Lewis, "A Response to Inequality," 361.

4. "Going Nowhere Immediate": Black Women of Hopelessness

1. Jeanne Noble, *Beautiful, Also, Are the Souls of My Black Sisters* (Englewood, N.J.: Prentice-Hall, 1978), 75–76.

2. Ibid., 75.

3. Ibid.

4. See Null, *Hollywood*.

5. Douglas Turner Ward, *Happy Ending* (1966), in Noble, *Beautiful, Also*, 83.

6. Louis D. Stone, "What It's Like to Be a Colored Woman," *Washington Post*, 13 November 1966, quoted in *Black Women in White America*, 217.

7. Noble, *Beautiful, Also*, 75.

8. Morrison, *The Bluest Eye*, 109.

9. Ann Petry, *The Street* (Boston: Houghton Mifflin, 1946), 127. Subsequent references to this work are given by page number in text.

10. Susan Brownmiller, *Against Our Will: Men, Women and Rape* (New York: Bantam Books, 1975), 5.

11. Abbey Lincoln, "Who Will Revere the Black Woman?" in *The Black Woman*, ed. Toni Cade Bambara (New York: New American Library, 1970), 82.

12. Marilyn French, *The Women's Room* (New York: Jove, 1977), 120.

13. See William Ryan, *Blaming the Victim* (New York: Pantheon Books, 1971).

14. "The Combahee River Collective: A Black Feminist Statement," in *Capitalist Patriarchy and the Case for Socialist Feminism*, 363.

15. Ruth Rosen and Sue Davidson, eds., *The Maimie Papers* (New York: Feminist Press, 1977), xxv.

16. Walker, "Interview with Alice Walker," in *Interviews with Black Writers*, 192.

17. Walker, *The Third Life of Grange Copeland*, 39. Subsequent references to this work are given by page number in text.

18. Elizabeth Schultz, "'Free in Fact and at Last: The Image of the Black Woman in Black American Fiction," in *What Manner of Woman*, ed. Marlene Springer (New York: New York University Press, 1977), 332.

19. Ibid.

20. Ibid., 335.

21. Joan Bischoff, "The Novels of Toni Morrison: Studies in Thwarted Sensitivity," *Studies in Black Literature* 6 (fall 1975): 21.

22. Ibid., 22.

23. Walker, "In Search of Our Mothers' Gardens," 66.

24. Franklin, *From Slavery to Freedom*, 620.

25. See E. Franklin Frazier, *The Negro Family in the United States* (Chicago: University of Chicago Press, 1939).

5. "Journeying from Can't to Can and Sometimes Back to "Can't": Black Women of Challenge and Contradiction

1. Robert Hayden in *Frances, Zora, and Lorraine*, ed. Juliette Bowles (Washington, D.C.: Howard University Press), 45.

2. Statement by Beulah Gloster of Morehouse College in a conversation on the condition of women in April 1974.

3. Carolyn Rodgers, "Poems for Some Black Women," in *How I Got Ovah*, 47–48.

4. Robert A. Bone, *The Negro Novel in America* (New Haven, Conn.: Yale University Press, 1958), 180.

5. Noel Schraufnagel, *From Apology to Protest: The Black American Novel* (Deland, Fla.: Everett Edwards, 1973), 42.

6. Addison Gayle, *The Way of the New World: The Black Novel in America* (Garden City, N.Y.: Doubleday, 1973), 196.

7. Beatrice Royster, "The Ironic Vision of Four Black Women Novelists" (Ph.D. diss., Emory University, 1975), 158.

8. Ibid., 154.

9. Petry, *The Street*, 7. Subsequent references to this work are given by page number in text.

10. James Ivy, "Ann Petry Talks About Her First Novel," in *Sturdy Black Bridges*, 198.

11. Vernon Lattin, "Ann Petry and the American Dream," *Black American Literature Forum* 15 (summer 1978): 69.

12. Ibid., 70.

13. Gayle, *The Way of the New World*, 194.

14. Richard Wright, *Native Son* (New York: Harper & Row, 1940; Perennial Classics, 1966), 215. For an interesting discussion of Wright's treatment of black women characters, see Sylvia Keady's study, "Richard Wright's Women Characters and Inequality," *Black American Literature Forum* 10 (1976): 123–26.

15. Royster, "The Ironic Vision of Four Black Women Novelists," 155.

16. Truth, quoted in *Black Women in White America*, 366.

17. Royster, "The Ironic Vision of Four Black Women Novelists," 171.

18. Bone, *The Negro Novel*, 187.

19. Ibid.

20. William H. Robinson, Introduction, in Dorothy West, *The Living Is Easy* (New York: Arno Press, 1948), ii. Subsequent references to this work are given by page number in text.

21. Bone, *The Negro Novel*, 188.

22. Ibid.

23. Ibid., 187.

24. Ibid., 188.

25. Ibid.

26. Janet Hyde, "Tomboyism," *Psychology of Women Quarterly* 2 (fall 1977): 74.

27. Wright, *This Child's Gonna Live*, 15. Subsequent references to this work are given by page number in text.

28. Wright, quoted in Thelma Rush and Carol Meyers, eds., *Black American Writers Past and Present: A Biographical and Bibliographical Dictionary* (Metuchen, N.J.: Scarecrow Press, 1975), 791.

29. Nella Larsen, *Quicksand* (New York: Alfred A. Knopf, 1929), 174. Subsequent references to this work are given by page number in text.

30. Claudia Tate, "*Corregidora*: Ursa's Blues Medley," *Black American Literature Forum* 13 (winter 1979): 140.

31. Gayl Jones, *Corregidora* (New York: Random House, 1975), 25. Subsequent references to this work are given by page number in text.

32. Tate, "*Corregidora,*" 140.

33. Ibid., 141.

34. Ibid., 139.

35. Ibid.

36. Steptoe, "Intimate Things in Place," 478.

37. Jones, quoted in Rush and Meyers, eds., *Black American Writers Past and Present,* 440.

38. "Gayl Jones: An Interview," *The Massachusetts Review* 18 (1977): 701.

39. Ibid.

40. Gayl Jones, *Eva's Man* (New York: Random House, 1976), 121. Subsequent references to this work are given by page number in text.

41. "Gayl Jones: An Interview," 700–701.

42. Ladner, *Tomorrow's Tomorrow,* 109.

43. Lerner, ed., *Black Women in White America,* 163–64.

44. bell hooks, *Ain't I a Woman?,* 59.

45. Tate, "An Interview with Gayl Jones," *Black American Literature Forum* 13 (winter 1979): 146.

46. Evelyn Heinz, ed., *Anaïs Nin: A Woman Speaks* (Momence, Ill.: Swallow Press, 1975), 44.

6. Giving Birth to Self: The Quests for Wholeness of Sula Mae Peace and Meridian Hill

1. Roseann Bell and Bettye Parker, "Introduction: The Analytical Vision," in *Sturdy Black Bridges,* 133.

2. Washington, "An Essay on Alice Walker," in *Sturdy Black Bridges,* 133.

3. Ibid.

4. Walker, in *Interviews with Black Writers,* 192.

5. Weems, "Artists without Art Form," 56.

6. Smith, "Toward a Black Feminist Criticism," 166.

7. Bischoff, "The Novels of Toni Morrison," 21.

8. Ibid., 22.

9. Morrison, *Sula,* 35. Subsequent references to this work are given by page number in text.

10. Steptoe, "Intimate Things in Place," 476.

11. Ibid., 480.

12. Smith, "Toward a Black Feminist Criticism," 168.

13. Ibid., 168.

14. Ibid. 170.

15. Steptoe, "Intimate Things in Place," 480.

16. Walker, *Meridian*, 88. Subsequent references to this work are given by page number in text.

17. Christian, *Black Women Novelists*, 209.

18. Ibid., 215.

19. Ibid., 218.

20. June Jordan, "What Would I Do White?," in *Black-Eyed Susans*, xviii.

21. Christian, *Black Women Novelists*, 207–8.

22. W. E. B. DuBois coined the term "double consciousness" in *The Souls of Black Folk*, 1898.

23. Christian, *Black Women Novelists*, 210.

24. Ibid.

25. Walker, *The Third Life of Grange Copeland*, 125.

26. Christian, *Black Women Novelists*, 235.

27. Ibid., 237.

7. The Space and the Enclosure: The Collective Vision of Black Women

1. Mary Helen Washington, ed., *Midnight Birds: Stories by Contemporary Black Women Writers* (New York: Anchor Books, 1980), xiv.

2. Tate, "Interview with Gayl Jones," 147.

3. Eisenstein, "The Relations of Capitalist Patriarchy," 47.

4. Tate, "Interview with Gayl Jones," 147.

5. Washington, ed., *Midnight Birds*, xiv.

6. Washington, ed., *Black-Eyed Susans*, xv.

7. See William Grier and Price Cobb, *Black Rage* (New York: Basic Books, 1968).

8. This word was used by Frederick Douglass for the rhetoric and images that the slaveholding culture of the South used to imprison the minds of blacks. It is an appropriate term for the rhetoric and myths that are used to imprison the minds of women and of men as well.

9. Kate Millett, *Sexual Politics* (New York: New American Library, 1969), 31.

10. Washington, ed., *Midnight Birds*, xvi.

11. Ibid., xvii.

12. Ibid., xvi–xvii.

13. Washington, ed., *Black-Eyed Susans*, xxxi.

14. Washington, ed., *Midnight Birds*, xvii.

15. Audre Lorde, "Black Women's Anger," *Essence*, October 1983, 90.

16. Washington, ed., *Black-Eyed Susans*, xxxi.

17. Nancy Hoffman, "White Women, Black Women: Inventing an Adequate Pedagogy," *Women's Studies Newsletter* 5 (spring 1977): 22.

18. Washington, ed., *Midnight Birds*, xx.

19. Ibid.

20. Washington, ed., *Black-Eyed Susans,* ix.

21. Washington, ed., *Midnight Birds,* xiv.

22. Janeway, *Between Myth and Morning,* 170.

23. Ibid.

24. Washington, ed., *Black-Eyed Susans,* xi.

25. Deborah McDowell, "New Directions for Black Feminist Criticism," 155.

26. Mari Evans, *I Am a Black Woman* (New York: William Morrow, 1964), 11–12.

SELECTED BIBLIOGRAPHY

Primary Sources

Brooks, Gwendolyn. *Maud Martha*. New York: Harper and Row, 1953.
Jones, Gayl. *Corregidora*. New York: Random House, 1975.
————. *Eva's Man*. New York: Random House, 1976.
Marshall, Paule, *Brown Girl, Brownstones*. New York: Random House, 1959.
Meriwether, Louise. *Daddy Was a Number Runner*. New York: Pyramid, 1970.
Morrison, Toni. *The Bluest Eye*. New York: Pocket Books, 1976.
————. *Sula*. New York: Bantam Books, 1973.
Petry, Ann. *The Street*. Boston: Houghton Mifflin, 1946.
Walker, Alice. *Meridian*. New York: Harcourt Brace Jovanovich, 1976.
————. *The Third Life of Grange Copeland*. New York: Harcourt Brace Jovanovich, 1970.
West, Dorothy. *The Living Is Easy*. New York: Arno Press, 1948.
Wright, Sarah. *This Child's Gonna Live*. New York: Dell, 1969.

General Works

Ahern, Dee. *The Economics of Being a Woman*. New York: Macmillan, 1976.
Aldridge, Delores. "Black Women in the Economic Marketplace: A Battle Unfinished." *Journal of Social and Behavioral Sciences* 21 (winter 1975): 48–62.
"Alice Walker Talks About Black Women." *Encore*, April 1973, 41–42.
Allen, Walter. "Family Roles, Occupational Statuses, and Achievement Orientation among Black Women in the United States." *Signs* 4 (summer 1979): 672–79.
Angelou, Maya. *Gather Together in My Name*. New York: Random House, 1974.

Bambara, Toni Cade, ed. *The Black Woman*. New York: New American Library, 1970.

———. "On the Issue of Roles." In *The Black Woman*, edited by Toni Cade Bambara, 101–10. New York: New American Library, 1970.

Bardwick, Judith, and Elizabeth Dowan. "Ambivalence: The Socialization of Women." In *Women in Sexist Society*, edited by Vivian Gornick and Barbara K. Moran, 85–90. New York: Mentor, 1971.

Baxandall, Rosalyn, et al., eds. *America's Working Women: A Documentary History, 1600–Present*. New York: Vintage Books, 1976.

Beal, Frances. "Double Jeopardy: To Be Black and Female." In *Sisterhood Is Powerful*, edited by Robin Morgan, 340–52. New York: Random House, 1970.

———. "Slave of a Slave No More." *The Black Scholar* 6 (March 1975): 2–10.

Bernard, Jesse. *Marriage and Family among Negroes*. Englewood Cliffs, N.J.: Prentice-Hall, 1966.

Billingsley, Andrew. *Black Families in White America*. Englewood Cliffs, N.J.: Prentice-Hall, 1966.

Bird, Caroline. *Born Female: The High Cost of Keeping Women Down*. New York: David McKay, 1968.

Bischoff, Joan. "The Novels of Toni Morrison: Studies in Thwarted Sensitivity." *Studies in Black Literature* 6 (fall 1975): 21–26.

Blackburn, Regina. "In Search of the Black Female Self: African-American Women's Autobiographies and Ethnicity." *Women's Autobiography*. Edited by Estelle Jelinke, 133–48. Bloomington: Indiana University Press, 1980.

Blackburn, Sara. "You Still Can't Go Home Again." Review of *Sula*, by Toni Morrison. *New York Times Book Review*, 30 December 1979, 2.

Blauner, Robert. *Racial Oppression in America*. New York: Harper & Row, 1972.

Bloch, Ruth. "Untangling the Roots of Modern Sex Roles: A Survey of Four Centuries of Change." *Signs* 4 (winter 1978): 237–52.

Bond, Jean Carey. "The Media Image of Black Women." *Freedomways* 15 (1975): 34–37.

Bone, Robert A. *The Negro Novel in America*. New Haven, Conn.: Yale University Press, 1958.

Brisbane, Robert H. *Black Activism*. Valley Forge, Pa.: Judson Press, 1974.

———. *The Black Vanguard*. Valley Forge, Pa.: Judson Press, 1970.

Brownmiller, Susan. *Against Our Will: Men, Women and Rape*. New York: Bantam Books, 1975.

Chafe, William H. *The American Woman: Her Changing Social, Ecomomic, and Political Roles, 1920–1970*. New York: Oxford University Press, 1972.

———. *Women and Equality: Changing Patterns in American Culture*. New York: Oxford University Press, 1977.

Chisholm, Shirley. "Race, Revolution and Women." *The Black Scholar* 7 (December 1971): 17–21.

————. "Racism and Anti-Feminism." *The Black Scholar* 1 (January/February 1970): 40–47.

————. "Sexism and Racism: One Battle to Fight." *Personnel and Guidance Journal* 51 (October 1972): 123–216.

————. "Women Must Rebel." *Voices of New Feminism.* Edited by Mary Lou Thompson, 207–16. Boston: Beacon Press, 1970.

————. *Unbought and Unbossed.* Boston: Houghton Mifflin, 1970.

Christian, Barbara. *Black Women Novelists: The Development of a Tradition, 1892–1976.* Westport, Conn.: Greenwood Press, 1981.

Clark, Joanna. "Motherhood." *The Black Woman,* edited by Toni Cade Bambara. New York: New American Library, 1970.

Cleaver, Eldridge. *Soul on Ice.* New York: McGraw-Hill, 1968.

Cole, Johnetta, "Black Women in America: An Annotated Bibliography." *The Black Scholar* 2 (December 1971): 42–53.

————. "Culture: Negro, Black, and Nigger." *The Black Scholar* 1 (June 1970): 40–46.

Cornelisen, Ann. *Women of the Shadows.* Boston: Little, Brown, 1976.

Cornillon, Susan, ed. *Images of Women in Fiction: Feminist Perspectives.* Bowling Green, Ohio: Bowling Green State University Press, 1972.

Cowley, Joyce. "Pioneers of Women's Liberation." In *Voices of the New Feminism,* edited by Mary Lou Thompson, 83–86. Boston: Beacon Press, 1970.

Dance, Daryl. "Black Eve or Madonna? A Study of the Antithetical Views of the Mother in Black American Literature." In *Sturdy Black Bridges,* edited by Roseann Bell et al., 123–32. New York: Doubleday, 1979.

Davis, Angela. "Rape, Racism, and the Capitalist Setting." *The Black Scholar* 10 (April 1978): 38–42.

————. "Reflections on the Black Woman's Role in the Community of Slaves." *The Black Scholar* 3 (December 1971): 7–9.

Dill, Bonnie. "The Dialects of Black Womanhood." *Signs* 4 (spring 1979): 543–55.

DuBois, W. E. B. *The Souls of Black Folk.* Boston, 1898. Reprint. New York: Fawcett, 1963.

Eisenstein, Zillah R., ed. *Capitalist Patriarchy and the Case for Socialist Feminism.* New York: Monthly Review Press, 1979.

————. "Some Notes on the Relations of Capitalist Patriarchy." In *Capitalist Patriarchy and the Case for Socialist Feminism,* 46–53. New York: Monthly Review Press, 1979.

Ellison, Ralph. *Invisible Man.* New York: Random House, 1952.

Evans, Sara. *Personal Politics: The Roots of Women's Liberation in the Civil Rights Movement and the New Left.* New York: Alfred Knopf, 1979.

Exum, Pat Crutchfield, ed. *Keeping the Faith: Writings by Contemporary Black American Women.* Greenwich, Conn.: Fawcett, 1974.

Fanon, Frantz. *Black Skin, White Masks: The Experience of a Black Man in a White World*. New York: Grove Press, 1967.

Ferguson, Mary Anne. *Images of Women in Literature*. Boston: Houghton Mifflin, 1973.

Fisher, Paul, and Ralph Lowenskin. *Race and the News Media*. New York: Praeger, 1967.

Foster, Frances. "Changing Concepts of the Black Woman." *Journal of Black Studies* (June 1973): 433–52.

Franklin, John Hope. *From Slavery to Freedom*. New York: Random House, 1969.

French, Marilyn. *The Women's Room*. New York: Jove, 1977.

Friedan, Betty. *The Feminine Mystique*. New York: W. W. Norton, 1963.

———. *It Changed My Life*. New York: Dell, 1976.

Gayle, Addison. *The Way of the New World: The Black Novel in America*. Garden City, N.Y.: Doubleday, 1973.

Giele, Janet Z. *Women and the Future*. New York: Macmillan, 1978.

Gornick, Vivian, and Barbara K. Moran, eds. *Woman in Sexist Society: Studies in Power and Powerlessness*. New York: Mentor, 1971.

Grant, Joanne, ed. *Black Protest: History, Documents, and Analyses 1619 to the Present*. Greenwich, Conn.: Fawcett, 1968.

Green, Marjorie. "Ann Petry Planned to Write." *Opportunity* 24 (spring 1946): 78–79.

Grier, William, and Price Cobbs. *Black Rage*. New York: Basic Books, 1968.

Hamer, Fannie Lou. "It's in Your Hands." In *Black Women in White America*, edited by Gerda Lerner, 609–14. New York: Random House, 1972.

Hare, Nathan. "Revolution without a Revolution: The Psychology of Sex and Race." *The Black Scholar* 9 (April 1978): 12–17.

Harley, Sharon, and Rosalyn Terborg-Penn, eds. *The Afro-American Women: Struggles and Images*. New York: Kennikat Press, 1978.

Hatch, James, ed. *Black Images on the American Stage: A Bibliography of Plays and Musicals, 1770–1970*. New York: Drama Books Specialists, 1970.

Hernton, Calvin. *Coming Together: Black Power, White Hatred, and Sexual Hang-ups*. New York: Random House, 1971.

———. *Sex and Racism in America*. New York: Grove Press, 1965.

Hoffman, Nancy. "White Women, Black Women: Inventing an Adequate Pedagogy." *Women's Studies Newsletter* 5 (spring 1977): 21–24.

Hood, Elizabeth. "Black Women, White Women: Separate Paths to Liberation." *The Black Scholar* 4 (April 1978): 8–13.

hooks, bell. *Ain't I a Woman? Black Women and Feminism*. Boston: South End Press, 1981.

Hornsby, Alton, ed. *The Black Almanac*. New York: Barron's Educational Series, 1972.

Hull, Gloria, et al., eds. *But Some of Us Are Brave: Black Women's Studies*. Old Westbury, N.Y.: Feminist Press, 1982.

Hyde, Janet. "Tomboyism." *Psychology of Women Quarterly* 2 (fall 1977): 73–75.

Ivy, James. "Ann Petry Talks About Her First Novel." In *Sturdy Black Bridges*, edited by Roseann Bell et al. New York: Doubleday, 1979.

Jackson, Jacquelyn. "Black Women in a Racist Society." In *Racism and Mental Health*, edited by Charles Willie et al. Pittsburgh: University of Pittsburgh Press, 1972.

————. "A Partial Bibliography on or Related to Black Women." *Journal of the Study of Behavioral Sciences* 21 (winter 1975): 90–135.

Janeway, Elizabeth. *Between Myth and Morning: Women Awakening*. New York: William Morrow, 1974.

Jeffers, Camille. *Living Poor*. Ann Arbor : University of Michigan Press, 1967.

Jordan, June. "All about Eva: A Review of Gayl Jones's *Eva's Man*." *New York Times Book Review*, May 1976, 36–37.

Joseph, Gloria, and Jill Lewis. *Common Differences: Conflicts in Black Feminism and White Feminist Perspectives*. Garden City, N.Y.: Anchor Books, 1981.

Kapai, Silla. "Dominant Themes and Techniques in Paule Marshall's Fiction." *College Language Association Journal* 16 (September 1972): 49–59.

Kaplan, Sydney Jane. "Review Essay: Literary Criticism." *Signs* 4 (spring 1979): 514–27.

Karenga, Ron. "In Love and Struggle: Toward a Greater Togetherness." *The Black Scholar* 6 (March 1975): 16–28.

Keizs, Marcia. "Themes and Styles in the Works of Paule Marshall." *Black American Literature Forum* 9 (fall 1975): 67–76.

King, Mae. "The Politics of Sexual Stereotypes." *The Black Scholar* 4 (March/April 1973): 12–23.

Klagsburn, Francine, ed. *The First Ms. Reader*. New York: Warner, 1973.

Klotman, Phyliss. "Dick and Jane and the Shirley Temple Sensibility in *The Bluest Eye*." *Black American Literature Forum* 13 (winter 1979): 123–25.

Koontz, Elizabeth. "Women as a Minority Group." In *Voices of the New Feminism*, edited by Mary Lou Thompson, 38–44. Boston: Beacon Press, 1970.

Ladner, Joyce. *Tomorrow's Tomorrow*. New York: Doubleday, 1972.

LaRue, Linda. "The Black Movement and Women's Liberation." *The Black Scholar* 1 (May 1970): 36–42.

Lattin, Vernon. "Ann Petry and the American Dream." *Black American Literature Forum* 15 (summer 1978): 68–70.

Lee, Don. *Don't Cry, Scream*. Detroit: Broadside Press, 1969.

Lerner, Gerda, ed. *Black Women in White America: A Documentary History*. New York: Random House, 1972.

Lewis, Diane. "A Response to Inequality: Black Women, Racism, and Sexism." *Signs* 3 (winter 1977): 339–61.

Lincoln, Abbey. "Who Will Revere the Black Woman?" In *The Black Woman*, edited by Toni Cade Bambara, 80–84. New York: New American Library, 1970.

Loewenberg, Bert James, and Ruth Bogin. *Black Women in Nineteenth-Century American Life*. University Park: Pennsylvania State University Press, 1976.

Lounsberry, Grace, and Grace Honet. "Principles of Perception of Toni Morrison's *Sula*." *Black American Literature Forum* 13 (winter 1979): 124–29.

Lynch, Acklyn. "Notes on Black Women Writers of the Past Two Decades." In *Frances, Zora, and Lorraine: Essays and Interviews on Black Women and Writing*, edited by Juliette Bowles, 45–49. Washington, D.C.: Howard University Press, 1979.

Lynch, Hollis R. *The Black Urban Condition: A Documentary History, 1866–1971*. New York: Thomas Y. Crowell, 1973.

Lyons, Harriet. "Female Eroticists: Stirrings of Sexuality." *The Village Voice*, 27 April 1972.

Mainardi, Pat. "The Politics of Housework." In *Sisterhood Is Powerful*, edited by Robin Morgan, 23–26. New York: Random House, 1970.

Mapp, Edward. "Black Women in Films." *The Black Scholar* 4 (March/April 1973): 42–46.

McCray, Carrie. "The Black Woman and Family Roles." In *The Black Woman*, edited by LaFrances Rodgers-Rose, 56–60. Beverly Hills, Calif.: Sage Publications, 1980.

Meriwether, Louise. "Half a Man: Emasculation of the Negro Man." *Negro Digest* 14 (October 1965): 4–13.

Miller, Loren. "Farewell to Liberals." In *Black Protest: History, Documents, and Analyses*, edited by Joanne Grant, 427–83. New York: Fawcett, 1968.

Millett, Kate. "Sexual Politics in Literature." In *Sisterhood Is Powerful*, edited by Robin Morgan, 311–36. New York: Random House, 1970.

Montagu, Ashley. *The Natural Superiority of Women*. New York: Macmillan, 1968.

Morgan, Robin. "Know Your Enemy: A Sampling of Sexist Quotes." In *Sisterhood Is Powerful*, edited by Robin Morgan, 31–36. New York: Random House, 1970.

Murray, Pauli. "Jim Crow and Jane Crow." In *Black Women in White America*, edited by Gerda Lerner, 584–88. New York: Random House, 1972.

———. "The Liberation of Black Women." In *Voices of the New Feminism*, edited by Mary Lou Thompson, 87–102. Boston: Beacon Press, 1970.

Myers, Carol. *Women in Literature: Criticism of the Seventies*. Metuchen, N.J.: Scarecrow Press, 1976.

Noble, Jeanne. *Beautiful, Also, Are the Souls of My Black Sisters*. Englewood, N.J.: Prentice-Hall, 1978.

————. "Negro Women and Their Education." *Journal of Negro Education* 26 (winter 1957): 15–21.

Null, Gary. *Hollywood: The Negro in Motion Pictures*. New York: Citadel Press, 1975.

O'Brien, John, ed. *Interviews with Black Writers*. New York: Liveright, 1973.

Ogunyemi, Chikwenye. "Sula: A Nigger Joke." *Black American Literature Forum* 13 (winter 1979): 130–34.

Olsen, Tillie. *Silences*. New York: Delta/Seymour Lawrence, 1965.

Pettigrew, L. Eudora. "Women's Liberation and Black Woman." *Journal of Social and Behavioral Sciences* 23 (spring 1977): 146–61.

Piercy, Marge. Review of *Meridian*, by Alice Walker. *New York Times*, 23 May 1976, 5–12.

Reid, Inez. "Together." *Black Women*. New York: Emerson Hall, 1971.

Rich, Adrienne. "Disloyal to Civilization: Feminism, Racism, and Gynephobia." *Chrysalis* 7 (1979): 10–27.

————. *Of Woman Born: Motherhood as Experience and Institution*. New York: W. W. Norton, 1970.

Roberts, J. R., ed. *Black Lesbians: An Annotated Bibliography*. Tallahassee: Naiad, 1981.

Rodgers, Carolyn M. *How I Got Ovah*. New York: Doubleday, 1976.

Rodgers-Rose, LaFrances, ed. *The Black Woman*. Beverly Hills, Calif.: Sage, 1980.

Rosenblatt, Roger. *Black Fiction*. Cambridge: Harvard University Press, 1974.

Rosen, Ruth, and Sue Davidson, eds. *The Maimie Papers*. New York: Feminist Press, 1977.

Royster, Beatrice. "The Ironic Vision of Four Black Women Novelists." Ph.D. diss., Emory University, 1975.

Ruby, Kathryn. "The Feminine Aesthetic: New Avenues." *Margins* 7 (August/September 1973): 3–4.

Rush, Thelma, and Carol Myers, eds. *Black American Writers Past and Present: A Biographical and Bibliographical Dictionary*. Metuchen, N.J.: Scarecrow Press, 1975.

Schraufnagel, Noel. *From Apology to Protest: The Black American Novel*. Deland, Fla.: Everett Edwards, 1973.

Schultz, Elizabeth. " 'Free in Fact and at Last': The Image of the Black Woman in Black American Fiction." In *What Manner of Woman*, edited by Marlene Springer, 337–47. New York: New York University Press, 1977.

Silberman, Charles. "Crisis in Black and White." In *Black Protest: History, Documents, and Analyses*, edited by Joanne Grant, 436–40. New York: Fawcett, 1968.

Sizemore, Barbara. "Sexism and the Black Male." *The Black Scholar* 4 (March/April 1973): 2–11.

Skeeter, Sharyn. "Black Women Writers: Levels of Identity." *Essence* 4 (May 1973): 3–10.

Smith, Barbara. "Beautiful, Needed, Mysterious." *Freedomways* 14 (first quarter, 1977): 69–72.

———. "Doing Research on Black American Women." *Women's Studies Newsletter* 4 (spring 1976): 4, 5, 7.

———. "Notes for Yet Another Paper on Black Feminism, Or Will the Real Enemy Please Stand Up?" *Conditions: Five* 1979, 12–18.

———. "Toward a Black Feminist Criticism." In *But Some of Us Are Brave*, edited by Gloria Hull et al. Old Westbury, N.Y.: Feminist Press, 1982.

Sochen, June. *Movers and Shakers: American Women Thinkers and Activists, 1900–1970*. New York: Quadrangle, 1974.

Stack, Carol. *All Our Kin: Strategies for Survival in a Black Community*. New York: Harper and Row, 1974.

Staples, Robert. "The Myth of the Impotent Black Male." *The Black Scholar* 9 (April 1978): 2–9.

Steptoe, Robert. "Intimate Things in Place: A Conversation with Toni Morrison." *Massachusetts Review* 9 (autumn 1977): 473–84.

Sternberger, Janet. *The Writer on Her Work*. New York: W. W. Norton, 1980.

Tate, Claudia. "*Corregidora*: Ursa's Blues Medley." *Black American Literature Forum* 13 (winter 1979): 139–40.

———. "An Interview with Gayl Jones." *Black American Literature Forum* 13 (winter 1979): 142–49.

———. *Interviews with Black Women Writers*. New York: Continuum, 1981.

Thompson, Daniel. *Sociology of the Black Experience*. Westport, Conn.: Greenwood Press, 1974.

Thompson, Mary Lou, ed. *Voices of the New Feminism*. Boston: Beacon Press, 1970.

Truth, Sojourner. "I Suppose I Am About the Only Colored Woman." In *Black Women in White America*, edited by Gerda Lerner, 566–71. New York: Random House, 1972.

U.S. Bureau of the Census. *The Social and Economic Status of the Black Population*, 1974. Washington, D.C.: Government Printing Office, 1974.

U.S. Department of Labor: *Handbook of Labor Statistics, 1978: Bulletin 3000*. Washington, D.C.: Government Printing Office, 1979.

Walker, Alice. "In Search of Our Mothers' Gardens." *Ms.* 2 (May 1974): 64–70, 105.

Wallace, Michele. *Black Macho and the Myth of the Super Woman*. New York: Dial Press, 1978.

Ware, Cellestine. *Woman Power: The Movement for Women's Liberation*. New York: Tower, 1970.

Washington, Mary Helen, ed. *Black-Eyed Susans: Classic Stories by and about Black Women*. Garden City, N.Y.: Anchor Books, 1975.

————, ed. *Midnight Birds: Stories by Contemporary Black Women Writers.* New York: Anchor Books, 1980.

Weems, Renita. "Artists without Art Form." *Conditions: Five* 1979, 8–13.

Woolf, Virginia. *A Room of One's Own.* New York: Harcourt Brace, 1929.

Selected Titles in Black Feminist Scholarship Written by Black Women, 1981–1995

Cannon, Katie. *Black Womanist Ethics.* Atlanta: Scholars Press, 1988.

Carby, Hazel. *Reconstructing Womanhood: The Emergence of the Afro-American Woman Novelist.* New York: Oxford University Press, 1987.

Christian, Barbara, ed. *Alice Walker: "Everyday Use."* New Brunswick: Rutgers University Press, 1994.

————. *Black Feminist Criticism: Perspectives on Black Women Writers.* New York and Oxford: Pergamon, 1985.

————. *Black Women Novelists: The Development of a Tradition, 1892–1976.* Westport, Conn.: Greenwood Press, 1980.

Cole, Johnetta, ed. *All American Women: Lines That Divide, Ties That Bind.* New York: Free Press, 1985.

Davies, Carole Boyce. *Black Women, Writing, and Identity: Migrations of the Subject.* London and New York: Routledge, 1994.

Davis, Angela. *Women, Race, and Class.* New York: Random House, 1981.

————. *Women, Culture, and Politics.* New York: Random House, 1989.

Davis, Marianna, ed. *Contributions of Black Women to America,* 2 vols. Columbia, S.C.: Kenday Press, 1982.

DeCosta-Willis, Miriam, ed. *The Memphis Diary of Ida B. Wells.* Boston: Beacon Press, 1995.

Foster, Frances. *Written by Herself.* Boston: Beacon Press, 1990.

Grant, Jacquelyn. *White Women's Christ and Black Women's Jesus: Feminist Christology and Womanist Response.* Atlanta: Scholars Press, 1989.

Guy-Sheftall, Beverly. *Daughters of Sorrow: Attitudes toward Black Women, 1880–1920.* Brooklyn: Carlson, 1990.

————. *Words of Fire: An Anthology of African-American Feminist Thought.* New York: The New Press, 1996.

Hill-Collins, Patricia. *Black Feminist Thought: Knowledge, Consciousness, and the Politics of Empowerment.* New York: Routledge, Chapman, and Hall, 1991.

Holloway, Karla. *Moorings and Metaphors: Figures of Culture and Gender in Black Women's Literature.* Brunswick: Rutgers University Press, 1992.

————. *The Character of the Word: The Texts of Zora Neale Hurston.* Westport, Conn.: Greenwood Press, 1987.

hooks, bell. *Black Looks: Race and Representation.* Boston: South End Press, 1992.

————. *Feminist Theory: From Margin to Center.* Boston: South End Press, 1984.

————. *Talking Back: Thinking Feminist, Thinking Black.* Boston: South End Press, 1989.

————. *Yearning: Race, Gender, and Cultural Politics.* Boston: South End Press, 1990.

Hull, Gloria. *Color, Sex, and Poetry: Three Women Writers of the Harlem Renaissance.* Bloomington: Indiana University Press, 1987.

————, ed. *Give Us Each Day: The Diary of Alice Dunbar-Nelson.* New York: W. W. Norton, 1984.

Jones, Jacqueline. *Labor of Love, Labor of Sorrow: Black Women, Work, and the Family—from Slavery to the Present.* New York: Random House, 1985.

Jordan, June. *Technical Difficulties.* New York: Pantheon, 1992.

Joyce, Joyce Ann. *Warriors, Conjurers, and Priests: Defining African-centered Literary Criticism.* Chicago: Third World Press, 1994.

Lorde, Audre. *Sister Outsider: Essays and Speeches.* Trumansburg, N.Y.: Crossing Press, 1984.

McKay, Nellie, ed. *Critical Essays on Toni Morrison.* Boston: G. K. Hall, 1988.

Morrison, Toni. *Playing in the Dark: Whiteness and the Literary Imagination.* Cambridge: Harvard University Press, 1992.

————, ed. *Race-ing Justice, En-gendering Power: Essays on Anita Hill, Clarence Thomas, and the Construction of Social Reality.* New York: Pantheon, 1992.

Pryse, Marjorie, and Hortense Spillers, eds. *Conjuring: Black Women, Fiction, and Literary Tradition.* Bloomington: Indiana University Press, 1985.

Rose, Tricia. *Black Noise: Rap Music and Black Culture in Contemporary America.* Hanover, N.H.: Wesleyan University Press, 1994.

Smith, Barbara, ed. *Home Girls: A Black Feminist Anthology.* Latham, N.Y.: Kitchen Table Press, 1983.

Smith, Valerie. *Narrative Authority in Twentieth Century Afro-American Fiction.* Cambridge: Harvard University Press, 1987.

Spillers, Hortense, ed. *Comparative American Identities: Race, Sex, and Nationality in the Modern Text.* New York: Routledge, 1991.

Tate, Claudia. *Domestic Allegories of Political Desire: The Black Heroine's Text at the Turn of the Century.* New York: Oxford University Press, 1992.

Townes, Emile. *Womanist Justice, Womanist Hope.* Atlanta: Scholars Press, 1993.

Walker, Alice, and Prathibha Parmar. *Warrior Marks: Female Genital Mutilation and the Sexual Blinding of Women.* New York: Harcourt Brace and Company, 1993.

Wall, Cheryl. *Changing Our Own Words: Essays on Writing by Black Women.* New Brunswick: Rutgers University Press, 1989.

Wallace, Michele. *Invisibility Blues: From Pop to Theory.* London: Verso, 1990.

Washington, Mary Helen. *Invented Lives. Narratives of Black Women, 1860–1960.* Garden City, N.Y.: Anchor, 1987.

Williams, Delores. *Sisters in the Wilderness: The Challenge of Womanist God-Talk.* New York: Orbis Books, 1993.

INDEX

Ajax, 172, 177–79, 206, 208
Angelou, Maya, 5, 48
artistic yearnings, 120, 175
Aunt Jemima (image of), 3–4, 24

Bambara, Toni Cade, 13, 34–35, 161 X
Bannie, Miss, 149
Beal, Francis, 199
beatings, 58, 93, 102, 124, 135
Bethune, Mary McLeod, 25
black male–female relationships, 69–71,
  73–76, 78, 82–96, 111–17, 123–24
black men, 69–71, 72, 73–76, 78, 82–96, 111– X
  17, 123–24, 133–34, 137, 139–40, 142, 144–
  46, 148–50, 152, 197–99
black men characters: Ajax, 172, 177–79, X
  206, 208; Boy-Boy, 82–85; Deighton
  Boyce, 74–76, 197–99, 211; Cholly
  Breedlove, 55–63, 123–24; "Daddy"
  Coffin, 69–71, 211; Brownfield
  Copeland, 87–95, 114–18, 136; Grange
  Copeland, 85, 114–18, 198; Truman
  Held, 185–87, 188–94; Bart Judson, 139–
  42, 145; Jude, 172, 174; Mutt Thomas,
  154–56; Jacob Upshur, 147–48, 152
Black Power movement, 16, 25, 33
black women: as daughters, 53–56, 63, 66,
  69–71, 73–83, 112, 117, 121–22, 140–45,
  153–60, 169–71; in the labor market, 18–
  23, 27–28; as lovers, 59, 87–88, 171–78; in

the media, 24–25, 40–41; as mothers,
  45–96, 127–38, 139–45, 146; in
  relationships with black men, 7, 8, 31–
  33, 41–44; in relationships with white
  women, 3–8, 23–24, 30–32, 39–41; in
  scholarship, 34–35; as wives, 45–96, 139–
  45, 146–53
black women activists, 20–26, 34–35, 37;
  feminists, 2, 9, 37, 39–44; politicians, 28,
  34, 36–38; writers, 9–14
black women novelists: Gwendolyn
  Brooks, 13, 197; Gayl Jones, 14, 153–58,
  162; Paule Marshall, 13, 71, 79, 197;
  Louise Meriwether, 14; Toni Morrison,
  14, 82–84, 94, 160, 165–73, 176–79, 197,
  205; Ann Petry, 13, 130, 131–32, 134, 197;
  Alice Walker, 12, 14, 85–96, 165–67, 198,
  204; Dorothy West, 13, 138; Harriet
  Wilson, 10; Sarah Wright, 14, 146, 150
Black Women Organized for Action
  (BWOA), 41–42
black women protagonists: Selina Boyce,
  71–76, 78–81; Pauline Breedlove, 53–68,
  119–24, 195, 198, 201–2, 207, 212, 214;
  Pecola Breedlove, 54, 62–64, 118–19;
  Francie Coffin, 69–71; Henrietta Coffin,
  69–71; Mem Copeland, 86–89, 91–96,
  196, 198, 201; Ursa Corregidora, 153–56;
  Meridian Hill, 50–54, 179–94, 201–2,
  208–9; Mrs. Hill, 50–54, 180, 183, 202,

black women protagonists *(cont.)*
206, 208; Lutie Johnson, 129–38, 197,
201, 205, 212; Josie, 86–88, 112–15, 118,
207, 208, 212, 214; Cleo Judson, 139–46,
208, 214; Maud Martha, 64–68, 197; Eva
Medina, 158–64, 199, 206; Min, 101–5,
107; Nel, 171–74, 184, 206, 207; Eva
Peace, 82–85, 169–70, 184, 194, 201;
Hanna Peace, 170–71, 214; Sula Peace,
167–81, 184, 193–94, 199, 201, 204, 206,
207–8, 210; Mariah Upshur, 146–52, 194,
197, 208, 210
black women's independence, 203
black women's loyalty to black men, 36,
198–200
Bluest Eye, The, 53–64, 119–26, 198, 209, 214
Boy-Boy, 82–85
Boyce, Deighton, 74–76, 197–99, 211
Boyce, Selina, 71–76, 78–81
Breedlove, Cholly, 55–63, 123–24
Breedlove, Pauline, 53–68, 119–24, 195, 198,
201–2, 207, 212, 214
Breedlove, Pecola, 54, 62–64, 118–19
Brooks, Gwendolyn, 13, 197
Brown Girl, Brownstones, 71–81, 197–98,
204–5
Brownmiller, Susan, 38

capitalism, 4, 197
childbirth, 61–62, 68–69
Chisholm, Shirley, 26, 34, 36–37
Christian, Barbara, 24, 54, 81, 85, 190
civil rights movement, 16, 26–28, 29–33,
42, 50, 183, 184–87
Cleaver, Eldridge, 26, 90, 186
Coffin, "Daddy," 69–71, 211
Coffin, Francie, 69–71
Coffin, Henrietta, 69–71
Combahee River Collective, 9, 41, 43–44, 107
Copeland, Brownfield, 87–95, 114–18, 136
Copeland, Grange, 85, 114–18, 198
Copeland, Mem, 86–89, 91–96, 196, 198, 201
Corregidora, 153–56, 204
Corregidora, Ursa, 153–56

Daddy Was a Number Runner, 68–71
Dance, Daryl, 48–49, 89–90

Davis, Angela, 4, 35, 39
de Beauvoir, Simone, 22, 45–46
domestics, 98–100, 120–22
double jeopardy, 2, 5–7, 10–12, 32, 195, 201,
209

Eisenstein, Zillah, 4, 38, 200
Eva's Man, 156–64, 199

"femininity," 205–6
Friedan, Betty, 22, 38

Guy-Sheftall, Beverly, 5, 35

Hamer, Fannie Lou, 37–38
Harper, Frances E. W., 24–25
Held, Truman, 185–87, 188–94
Hill, Meridian, 50–54, 179–94, 201–2,
208–9
Hill, Mrs., 50–54, 180, 183, 202, 206, 208
hooks, bell, 24, 31, 35, 38–39, 162

insanity, 64, 163

Johnson, Lutie, 129–38, 197, 201, 205, 212
Jones, Gayl, 10, 14, 153–60, 213
Jordan, Barbara, 33, 36
Josie, 86–88, 112–15, 118, 207, 208, 212, 214
Jude, 172, 174
Judson, Bart, 139–42, 145
Judson, Cleo, 139–46, 208, 214
Junto, 109–11, 133

lesbianism, 8, 15, 39, 43, 44, 154–56, 163, 176
Living Is Easy, The, 138–46, 214
Lorde, Audre, 210
love, 55, 62, 66, 87–88, 143

Mammy, 6, 7, 23
Marshall, Paule, 13, 71–72
Maud Martha, 64–68, 197
Maud Martha, 64–68, 197
McDaniel, Hattie, 23
McQueen, Butterfly, 23
Medina, Eva, 158–64, 199, 206
Meridian, 50–54, 179–94, 201–2
Meriwether, Louise, 14

Min, 101–5, 107
Morgan, Irene, 20
Morrison, Toni, 14, 82–84, 94, 160, 165–73, 176–79, 198, 205
motherhood as institution, 46–48
murder, 95, 116–17, 134, 163
Murray, Pauli, 29, 34

National Black Feminist Organization (NBFO), 41
Nation of Islam, 31
Nel, 171–74, 184, 206, 207
novels, black women's: *Bluest Eye, The,* 53–64, 119–26, 198, 209, 214; *Brown Girl, Brownstones,* 71–81, 197–98, 204–5; *Corregidora,* 153–56, 204; *Daddy Was a Number Runner,* 68–71; *Eva's Man,* 156–64, 199; *Living Is Easy, The,* 138–46, 214; *Maud Martha,* 64–68, 197; *Meridian,* 50–54, 179–94, 201–2; *Street, The,* 100–111, 129–38, 204; *Sula,* 82–85, 166–81, 193–94, 199, 205, 208, 210–12; *Third Life of Grange Copeland, The,* 85–96, 111–18, 198, 201, 214; *This Child's Gonna Live,* 146–53, 198

Olsen, Tillie, 11
Our Nig, 10

Parks, Rosa, 25
"passing," 14
Peace, Eva, 82–85, 169–70, 184, 194, 201
Peace, Hanna, 170–71, 214
Peace, Sula, 167–81, 184, 193–94, 199, 201, 204, 206, 207–8, 210
Petry, Ann, 13, 129–32
Pizzini, Mrs., 106–7
poverty, 5, 108, 146–49, 195–96
pregnancy, 51–52, 58–61, 112, 181–82
prostitution, 108, 110, 113, 126, 211

Rabinowitz, Lynn, 186–87, 212
rape, 54, 63, 134, 159
religion, 124, 148, 149
Republic of New Africa (RNA), 31
Rich, Adrienne, 38–39, 46
Rushing, Andrea Benton, 48

Sapphire (image of), 3–4, 24
sex, 59, 113–15, 142, 149, 161, 168–70, 174, 179–82
sexual abuse, 102, 133, 152–53, 157–58, 170–72
Shange, Ntozake, 9, 210
Shipley, Captain, 115
Sipuel, Ada, 20
Sizemore, Barbara, 42
Smith, Barbara, 11, 171, 176–77
Stanton, Elizabeth, 5, 39
Street, The, 100–111, 129–38, 204
Student Nonviolent Coordinating Committee (SNCC), 28–31, 37, 41–42
suicide, 76, 115, 212
Sula, 82–85, 166–81, 193–94, 199, 205, 208, 210–12

Tate, Claudia, 13, 154–55, 200
Terrell, Mary Church, 22, 25
Third Life of Grange Copeland, The, 85–96, 111–18, 198, 201, 214
This Child's Gonna Live, 146–53, 198
Thomas, Mutt, 154–56
Truth, Sojourner, 2, 43

Upshur, Jacob, 147–48, 152
Upshur, Mariah, 146–52, 194, 197, 208, 210

Walker, Alice, 12, 14, 85–96, 165–67, 198, 204
Wallace, Michele, 32, 34, 42–43, 83
Washington, Mary Helen, 196, 204, 210–13
Wells-Barnett, Ida, 22
West, Dorothy, 13, 138
white feminists, 3, 8, 22–23, 38–40, 41
white men, 109, 112, 114–15, 132, 135, 142, 174
white men characters: Junto, 109–11, 133; Captain Shipley, 115
white standard of beauty, 58–60, 62, 68, 108–9, 111, 119, 141, 197, 204–7
white women, 102, 106–7, 114, 116, 121, 132, 135, 137, 141, 149, 186–87
white women characters: Miss Bannie, 149; Mrs. Pizzini, 106–7; Lynn Rabinowitz, 186–87, 212
Wilson, Harriet, 10
women's movement, 16, 39–43
Wright, Sarah, 14, 146, 148

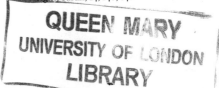